p. 59 Reg. Bugler
63
78
80 *
103
112
115
129 *
→ 131 * 132, 133
134
146-148
151-52 53
157
169
179

183
189

"Two Miserable Presidents"
Amazon

CHICAGO, 1903.

ARMY LETTERS

1861-1865.

BEING EXTRACTS FROM PRIVATE LETTERS TO RELATIVES AND FRIENDS FROM
A SOLDIER IN THE FIELD DURING THE LATE CIVIL WAR, WITH AN

APPENDIX

CONTAINING COPIES OF SOME OFFICIAL DOCUMENTS,
PAPERS AND ADDRESSES OF LATER DATE.

BY

OLIVER WILLCOX NORTON,

*Private Eighty-third Regiment Pennsylvania Volunteers,
First Lieutenant Eighth United States Colored Troops.*

PRINTED FOR PRIVATE CIRCULATION ONLY.

COPYRIGHT, 1903, BY O. W. NORTON.
ALL RIGHTS RESERVED.

PRINTED BY O. L. DEMING, CHICAGO.

TABLE OF CONTENTS

	PAGE
Introduction	6
Letters 1861	9
Letters 1862	39
Letters 1863	132
Letters 1864	196
Letters 1865	249
Recollections	280

APPENDIX

Record Escutcheon	302
Military Societies	305
List of Battles and Skirmishes	306
Letter from General James C. Rice	307
Letter from Captain John Hechtman	308
Order from War Department	309
Honorable Discharge from Eighty-third P. V.	310
Commission as First Lieutenant Eighth U. S. C. T.	311
Appointment as Regimental Quartermaster Eighth U. S. C. T.	312
Honorable Discharge from Eighth U. S. C. T.	313
Paper Read at Social Club, 1875	315
Two Bugle Calls	323
Corps Badges	330
Our Fallen Comrades, Address at Dedication of Regimental Monument, Gettysburg	337
The Third Brigade at Appomattox, Address by General Joshua L. Chamberlain	347

ILLUSTRATIONS

Portrait of Author, 1903	Frontispiece
Portrait of Author, 1861	8
Brigade Flag in Colors	153
Portrait of General Strong Vincent	163
Portrait of Author, 1863	193
Escutcheon	303
Music of Butterfield's Brigade Call	325
Music of Taps	329
Monument Eighty-third P. V. at Gettysburg	335
Position of Eighty-third Pennsylvania Volunteers on Little Round Top, Gettysburg	345

INTRODUCTION

THE AUTHOR of the letters in this volume placed his name on the roll of volunteers to answer the call of President Lincoln for seventy-five thousand men for three months' service, at Springfield, Pennsylvania, on the 10th of April, 1861. The volunteers from Springfield were formed into a company with those from Girard. This company formed part of a regiment which completed its organization at Erie, Pennsylvania, on the 20th of April, 1861. This Regiment, after serving three months, was re-organized and under the name of the Eighty-third Regiment Pennsylvania Volunteers entered the service of the United States for three years, or during the war. The author served as a private soldier in this regiment from its organization until November, 1863, when he was commissioned by President Lincoln as First Lieutenant of the Eighth United States Colored Troops, and served in that capacity until November, 1865.

During this period of four and one-half years he wrote, at short intervals, letters to relatives and friends, describing his experiences as a private soldier and officer. Some of these letters have been collected and printed in this volume with a view to preserving for his children and friends a record of a soldier's life in the time of the Civil War. They are printed exactly as written, without alteration or addition. Some paragraphs of purely personal nature, or which have no reference to army life, have been omitted. It may be thought that many others might have been left out with advantage, but the purpose of presenting as accurately as possible the life of a soldier, and the ideas and motives which actuated him as revealed in his letters, would not be so well served by such omission.

This volume is printed for private circulation only. The letters have no literary merit. Little will be expected in this respect from a young man whose education was limited to such instruction as he could obtain in district schools and village academies before completing his sixteenth year. No apology is made for crude or even coarse expressions, because to change the letters in any respect would be to destroy any value they may have.

Copies of some official documents, with some narratives and addresses of a later date, are given in an appendix. The author is indebted to General Joshua L. Chamberlain for the valuable paper "The Third Brigade at Appomattox," with which this volume ends.

O. W. Norton

CHICAGO, 1903

O. W. NORTON, April, 1861.
In uniform of Girard Guards.

LETTERS OF 1861

*Camp Wilkins, Pittsburgh, Penn.,
Friday, May 10, 1861.*

Dear Sister L.:—

I hardly know where to begin or what to write. My mind is, perhaps, in the same condition as yours—a good deal confused. It is a damp, rainy morning, so rainy that no companies will be out for drill until the weather is more favorable, so I have leisure to write. My health is tolerably good. I have been sick with a severe cold one day so I could not drill, but a wet towel cured that and I have had a turn of sick headache; beyond that I have been very well. I feel very well this morning. I had a good breakfast, had milk in my coffee, and last night we had butter.

The day I had the sick headache, I got nothing for breakfast but a piece of dry bread, and at noon we had a rice soup that was burnt so as to be nauseous. I ate a good quantity, however, and, consequently, *unate* it and ate no more till the next night.

We have fixed up our quarters first-rate. Four of us occupy a shed about ten feet by five feet. Plenty of lumber was furnished and we partitioned off a cabin, about half our room, and covered it all over except a little hole to crawl into. Inside we have a berth or bunk for one, and straw in the bottom for the rest, a first-rate camp. The front room we use for sitting room, parlor, reception room, reading room, writing room, etc., a place about five feet square.

We have lots of papers—New York, Philadelphia, Cincinnati, Cleveland and Pittsburgh dailies, four or five every day. I have sent some home. In the Dispatch you can see an account of our proceedings last Sunday.

I got a pass and went out into the city yesterday. I took the morning's mail down to the office. We had about one hundred papers and forty-eight letters. Our company has more letters and papers sent and received than any other three companies in the regiment. Our company has been selected to bear the regimental flag, as ours is the best flag in the regiment. In fact, I haven't seen a nicer flag anywhere than ours. Being about medium height, my place is very near the flag.

But I am digressing—I was going to tell you what I saw in the city. I walked through a good share of the trading part of the city, seeing the lions and big black buildings, then I went down to the river and followed that up some distance. I then jumped on one of the cars of the horse railroad and went up to the United States arsenal. I had full liberty to walk about the grounds, but I could not enter any building. It is the most beautiful I have seen this long time. The grass is about six inches high and beautiful gravel walks run through it in all directions. Shade trees in full leaf are set all around, and lilacs, which are in full bloom, are set round in tasty places. I was just picking some of them to send to you when a couple of sentinels charged bayonets on me and I let 'em alone. They said no one was allowed to pick flowers or go on the grass. All well enough, I suppose, but I wanted some. I counted two hundred and forty-four cannon lying round in the yard, about sixty ten-inch Columbiads, and the rest from twelve to sixty-four-pounders, and I should think twenty-five or thirty cords of cannon balls and bomb shells. I saw eight guns and a lot of balls that were taken in the Revolution. One of the guns was marked W. Bowen, fecit, 1747, two others ditto 1755, one 1776 and two made in Paris. I should think as many as two hundred cannon are set round about the grounds as posts. The small arms I could not see, as they are all in the buildings. They are making a gun nineteen feet long and four feet across the muzzle, to carry a fifteen-inch ball.

One of the boys who went down to old Ft. Duquesne brought up a piece of bark from a log in the old fort built more than one hundred years ago. I got a piece, which just for a curiosity I send to you.

H. B.'s enlisting is just about what I expected to hear. D. T. too, is in. Well, success to them! I have seen C. R.'s father two or three times; had an introduction. He came to my door yesterday. He said our quarters looked about as comfortable as any.

I heard yesterday that we were ordered to march on Harper's Ferry within ten days, but as nothing has been said about it publicly in camp, I don't much believe it. So many false rumors are about that no one knows what to believe. I think, however, that we shall leave for somewhere soon. Government is making active preparations for war. One piece of news that we received from Girard caused a good laugh in our company, viz.: that the young ladies of Girard had presented ex-Lieutenant S. with a wooden sword.

Camp Wright, Hulton, Penn.,
Saturday, June 8, 1861.

Dear Sister H. :—

You will see by the date of this that I have left Camp Wilkins and am now at the new camp called Camp Wright. We arrived here to-day. Oh, I tell you we have a splendid place, fifteen miles from Pittsburgh on the south bank of the Alleghany. The barracks of the Erie regiment are sheds seventy-five feet long and twenty feet wide. They stand in a row with an alley ten feet wide between each two. Each shed is divided by a partition running through the middle, making two long rooms ten feet wide. Each company occupies one room in one shed and one in the next shed across the alley.

At the head of the alley are the Captain's quarters, overlooking his whole company. The railroad runs between the camp and the river and on the other side of the railroad is the parade ground, a beautiful meadow of ninety acres. The barracks are built on a side-hill so that the upper end rests on the ground and the other is some six feet from the ground. The floor descends about seven feet in the seventy-five, making quite a slope. The tables are wide boards hung on hinges to the side of the wall. We are to sleep on the bare floor. We have just the best of spring water and it tastes good after drinking the nasty river water which we had so long in Pittsburgh.

There is a large orchard in camp and a grove of beautiful shade trees. A little brook runs through a shady hollow down on one side, and every one seems delighted at the change from the foul, dirty camp to this beautiful place.

But we are not to stay here long. Colonel McLane received a dispatch from Washington yesterday, saying that we were accepted by the Government, and were to be mustered into the United States service immediately, those who are willing for three years and the others for three months from this time, those who will not enlist for three months to be sent home. I shall not enlist for three years now. I will wait till my three months are up. We are to be uniformed and equipped immediately. We expect to be ordered to Western Virginia or Harper's Ferry, though, for good reasons, we are not told where we are going.

A large amount of cartridges were sent off from the arsenal Thursday night, and troops are moving south from all directions, showing that something is to be done and that soon, too. Perhaps the war movements will not be so interesting to you, so I will tell you of a visit I paid to a glass factory yesterday. I never was in one before and it was quite a sight to me. A dozen or more great furnaces were filled with boiling glass, and a boy would run up and stick in a long rod, give it a turn and take out a dumpling of the red-hot liquid and hold it over an iron die, when another would cut it off with a pair of shears and bring down a lever on it, pressing it into a mold, and then pull it back and turn out a beautiful salt-cellar or sugar-bowl like yours, or a tumbler, a lamp, a sauce-dish, or whatever the mold happened to be. At another place they were blowing bottles and glass jars, such as they have to hold candy in shop windows. A man takes a hollow rod, runs it in the furnace and brings out a little wad of glass, then blows it a little and it swells out just like a bubble. He then whirls it over his head a few times and blows a little more, rolls it round on an iron plate to make it round, clips it off with a pair of shears, and another man stabs a fork into the bottom of it, and heating it, passes it to another who shapes the neck and mouth. They would make twenty in the time it takes me to tell you how they make one. One of the workmen kindly handed me his pipe and told me to blow a bottle. I did, two or three of them, and blew some glass bubbles, a piece of one of which I send to you. I think you never saw thinner glass, at least I never did.

While I was down to the river yesterday, I saw a curiosity—a tree growing downwards. The roots were in the top of the river bank, and the trunk hung right down and the branches curved upward.

Camp Wright, Hulton, Penn.,
Sunday, June 9, 1861.

Dear Sister L.:—

I wish you could just step in and see us here, say on a dress parade. We are in just as beautiful a place as I ever saw. The lovely Alleghany rolls along at the foot of the hill, and the little country seats nestled in quiet nooks, the new buildings in camp, the groves and orchards, the lane that leads to the river, and the beautiful mountain rising up on the other side of the river, make a picture I never saw equalled.

I wrote to H. yesterday that we were accepted and were to be mustered in immediately. The Colonel received a telegram last night from the Secretary of War, saying that we would be taken for three years, unless sooner discharged, or we would be sent home. That you see materially alters the case. I don't know how it will work. Some whole companies say that they will not go. We shall know in a day or two. I hardly know what to do. It seems a long time to live such a life, but if I am needed, I must go. If our company goes as a company, I shall go too. If not, you may look for me home soon.

I just wish I could have seen you last night instead of reading your letter. I thought perhaps you were having a good time about the time I was reading that letter. I sincerely hope the choice you have made is a good one. Give my respects to C and tell him. I think, as matters stand, the sooner he and I become acquainted the better. I would like to have him write to me.

I think from what you write, that vegetation must be more advanced here than there. Potatoes and corn are six inches high, and clover in bloom. I saw strawberries and cherries in market yesterday.

H. B. wrote the other day that his folks had adopted a daughter about fifteen years old, and that L. C. was a secessionist. He had a big fuss with the boys who put up a Union flag near his house, threatened the life of some, sued others, and was bound over himself to appear at court to answer for his rabid conduct.

Well, I must stop. I hope you will not wait so long before writing again. I am so anxious to hear from you often. If there is anything you expected to see, that is omitted, you may hear it in the future. My address is Camp Wright, Pittsburgh.

Camp Wright, Hulton, Penn.,
Saturday, June 15, 1861.

Dear Father:—

Our camp this week has been the scene of a good deal of confusion and uneasiness. I clip an extract from this morning's Dispatch that explains the cause.

We have been told by some officers that "We were accepted; we were going to Chambersburg; we were not accepted; we were accepted for three years; those who would not enlist for the war would be sent home; they would be kept here till their three months expires; that Companies A, B, C, F and I only, would go for the war, and the rest would be disbanded," and within ten minutes Major Schlaudecker has told me "that none of the companies would go; that we would all go together, one way or the other."

Acting on the statement that our company would not go, I went this morning and put my name on Company B's roll for the war. Our Captain said "No man should leave his company till it was disbanded." The Colonel said "Any man who chose could enlist in any company in the regiment to go for the war, Captains notwithstanding." "Father said I might and mother said I shouldn't," and I concluded I would do as I was a mind to.

The statement that the companies could not be filled in time to report according to orders, is probably the true one, and so that performance will not amount to much.

Such a feeling pervades the minds of the soldiers that discipline is played out. Company K refused to turn out to roll call the other morning, and day before yesterday, not a man of them appeared on dress parade. Company F would not come out on parade yesterday.

Night before last a row broke out in a beer saloon near the depot and some of the Pittsburgh boys cleaned out the whole thing, broke in the doors and windows, smashed up the glass and furniture. A crowd collected and Colonel Grant was obliged to call out Companies B, G and I with their guns to disperse them. Company G charged down the road and across the railroad track through the thickest of them. They made quite a determined stand on the track, and some six or eight were wounded before they would leave. A man stood before me and I called to him twice to stand back. He did not move and I ran my bayonet into his side an inch or so. He started then. He was awful mad. The wound was not a serious one, only a flesh wound, but he swears he will shoot the man who stabbed him. He has been hanging round our quarters with a revolver several times lately, and pointed out a man who, he says, stabbed him, but he has got the wrong man. I think I am safe enough unless some one peaches. Only three or four in our company know who it was. M. W. Goold pricked one man, Godfrey, Wheeler and others pricked some, but none were seriously hurt. I have carried a revolver for a day or so, and I think I am all right.

The way we have been treated is enough to make a

preacher swear, almost. We are cheated in our rations about half the time. Our clothes are all dropping off from us. We don't know whether we are accepted or not, or that we will ever get any pay.

We have been practicing at target shooting lately. Our guns beat everything I ever saw to shoot. The balls are very heavy, eleven to the pound. We were shooting at "Old Jeff" yesterday, at forty rods, and over half the boys hit him. We broke his back, legs, arms, and knocked his teeth out. This morning, since I commenced writing, nineteen of us have been shooting at a target at twelve rods. Thirteen balls struck the board, nine inside the ring and four hit the center. I call that good shooting. I, of course, am not among the best, though I hit inside the ring. One ball went plumb through an oak tree, nine inches in diameter.

The orders this morning are that we must commence drilling again, and have every man attending to his duties or lying in the guard house.

I hope you will write as often as you can. It seems to me my letters are like "angels' visits." My health is excellent. It never was better. I am in the river every day. The river is about one hundred rods wide here, with a swift current. I rolled up in my blanket the other night and slept under an apple tree. I slept first-rate, did not wake till reveille, nor take the least cold. The boys are all getting considerably copper-colored in the hot sun. The weather is warm and dry. The Dispatch says the thermometer stood at 102 yesterday at noon.

P. S.—At 12 m. It is definitely settled now that we are to stay in the State service the remainder of the three months. No companies will leave the regiment. According to past experience, we expect this changed in a couple of hours.

Camp Wright, Hulton, Penn.,
Saturday, June 22, 1861.

Dear Mother:—

None of the boys have had any letters for a week. At last they begin to come and all bring news, "we heard you were coming home." Well, the origin of that story was this: Colonel McLane received orders to start for Harrisburg, where his regiment would be sworn in for three years. A vote was taken and not over half the men would enlist for that time, and it was reported that the remainder would be sent home, and the regiment filled from other companies in camp. As usual, the order was countermanded, and we are here yet.

Yesterday a dispatch was received saying we were to be armed and

Sunday morning, 23d.

I had got as far as that yesterday when I was stopped by the cry, "Fall in, marching orders are received, we're off by the first train," etc. I put away my writing, seized my gun, and was in the ranks in a short time. The cannon was booming out our joy, and amid the wildest cheers we marched to the guard house and reported to the "Officer of the day," who said the orders were to have everything packed and ready to leave by 2 o'clock. We returned to our quarters and commenced packing, when, as usual, the orders were countermanded. General McCall telegraphed, "Hold on, don't start till further orders." The further orders have not come yet. Here we are at 11 a. m., to-day, and three companies are detailed for guards, Companies E, F and K, showing that we will not leave to-day.

We are ordered to Harrisburg to receive uniforms and equipments, and we expect to go from there to Western Virginia.

That is the fourth time we have had marching orders countermanded. Colonel McLane telegraphed to Harrisburg that he should start for Harrisburg or Erie on Monday. If his regiment was not ordered off he would take them home. The arms were distributed to the regiment a few days ago, and we are having the most severe drill. The thermometer stands in the neighborhood of 100 most of the time and they take us out about two hours at a time and keep us marching till the sweat pours off in streams.

I think this severe drilling shows that we are to see

service soon, though when or where, we cannot tell. A soldier is a mere machine and has no business to know anything except his duty. His officers take care that he does not.

Camp Wright, Hulton, Penn.,
Thursday, June 27, 1861.

Dear Brother E. :—

We've had pretty spicy times in camp for a week or ten days. Marching orders are given and immediately countermanded. It's pack up, then unpack and make fun of it. One of the boys stuck up a picture—a courier driving at the top of his speed, shouting, "Hurrah! Marching orders;" and another following hard after, calling out, "Hold on, blast ye; they're countermanded." They call it, "The Erie boys' experience," and it is a pretty good hit.

The boys resort to all sorts of expedients to kill time. A good many of them are making clam-shell rings. It requires a good deal of work to make one, but they are the prettiest rings I ever saw. Some of them look like pearl, some are blue and some like carnelian. They take a high polish.

One of the Wildcats had a mud-turtle yesterday. He made a little *secesh* flag and tied it to his hind flipper and made him *trabble* with it, dragging it round in the dust. It made some sport.

The Armstrong Rifles had a veritable secession flag, hanging bottom side up, on their quarters, yesterday. It was captured at Philippi and sent up here. It was made of muslin, three stripes and seven stars, tin ones at that, an elegant thing.

I spend a good deal of time in the river. I am improving some in swimming. Swam across the other day at the widest place in sight. Some of our company found the body of a man in the river the other day. He appeared to have been in the water a long time. He was standing erect with his feet firmly bedded in the bottom, and his head about two feet under water. One of the feet broke off in pulling him up.

Well, I must stop. I do not know as there is anything in reach worth sending you as a curiosity. If I find anything, however, I will remember you.

Don't fail to write again soon. I think your last is the best letter I ever saw of yours. Write often and you will improve. Direct to Camp Wright, Hulton, care of Captain D. W. Hutchinson.

Camp Wright, Hulton, Penn.,
Thursday, June 27, 1861.

Dear Father:—

One of the items of interest in the editor's visit to Colonel McLane yesterday, is found in the Gazette of this morning, viz.: that throughout the whole day (yesterday) no marching orders or countermands were received. For a week or ten days the camp has been in a feverish state of excitement. First came the orders to distribute the arms and hold in readiness to march. The arms were distributed and then came the orders to start for Harrisburg, then the countermand—"Hold on, wait for further orders." Next day, "Grant no more furloughs, drill fast, you will be called soon." The orders stopped here and we "drilled fast" for two or three days, anxiously waiting for the "soon." It did not come, but, in its place, it was announced on Monday that the Governor was not dead, as before reported, only dead drunk, and that he and his aide would be here on Tuesday to dispose finally of the Erie Regiment, either order us to Harrisburg or home. Well, Tuesday came and the Governor didn't, so he was announced to come on Wednesday. Wednesday came and the Governor didn't, and it was then announced that the whole thing was a canard, started just to keep the boys quiet.

Some of the boys got a great demijohn and paraded round the camp with it, labeled in staring capitals, "The Governor's Aide."

Company E had a comic picture sent up from New York, representing a very *milingtary* man with a fierce mustache. When turned upside down, it was a complete jackass. That is just about our situation. No one knows what will be done with us. I think we will be kept here the rest of our time and then sent home with our clothes worn out, and no pay to buy more with. They will hardly uniform and equip us and send us into the field for three or four weeks.

Pay no heed whatever to the letters and telegrams saying we are coming home, but continue to write to us till you see us at home. A couple of wagon-loads of dead letters would be nothing compared to our uneasiness without letters from home.

Camp Wright, Hulton, Penn.,
Sunday, June 30, 1861.

Dear Sister L.:—

Major General McCall was here on Friday and organized two new regiments for the war. There are now in this camp and Camp Wilkins about five thousand men. We had a review of all the troops in this camp Friday afternoon. The General expressed himself well pleased with our appearance.

Last night our regiment was drawn up in line of battle and we had a game of—charge bayonet. We are all armed now, you know, and, at the word, the bristling points came down and we started across the plain. We kept close together in good line till we almost reached the enemy (a crowd of spectators, unarmed women and children) when they fired a volley of screams at us and turned and fled. We broke ranks and pursued them, but as they seemed to get the better of us, we gave up the pursuit and fell into line. We received a lecture for breaking ranks and then faced about and charged again, this time in first-rate order. We tried it two or three times, succeeding very well, and then came the tug of war. A crowd of spectators had gathered on the back side of the field towards the river. Colonel Grant saw we wanted some fun and he drew us up in front of their terrible battery of laughter. We moved on steadily till the command, "Double quick;" "Clear the field." Our Captain, who is not over nice in choice of words, sprang forward and sang out, "Forward boys, give 'em h—l." Oh, what a scene! Every man did his best to outrun the rest, and with the wildest whoops we brought up at the fence in a cloud of dust and the field was cleared. The "Charge of the Light Brigade" was nothing in comparison to that. We had but few mishaps. E. A. S. (the Reverend) lost one of his pearly false teeth and had to stop to find it, and Jack W. fell down and ran his bayonet into the ground.

We have got out of ball-cartridges and are practicing in skirmishing with blank-cartridges. You would laugh to see us fall flat on our faces and fire a volley and then roll over on our backs and load. We do this, however, and it is not so difficult as it might seem. Of course, we are not so liable to be hit by balls when lying on our backs. We just rise, so as to support the gun on our elbows, fire, and fall flat again, then tumble on the back and slide the gun down till the butt rests on the ground between the heels, and the muzzle is right over the face where a cartridge can be put in and sent home very easily. Company I is very expert in this. They will be running on double quick, and at the word, fall, fire and load in half a minute.

I have heard of no arrangements for the Fourth yet. Colonel McLane has gone to Erie, and some say he expects to have us there on the Fourth, but I think that's all camp talk. The paymaster is to be here and pay off Colonel Hay's and Colonel Jackson's regiments this week. Some say he will pay us, but I guess all we will get won't make us rich.

We have had considerable excitement in our company lately in regard to the conduct of our officers. It is ascertained that they are cheating us in a rascally manner. Each company is allowed seventy-seven rations per day for the privates and non-commissioned officers and musicians, and each commissioned officer is allowed four rations per day. Properly cooked and distributed one ration is all a man can eat and it almost always happens that some of the company are absent, and the law says, "That, if anything is saved from their rations the company may sell it and raise a company fund." In this way Company B has now a fund of $200. Well, our three officers, instead of drawing their own rations, have boarded themselves and servant, all this time, out of ours, thus keeping us half the time without enough to eat, and depriving us of selling any extra allowance when we have it. A ration is valued at thirty cents, and by this course, each one of the officers saves $1.20 per day, besides a ration for his servant, making $1.50 per day, amounting to the nice little sum of $45 per month for each one. Not content with this they go a little deeper. A rich old farmer named Black sent nine dozen of eggs and several pounds of butter marked especially for the privates of Company G. Not a private in the company got an egg, and only a little of the butter. Now I call that decidedly mean. Officers who are making $150 to $200 a month must cabbage the $11 privates' present. M. H. Goold gave the Captain a pretty good thrust about it yesterday. The Captain said he thought our talk about that had better stop, he was getting disgusted with it. Goold told him he thought the Captain was not more disgusted with it than the rest of us, or had more reason to be. The boys of Girard say they have not had a cent of the money that was put into the officers' hands for them and cannot get postage stamps of them without paying ten cents for three. I can't tell what has become of all the money for the Springfield boys. There are not more than thirty in the company and $150 would make $5 apiece, and I can't find one who says he has had a dollar. I have had twenty-five cents and seven stamps. What has become of the money? Any talk like that makes the officers d—n us up hill and down. There will be some talk about it though, if we ever get back to Girard. I must close. I hope you will write soon.

Camp Wright, Hulton, Penn.,
July 14, 1861.

Dear Sister L.:—

I spent the morning of the Fourth in writing letters. In the afternoon Colonel Grant read the Declaration of Independence, and Captain Porter delivered an oration to the soldiers and citizens in a neighboring grove, after which we had a review of the four regiments and a dress parade and adjourned.

Since the Fourth, there has been considerable excitement in reference to our pay. Orders to pay and countermands have been received in quick succession. Seven different days have been set, on which we were to receive our $17.23, which, probably is all we will ever get. Payment is now postponed to Tuesday. Our time, as made out on the pay-roll, closes one week from to-day (the 21st), but I doubt our getting home before the 1st of August.

The latest reliable news is that we are neither in the United States or State service, nor ever have been, and that we will all have to be mustered in for three months before we can draw a cent of pay. This will be done to-morrow.

The Erie Regiment is one grand fizzle out. We left home full of fight, earnestly desiring a chance to mingle with the hosts that fight under the Stars and Stripes. For two months we drilled steadily, patiently waiting the expected orders which never came but to be countermanded. We have now come to the conclusion that we will have no chance, and we are waiting in sullen silence and impatience for the expiration of our time. The State of Pennsylvania cannot furnish a better regiment than ours, and yet, where is it?

I try to look beyond this abuse and see a glorious government that must be sustained, and I feel as ready to enlist for the war to-day as I did on the 26th of April. I have written H. B. to find out what inducements there are to join his company. I would like to go back to old Ararat again and go in with him and D. T. I think if they raise any company there at all, it will be a sterling good one.

I am glad you write so much news when you write. Father's letters are just like newspaper articles. If any letters come there for me, please send them with the least possible delay.

Camp Corcoran, Arlington Heights, Va.,
Monday, Sept. 30, 1861.

Dear Sister L.:—

My soldiering now is not play, it is work. The last time I wrote you we were in Camp Casey, above Washington. Last Saturday afternoon we received orders to strike tents and be ready to march. We were ready in half an hour, and at sunset we started, no one knew where. We went down through the city, past the Capitol, and across the Long Bridge, and set our feet on the sacred soil of the "Mother of Presidents." After marching about eight miles, we halted on a piece of rough ground, evidently a pasture, stacked our guns and lay down to rest. We were hungry, but we had nothing to eat. D., H. and I had each a blanket. We spread one down and the other to cover us and tried to sleep, but it was so cold we could not sleep much. The dew wetted our blankets both through, and H. was almost sick, so we had rather a sorry night. I rose about 4 o'clock and stood by the guard fire till reveille, drying our blankets. Half an hour after sunrise we marched about half a mile to our present camp. We pitched our tents and had our dinner of bread and raw pork at noon. I could not eat raw pork and dry bread at home, but a fast of twenty-four hours, a ten-mile march, and a bivouac at night sharpens the appetite wonderfully. At night we got things arranged, and had a good supper. Our rations are of the best quality, except our salt beef, which is not sweet.

Now for our camp. We are on Arlington Heights, about four miles southwest of the Capitol. The Heights are ranges of hills running parallel with the river and overlooking the city. Fort Corcoran is about twenty rods from our camp, and another fort on the other side. As far as I can see in every direction, the white tents of our enemy dot every hilltop. The rebel camps are within two miles of us, their pickets and ours shooting each other every night.

Our whole regiment has been changed from light infantry to a rifle regiment. We are to have the short Minie rifle with sword bayonet. Our drill is changed entirely, but I am learning it very fast. The whole regiment is doing its best with the hope of soon meeting the enemy. We are drilling with old altered flintlocks.

As I came out of my tent yesterday morning, what was my astonishment to see the Reverend Mr. Reed of Pittsburgh standing before me in uniform. I looked at him and could hardly recognize him, but there was no mistake. He is the chaplain of Governor Black's regiment, twelve hundred strong. He said his regiment had gone to make a reconnoissance beyond Munson's Hill—that great fortification was taken without firing a gun, and a lot of wooden guns ingeniously painted showed how they were armed.

Regiments are moving every night, and though we are ignorant of what is to be done, the universal impression is that a great battle is on the tapis.

2 P. M. We have orders to be in readiness to march at a moment's notice. Forty rounds of cartridges are distributed. Lowe's balloon is in our camp. I would write more but must stop for want of time.

Address O. W. N., care Captain T. M. Austin, McLane's Regiment, Camp Corcoran, Washington, D. C.

Camp Leslie, near Falls Church,
Fairfax County, Va., Oct. 4th, 1861.

Dear Friends at Home:—

I last wrote from Camp Corcoran and once before from Camp Casey, and you see by date we have moved again. The Colonel here presented us to McClellan as a well drilled regiment and asked the privilege of taking a position in the advance, which, I suppose, is granted. You have read of the taking of Hall's Hill, in the late papers. Our camp is right there on the scene of the skirmish. Falls Church lies at the foot of the hill, to the southwest. We came here Wednesday last from Fort Corcoran. Munson's, of which we have all heard so much, is two miles to our left on the southeast. Mr. Reed is with his regiment on the same hill; the rebel pickets are about a mile from Falls Church, so you see we are not far from them.

My time is so limited that you must not wait for me to answer each letter individually, but I must write to all at once and hope each will write in return. I did not think you had forgotten me, but I have been five weeks from home and not a letter till to-day. I have been anxious to hear, full as much so as you, I presume. I hope you will write very often. The last letter I sent I did not pay the postage, because I could not. We can get no stamps here, and no one will take charge of postage not in stamps, so the letters have to be franked by the Major and sent on. I wish you could send a few stamps. My money is all gone, and although pay is due us now, I can't tell when we will get it.

General McClellan and his staff, General McDowell, General Porter, Prince de Joinville, Duc de Chartres and other notables visited us last night. They stayed only a short time. I heard McClellan remark as he rode up, "There, those boys haven't got their pants yet. That's a shame."

H. and I were selected as two of twenty from the regiment to go forward and lay out this camp. Lieutenant Wilson commanded. We lost our way and went some two or three miles to the right and beyond our camps, finally coming out right. The timber here is mostly small, scrub oaks, etc. In the woods near us we found any quantity of grapes and chinquapins (a small nut in a burr like a chestnut and tasting much like it). Chestnuts are ripe and plenty.

We are in Secessia and the meanest part of it, too, and anything the boys can forage they consider as theirs. A field of potatoes, five acres, was emptied of its contents in short order. H. and I got enough for a mess, and some parsnips. You ought to see us clean out the fences. The rails answer first-rate to boil our rations, and they have to do it. The country between here and Washington is in a sorry condition, the fences all burnt up, the houses deserted, the crops annihilated, and everything showing the footprints of war.

Virginia has acted meaner than South Carolina even, and I go for teaching her a lesson that she will remember. It will take years to recover from this blow.

We are very severely drilled and are improving fast. We are ordered to shoot any one who does not halt on being three times ordered to do so. I was on last night, and in four hours I think I challenged over fifty men. Our officers take every way to prove and try us, to accustom us to tricks, I suppose.

You need not envy us much our vegetables. They seem to be a failure. Our cooks don't know how to cook them and no one likes them. Persimmons are ripening now and they are delicious. . . .

Direct care Captain A., Colonel J. W. McLane's Regiment, Camp Leslie, Washington, D. C. . . .

Camp Leslie, near Falls Church,
Fairfax County, Va., Oct. 8, 1861.

Friend P—s.:—

In accordance with your expressed desire and my own promise, I have commenced writing to you. I intended to have written before, but an aversion to writing at all, which I have acquired in camp, is my only excuse. The inconveniences, or the total want of all conveniences, makes letter-writing in camp a very different thing from the same at home. If you find my letter written with a pencil, my paper soiled, my pencilmanship execrable, and the whole thing miserable, please don't set me down as one who knows no better or cares for nothing better, but excuse me as the victim of circumstances.

You will see by the date that I am in the advance army. Our Colonel has recommended us to General McClellan as a well drilled regiment, and we have been assigned the honorable position we now occupy. We reached Washington on Thursday evening, September 19th, and encamped on Meridian Hill, on the north side of the city, staying there long enough to get our arms, equipments and part of our uniforms, and see some of the lions (the Capitol, Patent Office, Arsenal, Old Abe and family, etc.), and then we crossed the Long Bridge and set foot on the "sacred soil"; the soil may be sacred, but we sacrilegious Yankees can't help observing that it is awfully deficient in manure. It is so poor that buckwheat or beans won't grow more than an inch high, and pennyroyal just sticks out.

We camped a few days near Fort Corcoran, on Arlington Heights, and then moved on to our present position. We are on Hall's Hill, lately the line of the rebel pickets. We are in sight of Falls Church and the rebels are just beyond in some force. We expect to move down there this week, when they will have to fight or leave. They will probably choose the latter.

You probably read in the papers so much of the details of camp life that I won't bore you by any lengthy description. Our regiment, I suppose, lives as all others do. Five of us sleep in a tent six feet by seven and keep our arms and accoutrements, too, in it. Our cooking is done in the open air, by swinging our camp kettles on poles over the fire. We live on salt beef, bacon, hard bread and beans.

Oct. 9th. I commenced writing yesterday, but was obliged to stop to attend drill, a very common incident in soldier life. The first thing in the morning is drill, then drill, then drill again. Then drill, drill, a little more drill. Then drill, and lastly, drill. Between drills, we drill, and sometimes stop to eat a little and have a roll-call.

General McClellan and staff, the Prince de Joinville, Duc de Chartres, General McDowell and other notables visited us the other afternoon. This morning eight of our company went out on picket. I expect to go to-morrow. We look on it as an honor to be selected for pickets. I saw a flake of snow this morning. Night before last we had a tremendous storm, a heavy shower accompanied by hail and a furious wind. Many tents were blown flat, our Lieutenant's among the number. We saved ours by holding it down, but were almost flooded out with the water. A baggage wagon, weighing nearly a ton, was lifted clear from the ground, and blown with its four horses some ten or twelve rods into the marsh. Our First Lieutenant was blown as much as twenty rods down into the edge of the wood before he could stop.

We are soldiering in earnest now. No Camp Wright work. I like it much better, and our men drill a great deal better when they feel that they are so near the enemy and see the need of improving their time.

I have had only one letter from home since I left. I am expecting one now, and have been for some time.

I do not think there will be any great battle here very soon, though I have no means of knowing to a certainty.

Camp Leslie, Hall's Hill,
Fairfax County, Va., Oct. 26, 1861.

Friend P—s. :—

To-day has been a great day with us. General McClellan and staff reviewed General Porter's Division, of which we form a part. Five brigades were reviewed. We are attached to General Butterfield's Brigade. Our regiment was very highly complimented by the General, as one of the best, if not the best, on the field. We had a sham battle, an exciting time.

My health is still good. I feel the effects of severe drill some. It is as much as I can stand, but, while many are getting sick, I am all right yet. One poor fellow in our regiment died last night. The first one that has died since we left home.

Many seem to think that this war is soon to close. I am fully satisfied, however, that it cannot be ended without the emancipation proclamation, and I think that will be made next winter. I am in for thorough work while we're at it, but I shudder for the results of the continuance of the war.

To-morrow we do guard duty. It is tiresome work. No sleep nights. Almost every time some fun occurs to relieve the monotony. An Irishman challenged a party the other night with, "Halt! Who goes there?" Ans.—"Grand rounds." "Och, to the divil wid yez grand rounds; I thought it was the relafe guard."

Camp Leslie, Hall's Hill,
Fairfax County, Va., Oct. 27, 1861.

Dear Sister L. :—

It is a beautiful Sabbath morning and I am on guard. I suppose you are now at church, but have you thought of me this morning and wondered where I was and what I was doing, whether I was well or sick, and how long since I heard from you, and when you meant to write to me again?

Have you thought that I have been gone from home just two months, and, in that time, I have had just one letter from you? Have those two months seemed long or short to you? Have you missed my society at all in that time? Have you known how close I am to the rebel rifles, and how many times I have been ordered to be ready to go at a moment's notice, and how many nights I have slept on my gun with my equipments buckled on, to be ready to fall in instantly? Have you thought of my standing guard at night in the rain when my clothes were soaked and my shoes full of water, and so tired I dare not stop walking lest I should fall asleep, which would be certain death? That is the way I live, and do you think I would like to hear from you often? You used to write when I was in Camp Wright, but lately I get no more letters. I don't know why. Can it be that you have to write so many letters to C. that you have no time to write to me? I am not jealous, but it seems to me that there might be room enough in your heart for a little love for me, if you do love him very much. There, I won't write in that strain any more. I know you will write, and often, too. And you want to hear from me, but what shall I write?

We are right here in the same camp that we have occupied for the last month nearly. We have received marching orders every three or four days, but they are always countermanded before we start. We are drilling very severely almost all the time. Two hours every morning with our knapsacks on, which is very hard work, and the rest of the day is mostly spent in battalion and brigade drill. Every time we go out we have some twenty or twenty-five pounds weight to carry, and carrying it so long is no boy's play.

I have not been sick but one day. I felt dizzy then and left the ranks. I was threatened with a fever, but I used a little cold water and drove it off. I am growing poor, I can't deny that, but still I am bony and tough. Many much larger men are giving out, while the small and slight ones endure best. H. is complaining considerable of the time. If he should live at home with his mother till he was gray, he would never be anything but a baby, but I guess we will break him of his notions here, partially, at least. He gets a letter almost every day, and isn't satisfied then. D. is tolerably well, though he and H., too, are troubled some with the prevailing disorder in camp, diarrhea. I am case-hardened; that don't affect me in the least. I can eat salt horse and wormy crackers and drink swamp water with impunity, the only fault being it don't give strength enough for our severe exercise. We expect our pay the 1st of November, which will be soon now.

Yesterday we had a grand review. General McClellan and staff reviewed General Porter's division, of which we form a part. Some eighteen regiments were present, besides several companies of artillery. We had breakfast at light, and had nothing to eat again until 4 p. m., and most of the time we were exercising pretty hard. I cannot tell you much about the parade, as the description would necessarily include many military terms which you would not understand. The troops were drawn up in three long lines and the artillery at one end of the lines. Each line wheeled into column and marched round in front and passed the general once in quick and once in double quick time, and the general and his staff rode along in front of, and in the rear of each line, each band playing as he passed its respective regiment. The review closed with a sham battle on one side. Our regiment was very highly complimented by the general, who said it was one of the best, if not the very best, on the whole field.

Everything is done with the strictest discipline. I cannot go to my quarters to-day or to-night without leave of the officer of the guard, nor can I take off a single article of clothing, but I must be here at the guard tents ready to fall in any time.

Camp of the 83rd Regiment, Penn. Volunteers,
Hall's Hill, Va., Nov. 13, 1861.

Dear Sister L.:—

I have been sorry many times since that I wrote in the strain I did in my last letter, because I see by yours that it caused you pain. I ought not to have written so, I know, but that morning I sat down and wrote just as I felt. I could not help it. The fact is, most of the boys, when they write home, write in as cheerful a strain as possible, knowing that their friends will magnify all their news that is at all unfavorable and dwell on their hardships, when it can do no good. I did not think that you had forgotten me and have not at any time, but I wanted to have you write.

You will see by my letter to Mother that we have been busy lately. We have drilled a great deal, and when I come in from drill I feel so tired it seems as though I could not think clearly enough to sit down and write. We have achieved a great victory in a peaceful way, and I expect the consequence will be that we will be ordered south. If the southern expedition is successful it will probably be followed by sending an army south to follow up its success by ours, and a good many of the troops here will be sent off there, and we among the number. I shall be glad of that. I would rather go further south than to winter here. It has not been very cold here yet. To-day is uncomfortably warm. We are having some beautiful weather, Indian summer days, and clear, moonlight nights.

Our last Sunday on guard we had a good time. One of the guards down by the woods heard a noise like some one coming through the bushes. He challenged, "Halt! Who goes there?" No answer. "Halt!" again. He did not stop, and after challenging again, he raised his gun and fired at the noise. The report rang all over camp, and there was a crowd there soon. An awful squeal greeted his ears immediately after his fire and the guards soon found the *secesh* to be a great hog that was wandering round in the woods. He was not killed, but his countenance was awfully disfigured. He squealed his best till another load through his head stopped his noise.

Three of us rigged ourselves out in our most horrible shape the other night when we got the countersign, and went over to the Michigan regiment. We approached the sentinel, when he halted us and demanded. "Who goes there?" I replied in a theatrical voice, "The devil with the countersign." The poor fellow was some dashed, but he finally recovered and replied, "Advance, one devil, and give the countersign. The countersign's correct. Pass devils." To the next challenge I replied. "A flock of sheep." The guard was up to time then and immediately replied, "Advance, old buck, and give the countersign." We made quite a round and had a lot of fun and came back with something to laugh over. One poor fellow shot off his middle finger the other night. He will have a sore time of it.

Camp of the 83rd Penn. Volunteers,
Hall's Hill, Va., Friday, Nov. 15, 1861.

Dear Friend P—s:—

We are still rusticating in the same camp where we have been since the first of October. There have been no movements of importance in this part of the army since then. The troops have been employed very busily in the meantime in perfecting themselves in all the duties of the soldier. Our regiment has earned the reputation of being the best in General Porter's division. A suit of fancy uniforms (Zouave) was lately presented to General P. with instructions to give it to the best drilled regiment in his division. A committee was appointed from General McClellan's staff who were to award the prize at a review of the division. Last Friday the trial came off. The weather was rainy and every way unfavorable, but some fifteen or twenty thousand troops were on the ground to compete for the prize. General McClellan said he was highly gratified with the discipline of the troops. He never saw better movements in his life. The committee were unanimous in awarding the uniform to the 83rd Regiment, Pennsylvania Volunteers. What do you think of that? It is no small thing for a new regiment to beat a number of regiments that have been in the field all summer, and the farfamed "Ellsworth Avengers," but we have done it. We have earned a good reputation and we mean to keep it. We are now to have the post of honor and of danger—that of rifle skirmishers to be thrown out in advance of the army in action. It is expected by many that we will be sent south soon, to follow up the successes of the naval expedition by more and greater victories. At last our government has begun to show its hand and a policy to work with vigor. The papers teem with our victories in small battles, and the rebels are beginning to see that we have a government yet.

a fact that they will find to their cost before we are done with them.

Camp of the 83rd P. V.,
Hall's Hill, Va., Dec. 4, 1861.

Dear Sister L.:—

I have just returned from picket. Monday morning six companies of us started for the picket lines. Each carried his knapsack packed, with overcoat on top, haversack with two days' provisions, canteen of water, cartridge box with forty rounds and the ever present gun, in all about fifty pounds. We set out at a pace of about four miles an hour, over hills, down through the woods, passing the charred ruins of Major Nutt's residence (once a splendid establishment, but now burned to the ground), across the railroad, and we reached Falls Church. This is a small Virginia village. A few good looking houses, one church, and one store, a one-story building with the glass half broken out, and three apples, two cakes and one paper of tobacco on the window sill, seemed to be the stock in trade. A charcoal sign "STORE" over the door was all that would lead any one to suppose it was a mercantile establishment. We struck the Leesburg turnpike here, and followed it about two miles. We stopped at a *secesh* house. This is the first time I have been an actual picket, and as it may be interesting I will give you a short description of what we saw and did. The house I spoke of is owned, or was, by a man in the rebel army. The only occupant was an old negro slave. He was closely guarded by our men. I do not know why, but I suppose to prevent his master from getting any information from him. We were here divided into reliefs and placed on our posts. These are little huts made of rails and covered with brush and leaves. During the day we kept concealed as much as possible, keeping a sharp lookout for the enemy, and at night we patrolled our beats, challenging every one who approached and demanding the mystic word that none but a friend can have. Last night the countersign was "Palo Alto," the night before "Lodi." After staying on post two hours, another relief takes our place and we return to headquarters.

Mr. Secesh had a large pile of brick, evidently designed to build him a house. We wanted to keep warm, so we pitched into the pile and built a lot of furnaces. We put in considerable fence and made good fires, and then took possession of a stack of wheat and made us good beds and slept well. We dug *secesh* potatoes to roast and popped *secesh* corn and pulled *secesh* cabbage. We don't care much for their *phelinks* when we get out of camp and into a rebel's potato-field.

I went out yesterday to get something to eat. I stopped at a house near the railroad. A respectable colored woman with her family seemed to be the only occupants. She said she had some pies and cakes, and set out some for me. While eating I entered into conversation with her. She told me that she and her children (a bright looking group of five) were all slaves, and her master in the rebel army. Her husband was hired to the rebels as teamster and escaped at the battle of Bull Run and is now in the north. I asked her if she did not want to escape. She said she did and would have done so long ago, but for her children. One was a babe and the eldest only nine. She will be after him yet. I was much interested in her, so earnest and deep, she seemed intelligent and understood well the causes of the war. I need not say, she was not *secesh*.

I wrote to E. last Saturday and told him we had not got our uniforms yet. I am happy to say that part of them have arrived, and the rest are coming as fast as the teams can bring them. I have not seen any more than I can through the broken sides of the boxes. Everything is complete—two new suits, new tents with a stove and table in each one, new knapsacks, canteens, haversacks, two pairs shoes, mess pans and a complete outfit of everything we need. This was sent to our government by a firm in France, as a sample of what they would furnish. We are anxious to have the boxes opened, and probably will see their contents at inspection next Sunday. I can then tell more about them.

Camp of the 83d P. V.,
Hall's Hill, Va., Dec. 8th, 1861.

Dear Sister L.:—

To-day (Sunday) has been a beautiful day. We had inspection this morning at 8 o'clock. At 10 I went to the colonel and got leave to go to the New York Forty-ninth. I found a number of friends that I had not seen for a long time. Nehemiah Sperry, Sherman Williams, Rollin Hart and a number from Mina that you do not know. You may blame me for going on Sunday, but remember I have no time beside when I can possibly go, and that I have not entered another camp, not even the Forty-fourth, within a rod of our own, since I have been in Virginia, and you will not be surprised.

The past week has been a week of lovely weather. Monday and Tuesday were cold, but clear, and the rest of the week has been mild and summer-like.

We have had the usual amount of drill. Governor Morgan reviewed us day before yesterday.

Our new uniforms have at last arrived. Fifteen wagons, with six mules to each, brought the last installment last night. It comes from France, even to the pins for staking the tents. We expect they will commence distributing them to-morrow. An agent of the French government is here and will fit each man with his uniform. We are not thought capable of fitting the outlandish things ourselves. He has measured all the officers and the measures are to be sent to France and exact fits made for the officers. They will arrive, he says, in less than six weeks. We are to have the most complete outfit ever seen in this country. Our tents are large enough to hold ten. A pole runs up in the center and a round table clasps right around it. We are to have folding chairs. Our knapsacks are a curious contrivance. A wooden frame is covered with calfskin with the hair on. This can be taken off the frame and used as a blanket to spread on the ground to sleep on. There are also little skirmishers' tents to be carried on the march. They can be taken apart and carried by two men, who can put them together and sleep in them anywhere. Our boys are overjoyed at their good fortune and the colonel says we will have to work hard to keep up our reputation.

We are all well in our tent. Well, I say, H. is not, either. He is suffering from a cold. I guess he will conclude the best medicine is books. It is almost time for tattoo and I must close.

Hall's Hill, Va., Dec. 19th, 1861.

Dear Sister L.:—

This has been a busy week. We've been moving into our new tents and fixing ourselves comfortable for winter. Our tents are round, with two doors that can be closed tight, and a pole in the center with two tables, one above the other on the pole. We have some twelve or fourteen in ours. We have bunks made so that we can sleep in one-half of the tent, and not sleep on the ground, either. On the other side we have a rack for our guns, a table and a stove. Think of that—a stove, a little sheet iron one, with two griddles! The stove and pipe cost four dollars. It warms up the tent, and we think it a first-rate institution.

Our new uniforms are distributed and they improve the looks of the regiment wonderfully.

Bancroft, the great historian, came to see us the other day. We donned our "baglegs" and went out with the rest of the brigade and went through with a sham battle for his amusement. Martindale's brigade was out this afternoon doing the same thing. Infantry, cavalry and artillery were doing their best. The regiment of infantry were blazing away at each other when a squadron of cavalry dashed round a piece of woods and charged down on them with the wildest yells. Then the artillery commenced firing on them (the cavalry) and they gave it up, wheeled and retreated. I was out in the woods after brush and came across the field. Quite a number of carriages were up from the city and I saw ladies watching the sport with a good deal of interest. They would start at the report of the cannons and give a nice little city scream, as ladies will.

I wish you could be here a few days to see the sights. It would do you so much good. I am getting some accustomed to the smell of powder. We go out every day target shooting, the whole regiment together. When we all get at it we make some noise. It would be quite a sight at home to see three or four hundred firing at once.

H. is in the hospital sick with the measles. He is doing first-rate, but he is so babyish that he makes a laughing-stock of himself. I do not blame him much. Such letters as he gets from home from his mother and Mary, commencing, "My very dear, absent, brave, soldier boy," or something like that, all of the "muzzer's pressus darlin'" order. He is a first-rate fellow, but I do wish he had more of the stiff upper lip and stoical bearing of the soldier. D. and myself are well. I am gaining. I weigh one hundred and thirty-five pounds.

I must tell you something about our new camp, for, though we are on the same ground, we have altered the looks of it materially. Each company's tents are in a line, and we have good wide streets between. These are all nicely graded and a trench dug round each tent and on each side of the street. Each side is set out with pine and cedar trees, and many of the tents have arches and bowers of evergreens before the doors. At the head of each street a grand arch is made with the letter of the company or some other device suspended, all made of the evergreen trees and branches. Company E, in the center, has the widest street and a little the nicest arch, as they have the colors.

Company E has two side arches, for little doors, I suppose. I tell you these embellishments make our camp look very nice, and the streets are graded so nicely, and the ground in front of our camp is worn smooth and bare, so we have a splendid parade ground for company or battalion drills.

Everything looks as though we were to winter here. We are having delightful weather. I never saw such in December. Such glorious moonlight nights. Now, don't tell, but I did wish I could be up in the land of snows long enough to have one evening's sleigh-ride, but I am content.

LETTERS OF 1862

Camp Porter, Hall's Hill, Va.,
Tuesday, Jan. 7, 1862.

Dear Sister L.:—

I had almost settled down to the conviction that we would see no fighting, that we would winter here, but at last we have a change. Orders have come that show we are to march in fighting order. We have two knapsacks. In one we pack the things we do not need, and in the other we put two blankets, a change of clothes, etc. We have orders to hold ourselves in readiness to march at ten minutes' notice. We are ready. We have our new rifles and they are splendid guns. Our regiment is drilled so that we will throw down the glove to any regiment in the service. General McClellan says we are equal in proficiency to any regulars in the army, and now he is ready. We are ready and we only wait the word go. Give McLane a chance and I feel confident the Eighty-third will be heard from. I know nothing of the plans. I am only a machine and am not expected to know anything. The papers say we are going down the river to take the batteries on the shore and outflank the rebels at the Junction. It may be so and it is just as likely to be nothing like the plan. It may be like all the alarms we have had before. But every one seems to think we are sure to go this time. H. is not well enough to do full duty, but will go as a wagon guard and have his knapsack carried.

Camp of the 83rd P. V.,
Hall's Hill, Va., Jan. 14, 1862.

Dear Friend P—s.:—

You inquire about our probable stay here in this camp. I suppose you know just as much as I do about it, or at least I know nothing and I don't believe you know any less.

We have orders to be in readiness to march at an hour's notice and have had this two weeks. Everything that we did not absolutely need on a march has been packed in our old knapsacks and sent to Georgetown. We are all ready and some think we will leave soon, but I am so skeptical that I don't believe it. I do not know as I told you that we had got our new rifles. They are the Minie, the best gun made, and our boys are very much pleased with them. We are practicing at five hundred yards almost every day and make some good shooting.

The Westfield cavalry is still on the other side of the river. I think they have not got their horses yet. Conway Ayres (you saw him at Ashville) has been over to see me. He is the adjutant. I had not heard much about their health. Since we got into our French tents we have not had much sickness. There is little sleeping on the ground, as all or nearly all have bunks made of pine poles.

We have the most changeable weather I ever saw. On Sunday the air was warm as summer, and to-day we have two inches of snow.

How am I enjoying myself? Well, as philosophically as I can. We have rather dull times, but evenings we write letters or sing, and we have started a debating society with considerable interest.

Hall's Hill, Fairfax County, Va.,
Friday eve., Jan. 17, 1862.

Dear Sister L.:—

"The long and weary months pass by" and still we camp in old Camp Porter, or, as it was called before our new tents were up, Camp Leslie.

For several days the weather has been so stormy that we have had but little drill. We have had some two inches of snow and then rain and sleet, making everything so slippery that it stopped all military operations.

You will ask what we have busied ourselves about. In the daytime we sit round the tents, reading, telling stories, grumbling about the rations, discussing the prospects of marching, cursing the English about the Mason and Slidell affair, expressing a willingness to devote our lives to humbling that proud nation, and talking of this, that and the other. Those whose tastes incline them that way are playing with the "spotted papers," but you will be glad to know that not one game of cards has been played in our tent since I lived in it, or in the old one, either, and more than that, I have not played a game since I've been in the U. S. service. I don't know as I am principled against it so much, but I don't know how to play and don't care to learn. I spend much time in writing. The boys laugh at me for writing so many letters, but I think it is as good a way of spending time as many others.

I have thought I would send you a present. Nothing less than my French comb. It is a singular thing, according to our notions, but I have no doubt it is a good one. Its value is nothing, however, except that which attaches to it as a soldier's comb and all the way from France. I don't know but some young ladies might consider it an insult for a young man to send them a fine comb. You can feel just as you please about it.

The individual, if there be any one in the army more thought of than any other, the one so long waited for by the boys with emaciated portemonnaies, has arrived. We were called to sign the pay-roll about 4 p. m. yesterday, and by midnight seven companies were paid and the rest of us by 9 o'clock this morning. That is rather quick work I call it.

I little thought when I crossed the Long Bridge last September that I would be so long here with no chance of meeting the enemy. But so it is. It seems to us very slow business, this crushing out the rebellion. I do not know but our leaders know best, but it seems to us very dull business, waiting for the rebels to be conquered by kindness. Our President is altogether too tender-hearted, too much afraid of touching the rebels in their tender spot—their niggers. General Sherman, whom he has sent to South Carolina, is such another bugaboo. He has done nothing except to land there. If Jim Lane had been sent there with permission to whip them the best he could, he would have had South Carolina used up by this time,

Charleston and Savannah in our possession and a good foothold for our forces. But no, it would not do to go to work so. This is not a war against slavery, but for the Union. We must preserve the Union, but not touch slavery. Away with such nonsense, I say, and the soldiers all say so. Give us a haul-in-sweep of their niggers, their houses, towns, and everything, only conquer them quickly.

Camp Porter, Va., Jan. 28, 1862.

Dear Cousin L. :—

I returned from the picket lines yesterday and found your pleasant letter of the 24th awaiting me. If you were in Camp Porter about 5 p. m. when that plastic individual that the boys call "Putty" arrives with the daily mail, and could see the interest with which his proceedings are watched as he distributes the spoils, your fears of burdening me with an extensive correspondence would soon vanish. I never thought so much of letters as I have since I have been here. The monotony of camp life would be almost intolerable were it not for these friendly letters. We do not expect much news, but they are like the delightful small-talk that does so much to make time pass agreeably in society. The worst feature of camp life is its influence upon the mind and character. The physical discomfort, hard fare, etc., I can endure very well, but I sometimes shrink from the moral or immoral influences that cluster round the soldier. The severe physical exercise is so fatiguing that but little disposition is felt to exercise the mind in anything that is beneficial. Everything that requires close or long-continued thought is excluded from the common soldier's tent and he usually settles down to the conviction that all he needs is enough to keep himself posted in the news of the day and a little light reading. Thus the stronger mental faculties are unused and of course they rust. Another evil is the absence of all female society. The roughest characters are always to be found in the army, and, the restraint of home and more refined friends removed, those who are better disposed are exposed to the influence of such characters without remedy. Our associations go far to mould our characters, and as a constant dropping wears away the stone, this influence must have its effect. The cultivation of the finer feelings of the heart is neglected and they too are not developed. The pure and elevating influence of music is lost. I am passionately fond of music (although a poor singer) and I miss this as much as any one thing. The music of the field is the fife and drum or the brass band, and the songs sung in camp are not at all remarkable for beauty or purity.

With all these drawbacks there are many pleasant times in the soldier's life. One of these is when he is the recipient of letters like yours; they speak to him in louder tones than those of the press or pulpit and bid him resist these evil influences and keep himself pure; they atone in a measure for the absence of friends and remind us that they are watching to see if we do our duty, and feel interested in our welfare. You need never fear burdening me with letters.

I fear that, if all the guide you had was my most graphic description of myself, I might pass you in Broadway ten times a day without recognition. I might say, however, that I am of the "tall and slender" order. Five feet nine is about my height, and one hundred and thirty-five pounds my weight. I am set down in the army description book as having brown hair and blue eyes, and, I might add, of very ordinary appearance.

I see you are a thorough abolitionist. I am glad of it. I thought I hated slavery as much as possible before I came here, but here, where I can see some of its workings, I am more than ever convinced of the cruelty and inhumanity of the system. It has not one redeeming feature. I was on picket duty last Sunday and some seven of us went out a mile or so beyond the lines on a little scouting party. I stopped at a little cabin near the Leesburg turnpike to get some dinner. I found an intelligent and cleanly mulatto woman in the house, surrounded by quite a number of bright little children. She promised me the best she had, and while she was preparing some hoecake and bacon, I entered into conversation with her and she was quite communicative. She was a slave, she said, so was her husband

and the children. Her master was in the rebel army and she was left in charge of her mistress, who lived in a respectable house across the way. Her husband had been taken about a month ago to work on the fortifications at Leesburg. He had, at first, refused to go with his master and was most brutally beaten. She showed me the post where he was tied up and told the story with an earnestness that nothing but actual experience can give. I talked long with her and told her I hoped this war would result in giving her and all of her class their freedom. "I hope so, Massa," said she, "but I dunno, I dunno." I had a little Sunday-school paper that I took out with me from camp. I read some of the stories to the children and gave them the paper. How their eyes sparkled as they saw the pictures! But the reading was Greek to them. The mother said: "I would study ten years if I could read like you, Massa; a black woman taught me some letters, but Massa Blaisdell took my spellin' book away and whipped me and he said 'larnin' wasn't for niggers.'" This is "the land of the free and the home of the brave."

We are still at Hall's Hill, and as far as I can see likely to stay here. No movement can be made while the roads are in such a state.

Hall's Hill, Va., Jan. 29, 1862.

Dear Sister L.:—

I suppose I might relieve your fears about my being killed or wounded at that great battle when I tell you that we are still here and likely to stay till spring. It is true we had marching orders, or orders to be ready to march at any time, but I do not now believe it was ever intended we should go. This large army is lying here, and, if there were nothing to keep up the excitement, they would soon become demoralized and care nothing for drill or discipline, expecting that they would have no use for it. So every little while they get up some marching orders or something of the kind to keep the men on the *qui vive*, always expecting some great thing that never comes. It is just so when we go on picket. The first time I was out, the officer told us that two men had deserted from a regiment down near Alexandria and they would probably try to cross the picket lines and get over to the rebels, and they wanted us to be very vigilant and arrest them if they came near us. Now I cannot certainly say that no such men deserted, but I will say that I believe it was just a story trumped up to make us watchful. Another time they told us that a large force of rebels had been seen near the lines and they expected an attack in the night. It seems to be a part of the tactics to use such means to keep up the spirits of the men, constantly holding out hopes that never are to be realized. I have got so case-hardened by such treatment that I will not believe anything until I see it with my own eyes. I did think when we had our marching orders about New Year's that something was to be done. Officers packed up their extra baggage and sent it off and everybody seemed in a bustle of preparation to leave. Well, they have kept it up about a month and nothing done yet, so I begin to believe that this is another sell. They found it would not work to humbug the men alone, so, as a last resort, they have to bring in the officers. They can make that work two or three months, but I believe that will "play out" in time. I know it has with me now. I suppose the battle you refer to was that of Somerset, in Kentucky, but that is a long way from here. That battle was a hard blow to secession, and I hope it will be followed by others.

Camp of the 83rd P. V.,
Hall's Hill, Va., Feb. 3, 1862.

Dear Friend P—s.:—

It is just such a morning as would make a misanthrope happy. Byron's bitterest and most sarcastic strains were, I believe, written in just such weather. It snowed last night and rains this morning and now two or three inches of slush cover unfathomable mud. Great black clouds roll up heavily from the west and slowly drizzle down discomfort in the camps. The evergreens that made our camp look so bright and homelike about the holidays are giving way under the abuse heaped upon them and now they stand leaning at every angle but that of 90 degrees, covered with ice and weeping great pearly tears of grief at their cruel treatment. The smoke curls slowly from the myriad pipes of the camp and makes a desperate effort to rise above the tents, then sinks despairingly to the ground. The cooks stir up their sputtering fires in vain efforts to make their kettles boil, and, as the rain drips off their ponchos, they look as if they would cook one more meal and die. I have been lounging on my bunk since breakfast, drawing the Spanish out of my cigar and working off the fatigue of yesterday's guard duty, and now I have taken up my pen to answer your letter of the 24th of January. What I shall write, I can't tell. There is no news beyond what you have in the papers. "All is quiet along the Potomac." Our marching orders are "played out." The boys are getting so that they won't believe anything now. They sit around the fire and while away these dull days the best they can. How time does pass away, though! Here it is the 3rd of February. Seems to me I never knew a winter to pass so quickly.

Camp Porter, Feb. 8, 1862.

Dear Sister L.:—

"All quiet along the Potomac" has become a by-word, it is used so often. Nothing stirring. Mud is triumphant and all business except guard and picket duty is suspended, unless I should mention a little target practice. Last night just after roll-call we heard tremendous cheers up at the right of the regiment. Company after company seemed to vie with each other to see which could cheer loudest. Finally, when half our boys had got to bed, the orderly came into the street with "Fall in, Company K, fall in." Out they tumbled and into line, when Captain A. said the general had just received a dispatch containing such good news that he had sent his orderly down to read it to the boys. He read a telegram stating that a fleet of gun-boats had gone up the Tennessee river, bombarded and taken the rebel Fort Henry and captured General Floyd, Tilghman and staff, twenty cannons and sixty prisoners. Captain A. proposed nine cheers for the Union victory. They were given and the Zouave tiger to close on. Every one thought that the ex-Secretary Floyd had been taken, but this morning's papers disclose a cruel sell. Instead of Generals Floyd and Tilghman, it was General Lloyd Tilghman, commandant of the fort, who was captured. It was a great victory for us, but we were very much disappointed after all. There is no other man whom I would be so much pleased to have taken as that "thafe o' the wurreld" Floyd. Jeff Davis wouldn't begin.

General Porter commands our division, containing twelve regiments or three brigades, thus:

GENERAL FITZ JOHN PORTER'S DIVISION.

FIRST BRIGADE, GENERAL MORELL.

Sixty-second Pennsylvania, Colonel Black.
Ninth Massachusetts, Colonel Cass.
Fourteenth New York, Colonel ———.
Fourth Michigan, Colonel ———.

SECOND BRIGADE, GENERAL MARTINDALE.

Twenty-fifth New York, Colonel Kerrigan.
Second Maine, Colonel ———.
Twenty-second Massachusetts, Colonel Henry Wilson.
Eighteenth Massachusetts, Colonel Lee.

THIRD BRIGADE, GENERAL DANIEL BUTTERFIELD.

Sixteenth Michigan, Colonel T. B. W. Stockton.
Eighty-third Pennsylvania, Colonel John W. McLane.
Forty-fourth New York, Colonel Stryker.
Seventeenth New York, Colonel Lansing.

ARTILLERY.

Sprague's Rhode Island Battery.
Griffin's Battery D, Fifth United States.
Follett's Battery.

CAVALRY.

Averill's Regiment.
Gorham's Regiment.
Eighth Pennsylvania Regiment.
Third Pennsylvania Regiment.

This is the force under Porter; quite a little army in itself. The Massachusetts troops are fine fellows, three regiments in the division. The "Farmers Regiment" raised by Senator Wilson is among them. He (Senator Wilson) is not the acting colonel at present, however, having returned to the Senate. The Ninth Massachusetts are mostly Irish Catholics. They will fight, I think, like the old Sixty-ninth New York at Bull Run. The Twenty-fifth New York is composed of New York roughs, Bowery boys, "Dead Rabbits," etc. Their colonel has been court-martialed on charge of treason, communicating with the enemy, drunkenness, etc. He is deprived of his command. They seem to keep to themselves and have nothing to do with any other regiment. I never saw but one of them in our camp. The Sixty-second Pennsylvania was raised at Pittsburg and is twelve hundred strong, commanded by ex-Governor Black of Nebraska, formerly of Pittsburg. The Forty-fourth New York (the Ellsworths) you have heard enough of them to know them by this time—their camp is next to ours, and the two regiments are as united in feeling and everything as brothers. We are like one great regiment. The Seventeenth New York in our brigade seems to have a grudge against both of us.

Camp Porter, Virginia,
Tuesday, Feb. 11, 1862.

Dear Cousin L. :—

"Norton, 'Putty' has brought you a valentine this time, I'll warrant," said one of my messmates, as I entered the tent last night and flung down my axe (I had been out on fatigue duty all day, making a government road to Washington, for the old roads are impassable on account of the mud). "Well, let me look at it," said I, and he handed me your letter of the 7th. It was not a valentine, but it pleased me much more than one of those sentimental things would have done.

I presume I do have considerable more time for writing than you do, but your remark about your household cares, etc., made me think of what Mother often says: if she had only one or two children to care for she might have a little time to herself. I see that any one who has a family to care for has enough to do to be constantly busy. From morning till night there is always something to do. I have commenced writing, but that ever recurring question comes again. "What shall I write"? It seems to the soldier when he takes up the pen as though there was nothing to write unless he has something to tell of gallant exploits in his own occupation, a brilliant victory over superior numbers of the enemy, in which he was one of the heroes. With something like that for a text he can write. Pages of foolscap are far too small to contain all he has to relate to his friends then, but, ah me, I've no such resource. A man is not a hero till he is shot at and missed. He who is shot at and killed is covered with the sod and forgotten by all but the narrow circle of his immediate friends. His name is once seen in the list of killed at the great victory, but lightly passed over, while the readers turn to honor the heroes who participated in the victory but were shot at and missed.

You want to know something of our "arrangements, beds, meals, etc." I might describe the interior of our tent in my poor way, and that will serve as a specimen of the whole, though each mess arranges its own tent in any way to suit the members. We have the large round tent, about eighteen feet across the bottom and tapering to a point at the top. A round pole in the center supports it, and, on this pole, two tables are suspended by ropes, one above the other, and so arranged that we can lower them to use as tables or raise them up above our heads. As to beds, we have every style and form that never were seen in a cabinet shop. We used to sleep on the ground or on pine boughs when we had the small or wedge tents, but when we obtained these we concluded to be a little more extravagant. Lumber in Virginia is out of the question. A very patriotic Union man about two miles from here refused to sell me a couple of fence boards six inches wide for $1.50, so I made up my mind to be my own saw-mill. At the time we encamped here, there were hundreds of acres of worn-out tobacco lands grown up with small pines in the neighborhood. They grow very close together, slim and straight.

"Necessity is the mother of invention," says the old adage, and so it proved with us. We cut down any number of the poles, peeled the bark, got a few pounds of nails at the sutler's and made our bedsteads, or bunks, we call them. They are like berths in a steamer, one above another, room for two above and two below, and for another back under the side of the tent. This, for one side of the tent, accommodates six men; another like it on the other side, six more. For the "mattress," or "downy bed," we hewed the poles flat and rather thin so they spring some and laid them side by side as close as possible. At night we spread our overcoats on the poles, take our knapsacks for pillows, and, covering ourselves with our blankets we enjoy such sleep as many a one who rests in the most luxurious bed might envy. Our *robe de nuit* is very simple, merely our every day dress, minus cap and boots. My rifle and cartridge box hang by my side, my cap lies on my knapsack, and my boots stand on the ground within my reach every time I sleep, so that, if the long roll beats, I can be with the company in line of battle in two minutes. We retire early, not so much from choice as necessity. At 9 o'clock the "taps" are beaten and all lights must be extinguished. It is rather uninteresting sitting in the dark, so that hour generally finds us "coiled up," as the boys express it. At daylight the "reveille" is sounded, the men turn out and the roll is called. Soon after breakfast is ready, consisting of bread, meat (pork, bacon or beef) and coffee. We now have our soft bread baked in the regiment, but we have eaten a great many of the crackers, or pilot bread, as it is called. Some of this was good, but the greater part very poor, moldy, wormy, and made of poor flour, etc. Several barrels had crackers stamped "T. Weld & Co., Boston, 1810"; Company I say they had a barrel marked "B. C. 97." I don't know whether the crackers or the barrel was made before Christ, but I think it must have been the barrel. We finally concluded that fresh bread, although lacking so many romantic associations, would be more nutritious, so we brought in a fine lot of brick that a *secesh* had provided to build for himself a fine house, made some splendid ovens, and now we have good bread. We have a little sheet-iron stove in our tent that does very well when it is not too cold, and we can cook a good many little extras, stew dried fruit, etc., and we manage to live quite comfortably.ˣ The paper you sent I have not received. It will probably arrive to-night. We have a great many papers. The Washington papers are here before breakfast every morning, the New York papers, "Erald," Tribune and Times, the day after they are published; Baltimore and Philadelphia papers the same day, and then we have Frank Leslie's, Harper's Weekly, Illustrated News and Forney's War Press. Friends at home send us the Independent and the Evangelist, the Advocate, the Guardian, etc., so that generally we are well supplied, but we devour papers with a rapidity that would astonish them that have less leisure time.

Last night a man died at the hospital. I can hear the band as they are paying their last respects to his remains. We have lost but one from our company. Poor Pickard died at the hospital in the latter part of January. I have sometimes thought that I could die on the battlefield and be content, but to die in a military hospital, away from my dearest friends, with only the rough hand of a fellow soldier to close my eyes to their last sleep, would be hard to bear. It was a gloomy day when we buried Pickard. Great piles of black clouds came rolling up from the west, and now and then a flake of snow came sailing down, mingling with the dead leaves as they went whirling over the frozen ground till they dropped together into some hollow to lie and be forgotten. I was one of the eight selected as the escort for the body, and I was much impressed with the solemnity and beauty of the military burial. The procession was formed at the hospital, the escort first with arms reversed, the pall-bearers with the body, the chaplain, the band, and the company and friends of the dead. The band played a beautiful but mournful dirge, and we moved slowly to the grave. We buried him under a large oak tree on an eminence overlooking a wide prospect of this once beautiful country. Arrived at the grave, the coffin was set down and the chaplain read the beautiful burial service and the body was lowered to its last rest. We fired three volleys over the grave, the drums meanwhile beating a low muffled roll, and then we turned back to camp. Thus rests on the soil of the "Old Dominion" a humble, honest man and a good soldier. Half a dozen miles off sleep the ashes of the "Father of his Country." The world admires and honors him, and weeps over his grave, and yet, who can say that Adam Pickard, in his humble sphere, did not his duty to his country as well as the immortal Washington? He left his wife and little children when his country needed him, and now his wife is left a widow and his children fatherless. It was a stern fate, but he looked it sternly in the face and died like a true soldier, leaving his family to God and giving his life to his country.

Hall's Hill, Va., Feb. 21, 1862.

Dear Sister L.:—

We have most glorious news every day. Fort Henry is taken, and immediately followed by the surrender of Roanoke Island. We haven't done cheering over that victory, before we hear of another and greater, the fall of Fort Donelson and the capture of fifteen thousand rebels. Right on the heels of this comes the evacuation of Bowling Green, defeat of the rebel cavalry near Winchester, and last the capture of Price and his army in Missouri. We have also a report of the surrender of Savannah without firing a gun. This came from the rebels, and, as they have prohibited the passage of any more news from Norfolk, I am inclined to think there's something in it. We will soon hear direct from the fleet. The rebels are beginning to feel heartily sick of their madness, if we may judge by their acts. We hear that Vice President Stephens has resigned and advised the rebels to lay down their arms and surrender. Governor Letcher has done the same. The rebels are evacuating Columbus to escape the fate of their friends in Fort Donelson, and to-day's Press says that they are leaving Centreville and Manassas to protect Richmond. If this is true we may be following them up in a very short time and completely whip them by the middle of March. Things certainly look brighter every day. The boys are already talking of what they'll er every day. The boys are already talking of what they'll do when they get home. I think I shall go home by way of New York and stop there for a short visit, and perhaps call at Ararat. What do you think of that for counting chickens before the process of incubation is completed?

It's a pleasant day and the "old tiger" has got the battalion putting them through the tallest kind of double quick steps. A somewhat distinguished (in his line) votary of Terpsichore said to me the other day, "I always liked a quick step, but hang your double quick. Single quick is fast enough for me."

Camp of the Penn. Mudturtles,
Hall's Hill, Va., Feb. 27, 1862.

Dear Cousin L.:—

Your letter came last night and with it rain and marching orders. I had just read it and the rain had just commenced drumming on our cotton houses, when a drum of another sort called the orderlies to headquarters and they soon returned with orders to pack up every thing and be ready to march at a moment's notice. This was welcome news, though the style the weather put on was not so welcome. We packed up everything and lay down on the bare poles to wait the moment's notice. The rain continued through the night and we were not called out. This morning two days' rations were issued and the orders repeated to be ready to move at any moment. I improve the time while we are waiting to answer your letter. You will excuse my writing with a pencil, as my portfolio and writing materials with your letter are in my knapsack under a pile that I dare not undertake to repack at a "moment's notice." I stepped out into the street this morning and one of the boys who stood there said to me: "Norton, there's something on my back; brush it off." I looked, and what do you think it was? "Couldn't imagine." He had his knapsack packed and on the outside two woolen blankets, one rubber ditto, one picket tent, pole and ropes, overcoat, pair of boots, haversack with two days' provisions (Hardees and tiger), canteen with two quarts of coffee, cartridge box with forty rounds and a thirteen-pound rifle. I can only say I didn't attempt to brush it off, but went back to my tent and found the same thing ready for my back with a bugle for a balance weight. All the regiments in the vicinity have the same orders, and last night the cook-fires on all the hills in sight were spluttering in the rain all night, cooking the rations.

There are many speculations as to where we are going. Some say a general advance is to be made on Centreville and Manassas, some that nothing more is contemplated than moving the camps a few miles further to better situations, others that the division is to go via Washington and Baltimore to Harper's Ferry. My own opinion is different from all these. I think we are going to—stay here. Cotton has abdicated, corn never was much of an absolute monarch, but "King Mud" is king yet. We have had two days this week of drying weather. One, Monday, I think, we had a gale, a very severe one, that dried up the mud considerably. It was the strongest wind we've had in Virginia since I've been here. It blew down a great many tents in all the regiments. Ours are so large and well staked down that only six or eight blew down, but in the Michigan and the Ellsworth regiments some companies had not a tent left standing. I was over in the Forty-fourth New York when the gale commenced and tents began to fly about. I saw one whisked off the foundation and blown into the next street, carrying with it three guns, coats, caps, bottles, etc., and as it struck a watch bounded out and dropped in the mud. The jewelry had a perilous voyage, but wasn't injured. In another tent the boys had dug a basement and fixed it up very nicely. They were busy at a game of cards when the wind unroofed their cave. Nothing disconcerted, they kept on, saying, "Let her go, we won't stop for a little wind—it's nothing to the lakes."

I see L. must have told you of her expected marriage. I can tell you but little of her intended. He is a farmer, and, from what I have seen of him, I think him a fine young man and I think you would like him, at least in one respect, he don't use tobacco. He tried a cigar with me once, smoked an inch of it, and, wise young man, his sensations requested a discontinuance of the operation. I'm sorry you feel so bad about my smoking. I think, after you had spent a night or two on picket and saw the comfort the soldiers draw from a pipe or cigar as they sit round the fire, you would say, "I forgive you—smoke, at least while you are in the army."

I received the Atlantics you sent. I was very much interested in reading them. I like the character of that magazine better than any other I am acquainted with. My friends in the tent unite with me in thanking you, for everything of the kind has to go the rounds, you know. There hasn't been an hour in the day since they came but some one has been reading them.

You inquire what delicacies I am most in need of and speak of sending me a box. I hardly know what to say. I have become so used to a soldier's fare that I do not need any delicacies. We have a nuisance in every regiment called a sutler, who generally has a supply of knick-knacks ready for us for a consideration, and when we tire of hog, hominy and hardees, we get a little something of him to make our rations relish. A good many of our boys have received boxes from home, but they generally came from farmers and contained butter, cheese, dried fruits, pickles, etc., that cost them little and were very welcome in camp. In New York every such thing must be bought and at high prices, too. I have done very well so far without them, and I should not like to have you go to much trouble or expense on my account. If you do have a few things that you want to send, I suppose if sent by express to the same address as my letters, they would come to me all right, as boxes are brought up almost every day by our teams from that office.

2 P. M.—We haven't marched yet, and are still expecting orders at a "moment's notice."

If there are any questions I have not answered please excuse me, as I have your letter packed up.

Camp of the 83rd P. V.,
Secesh, Va., March 5, 1862.

Dear Friend P—s.:—

I received your letter of the 24th ult. last night. We are still here on Hall's Hill with no prospect that I can see of leaving very soon. To be sure we have marching orders occasionally, were under orders last week. They kept us two or three days with everything in readiness to leave at a moment's notice and turned us out into ranks several times, but the whole thing flashed in the pan, as it always does. I think the spring will find us here. It does not seem to be any part of the plan to attack the rebels at Manassas till they are forced to abandon their position, partially, at least, by some other portion of our forces. The intention may be to turn their left flank and so get in their rear. General Banks made a movement looking towards that last week, by taking his division across the river at Harper's Ferry. He met no opposition, though report says the rebels immediately concentrated a large force at Winchester, their extreme left position, evidently to prevent his turning their flank. Everything is managed so secretly now it is impossible to tell what will be done two days in advance.

The weather is so extremely changeable that no reliance can be placed on its favorableness till spring is fairly open. For example, Sunday morning was clear and warm, at noon it rained, before night we had five inches of snow, during the night it rained and in the morning it was all slush, before noon the snow was all gone and last night it rained in torrents, washing great gullies in the streets. This morning it was frozen as hard as a stone and the sun is shining clear again. Now in such weather an army cannot move, the roads are so bad that artillery and baggage cannot be transported and we are forced to wait for better weather. In the west the army is doing wonders. Every day we receive news of the success of our arms and the total defeat of the rebels. While things work as well as they are doing now I am content to wait in patience the time for us to do our share in crushing the rebellion. I know the North is impatient and wondering why the Army of the Potomac don't move. It's just because we are to have no more Bull Runs. The time has not come yet, but when it does, I am convinced that the boys here will show as good fighting qualities as our western army. The fight at Dranesville, though but little was said of it in the papers, showed what stuff our boys are made of. They seem to care nothing for the rebels, but are ready to pitch into any number who show themselves.

Hall's Hill, Va., March 6, 1862.

Dear E.:—

As far as advice is concerned about what you are to do in the future I do not know as I can give any. Mother's idea of your learning a trade depends upon just what you intend to do through life. A blacksmith's trade is a very good one if well followed, and, if you ever intend to be a blacksmith, now is the best time for you to commence. By the time you are of age you will have a good capital to begin with, for I consider almost any business well mastered a capital. You can earn a good living and make property, too, always provided your heart is in it and you like the business. If you ever intend to learn any trade, now is just the time for you to begin. Your education is sufficiently advanced for the purpose, and it need not entirely stop on account of your having steady employment. On the other hand, if you have determined to adopt one of the professions and feel that you can succeed, and have made up your mind just what you will do and how you will do it, I say go ahead and do it. My advice is—determine now what you will follow through life and then shape your conduct accordingly. You doubtless have the idea that a good education is of great advantage to a man in any business. This is true, but you and I have to depend upon ourselves without help from relatives and commence life immediately on coming of age. We must look this fact squarely in the face and act accordingly. Now, if you mean by getting an education, completing a college course, how are you to do it? You can get along by working on a farm part of the time and fit yourself to enter college. Then you must have five or six hundred dollars to take you through and graduate. Then you are ready to commence the practice of your profession. You have years of patient industry after you begin, before you attain a profitable business. Now after you are fitted for college you have the means to earn to take you through. Look at that and meet it squarely. If you have health, patience, perseverance and firm self-reliance, you may accomplish it and obtain a good profession. On the other hand, if you learn a trade, you may be settled comfortably in life in a few years. But, if you adopt a business against your will, ten chances to one you will be unsuccessful. So if you decide on a trade pitch into it heart and soul and you may succeed. You say Father does not favor your learning a trade. Well, what does he advise? To get an education? Yes, but for what? What kind of an education, for that's the question? At the best he can assist you but a year or two longer, and he can scarcely do that. Now my opinion is that the best assistance he can give you is to help you fix your choice on some calling and then take the proper steps to secure success in that calling. You have the material in you for a first-class man, and I hope you will prove yourself to be one. Prove yourself to have one of the first qualities of such a man—decision of character—by marking out your path and then steadily following it. It is just the turning point of life with you, and I know just about how you feel. You look away down into the dim future of coming years and imagine yourself a man, a prosperous business in your hands, a splendid home, a good wife, and yourself rich and respected. Such is your ideal. It lies within your reach, but it will never come by your wishing for it. You must grow into it. You cannot begin too soon to select your road to it. There are many roads, but you can travel but one, and the sooner you set out the sooner you will reach the goal. I cannot advise you which to take, but only say take some one and act the man in your choice, show that you have judgment like a man and look at all sides of the question. Perhaps I have now written more than enough on this subject, but I see it is occupying your thoughts, and, as you asked my advice, you have it for what it is worth.

Alexandria, Va., March 17, 1862.

Dear Cousin L.:—

The "grand army" has at last moved. Our brigade left Hall's Hill at daylight last Monday morning and marched to Fairfax Court House. The whole army advanced the same day. On arriving at Fairfax we heard that our cavalry had been to Manassas Junction and found it evacuated and the barracks of the rebel army a mass of smoking ruins. The three terrible forts at Centreville were mounted with pine cannon and sheet iron mortars, so the great Manassas humbug is exploded. "Now what is to be done?" was the question we asked as soon as it was satisfactorily ascertained that these reports were true.

We rested at Fairfax, waiting for another rainy day, which did not come till Saturday. Then we marched to Alexandria. Our regiment has never moved yet without marching in the rain. It commenced raining just as we marched out of camp on Monday and rained till we halted at Fairfax. We had a hard march. After we had gone some three or four miles the men began to throw off blankets, coats and knapsacks, and towards night the road was strewed with them. I saw men fall down who could not rise without help. The rain soaked everything woolen full of water and made our loads almost mule loads. As for myself, I stood it well, at least as well as any, but I never was so tired before. I am acting as regimental bugler, but I could not blow a note when we stopped at night. We pitched our picket tents which we carry with us on the ground lately occupied by a *secesh* regiment. We built fires, boiled our coffee and roasted our bacon and then lay down on the ground to sleep. Oh, how we slept! The reveille at sunrise woke us, stiff and lame, but the sun came up warm and clear and a couple of days rest made us all right. Then on Saturday we were ordered to Alexandria. We marched eighteen miles, every step in the rain, but we had a good road and the men stood it much better than they did the other march. We halted at the camp of the Irish brigade under command of General T. F. Meagher. They had gone to Centreville and we took possession of their camp and made ourselves as comfortable as possible. I was fortunate enough to get into a line officer's tent. There were ten of us in a tent designed for one, but we built a fire, made coffee, swept off the floor and "coiled up" for the night. Oh, how we did steam! It was better than any sweat ever advocated by hydropaths. This morning we had to leave, as the Sixty-ninth was coming back to camp. We moved over on a hillside near Fort Ellsworth, and about half a mile from the river and the same from Alexandria.

General McDowell's corps, comprising his own and Generals McCall's, Smith's and Porter's divisions, in all about sixty thousand men, are here waiting for transports to take us off on another expedition. The destination is of course unknown to us, but we shall in all probability be sent against what remains of the rebel army between here and Richmond. There were one hundred and fifty vessels here yesterday, and troops embarking all the time. I think our time will not come for two or three days at least.

This is naturally a beautiful country, but either the war has made sad havoc here or the few inhabitants are greatly deficient in enterprise, for it looks almost like a desert now. There are a few splendid buildings here, but the majority are miserable huts. I called yesterday at the house of a northern man who had married a southern wife and adopted southern institutions. He had a good farm and excellent buildings all under the protection of the government. He has proved a loyal citizen, although a slaveholder, but his wife and daughter are rabid *secesh*. The daughter is a fine looking young woman, about twenty, I should think, and quite sociable. She commenced conversation by inquiring if I thought it was right to try to force the South to remain in the Union against their will. Of course I did, you know, and I was obliged to say so. She waxed quite warm in the defense of the rebels, but finally stopped by remarking abruptly that we had better change the subject, as we were friends now but would not be if we continued to talk about the war. She was in the Mansion House where Ellsworth was shot at the time of his death, and said, "He ought to have been shot, for he had no business to meddle with a flag that a man put on his own dwelling." It amused me to see a woman so gritty, but, if she does nothing but talk, I suppose she must be allowed to do that. She was very different from one I met when I was on picket duty in January. She was born in New York, but had lived here so long it seemed like her home. She, too, was very sociable and seemed to think there might be soldiers who were not ruffians. I believe you asked in a former letter if the government furnished postage or stationery. It does not. We furnish our own, and it is often hard to get. We're not much troubled with peddlers now, for we have not received any pay since December 31st, and money is too scarce to offer inducements to that gentry.

Hampton, Va., March 26, 1862.

Dear Sister L.:—

I received your letter of the 16th at Alexandria, but there has been no opportunity to send letters till now.

We have had so much of the checkered experience of life in the field that I cannot write the tenth part of what I could tell you if I could have a talk with you, but, as it is, I don't know as I could do better than to write a few extracts from my diary: "Friday, March 21st. Porter's division embarked at Alexandria on board a fleet of thirty steamers and transports. Saturday, 22nd, got under way at 12 m. and steamed down the Potomac. Passed Mount Vernon at 1 p. m.; had a good view of all the rebel batteries on the Virginia side; slept on deck under our little tents; woke in the morning in a puddle of water that ran down the deck. Sunday, 23rd: Had a splendid ride down Chesapeake Bay, and arrived at Fortress Monroe at 4 p. m.; anchored in Hampton Roads alongside the Monitor and opposite the country residence of ex-President Tyler. A French man-of-war lay near by and our band entertained the *messieurs* with the "Marseillaise," and afterward with schottisches, polkas, cotillions, etc., the marines dancing to the music on their quarter-deck.

Monday, 24th: Undertook to land, but the Columbia ran aground and the Nantasket took off four companies.

We then got off at Hampton landing, marched through the ruined village of Hampton and bivouacked in the fields southwest of the town. I saw the walls of the old stone church in which Washington used to worship. It was burned with the town, by Magruder. Hampton was a beautiful old town built almost wholly of brick and stone, but it looks now like the pictures of ancient ruins.

Tuesday, 25th: Broke camp at 8 a. m. and took the road to Great Bethel. After marching about four miles, our advance skirmishers reported that the rebels were posted two miles ahead in force that it would not be prudent for us to meet. We then turned into the pine woods west of the road and pitched our bivouacs—the whole division. This was done so that if the rebel scouts discovered us they could not estimate our numbers. Our pickets are half a mile ahead. They captured fifteen rebels just after sundown. H. is out with them and forty-five men from our company. The news was brought from the Fortress that our mortar-fleet had taken New Orleans with all the shipping and $10,000,000 worth of cotton. Also that the rebels were evacuating Norfolk and burning the town.

This takes me up to to-day, and my diary isn't made out any further.

Last night was cold. We had a little frost. T. and the Rabbi froze out at midnight and got up and made a big fire and snoozed by that the rest of the night. The weather is very changeable. Grass begins to grow here and peach trees are in blossom. The country here is very low and swampy. We are bivouacked in a pine swamp. The woods are full of vines and trees that I have never seen before, and the pine is a kind that I never heard of. The leaves are many of them nearly a foot long and as shaggy as they can be. They make splendid beds.

My health continues excellent. I march easier every day, and the last march I scarcely felt my knapsack.

We have not had a letter or paper since we left Alexandria, so we don't know anything about what is going on. I guess my letter-writing is about "played out," for my last stamp pays this postage and I haven't had a cent of money this fortnight.

In the Woods before Great Bethel,
Saturday, March 29, 1862.

Dear Sister L.:—

I had to stop right there and report to the general with my bugle, to teach me new calls. We have received no mail since we left Alexandria and none has been sent further than the Fortress. I don't know when you will get this, but I will write and perhaps they will send it some time or other. My last stamp got wet and spoiled, but D. gave me a stamped envelope, one of the last he had, so I am all right yet. He is just one of the best fellows that ever lived.

On Thursday General Porter's division made a reconnoissance two miles beyond Great Bethel. Our brigade with a battery took the lead. It is ten miles from here to the fortifications. The road is perfectly level and sandy all the way. The two regiments of Berdan's sharpshooters are in our division now and a company of them went with us as skirmishers. A spy had reported the rebels two thousand strong at the forts. These are a line of earthworks in the edge of a pine woods. In front of these is a large level field or two or three hundred acres, and in front of the field an extensive swamp full of wet holes, thickets, briars and vines. The road leads through the middle of this swamp to the field. Here was the place where so many of our brave boys fell last spring. We halted as we came up to the swamp. The colonel came along and told us to watch the colors and stick to them, that Great Bethel would be ours before night. We then commenced to move. The artillery took the road, the Seventeenth and Twelfth New York the swamp on the right, and the Forty-fourth and Eighty-third the left. We had just entered and were forcing our way through when we heard the crack of rifles in the woods ahead. The word was passed along to hurry up. I thought the ball had opened at last. You ought to have seen us go through those thickets then. Pell-mell we went, over bogs and through vines and places I never would have thought a man could get through under ordinary circumstances. As we came out to the field the firing ceased. We formed in line of battle instantly and moved toward the works. I expected to see a line of fire run along their breastworks, but not a sound came from them and not a man could we see. We came up to the front and our color guard leaped the ditch and planted the flag of the Eighty-third on the fortifications so long disgraced by the rebel rag. Great Bethel was ours and not a man hurt. They had pickets there who exchanged shots with our skirmishers as they came in sight and then retreated. We then turned to the left and went about two miles to another fortification. They had a dam here to fill a ditch in front of the works, and below the dam a bridge. As our skirmishers came out of the woods they saw three men tearing up the planks on this bridge. They fired and shot two of them. Some others ran out of the woods and carried them off, so we don't know whether they were killed or not. The main body of rebels had left in the morning. They have gone to Yorktown. We have orders to have three days' cooked rations on hand, so I think we shall be after them soon. When we came back we burned all the log barracks and brush houses at the forts. All the houses here are burned and the whole country is a desert. It is one of the most beautiful sections, naturally, I have ever seen. The soil is very rich and the surface perfectly level. The corn fields have only one stalk in a place, showing that it must grow very large.

We have been resting since Thursday night. We don't drill as much as we did at Hall's Hill.

Camp near Yorktown, Va.,
Monday, April 14, 1862.

Dear Cousin L.:—

I scalded one of my feet yesterday and was not able to go with the company which went out this morning to work on a road. I was sitting by the fire with several others making coffee. Each of us has a small tin kettle holding three pints or so, fitted with a tight cover. We call them muckets for want of a better name. By the way, I believe almost any of us would throw away a blanket before he would his mucket, they are so indispensable. The cover of one was crowded down so tight that there was no room for the steam to escape. It swallowed the indignity with commendable patience for a time, but finally it lost all self-control and exploded, throwing hot coffee in all directions, but particularly in the direction of my left foot. It was not very badly scalded, and I hope will be well in a few days.

I believe with you that our idle days are about over, at least we have been tolerably busy since we arrived at Fortress Monroe. We landed the 24th of March. You have much better opportunities of learning what is done in the army than we, for we depend for news on the New York papers and they are two days old before we get them. All that I can write then is to tell what falls under my immediate observation.

You have undoubtedly learned that the main body of the Potomac army is in the vicinity of Yorktown; that the rebels are concentrating all the troops they can to oppose us, and that they seem determined to make a desperate stand here, to keep us back from Richmond. By the time we are ready to attack them they will probably have 100,000 men very strongly intrenched with which to meet us. We have a still larger force and are working night and day to get our guns in position and leave nothing undone that will lead to a sure and decisive victory. We have McClellan to lead us and the prestige of victory on our side, which is a great help. What the French call the *Esprit de corps*, is excellent. The army seems to feel that a well fought battle here will crush the rebellion and send them home all the more speedily. They hear of the victories in the west and the determination seems universal that the honor of crushing the rebellion shall not rest wholly with the army of the Mississippi. We shall go into the fight with "Remember Fort Donelson and Pittsburg" on our lips and in our hearts. The traitors have no such thoughts to inspire them with confidence. If they know any thing at all of what transpires. it will only fill them with forebodings of their own fate. They may fight, and undoubtedly will, but it will be like the desperate fighting of cornered rats. They must fight or give up everything. It will be the greatest battle ever fought in America. It will be worth a year's soldiering to have been in it or to have fallen there under the Stars and Stripes.

It will be a year on the 26th since I enlisted. We have as yet seen but little fighting, though I think we shall see as much as any of the rest do here. Our division has been the advance so far. We frightened the rebels of Great Bethel and Union Mills, but I'm afraid Butterfield's brigade would hardly prove strong enough to drive them out of Yorktown. We arrived here a week ago yesterday. You may wonder why we have done so little apparently in all this time. I think we have done as much as could be done under the circumstances. Last week it rained four days and nights. This materially interfered with our operations. It is twenty-four miles to Fortress Monroe, our nearest shipping station. The latter part of the road is through swamps that were almost impassable even for troops. The provisions for 150,000 men, in fact every thing had to come this way. It was found necessary to select some point nearer where provisions and artillery could be landed. Two or three wharves have been built, as near as I can learn somewhere near the mouth of the York river, and roads are being made as rapidly as possible to different parts of the camps. These forts cannot be taken with light artillery, and siege guns have to be brought and put in position. Our regiment and the Avengers have made nearly six miles of corduroy road beside doing picket duty every four days, reconnoitering, etc. I assure you the work is being pushed forward with all the speed that is possible.

It has been impossible to supply the army with full rations a considerable part of the time since we have been here, and we have had to live on short allowance. I have not heard a word of grumbling, however. Men who have marched over the road from here to Fortress Monroe know why provisions cannot be got through fast enough. Our boys didn't come here to starve, however, because Uncle Samuel got out of hard tack. There were numbers of white rabbits in the vicinity when we arrived here. They are very large with short ears and their flesh tastes strangely like mutton. I have a faint recollection of using my bowie in the woods in preparing one for eating that took two of us to carry to camp. Large, ain't they?

Our company spent a night last week down near the river. We went down to be ready to work on the road next day. We had no tents and it was pretty cold, so half a dozen of us started out about midnight to look round a little. We finally came out near a house and barn. I snatched a turkey off the fence and one of the others a rooster, and made back into the woods. We stopped to secure them when the others came up, saying they had found a pig, but did not dare to kill him for fear of his making a noise and waking up the wrong passenger. Bowen, who is not afraid of trifles, however, finally opened the door and went in. He knocked him, but the inconsiderate rascal squealed terribly. He seized him, however, and made off, the pig still squealing. Just as was expected, he woke up the rebels and we had just got into the woods when a ball came whistling over our heads. Nobody was hurt. I suppose the man shot at the squeal, for that was immediately stopped, and we heard no more guns. Just about daylight, before there was much stir, we came to the camp with the pig all dressed, turkey and rooster ditto. The colonel, who is always astir early, came riding down, and stopping suddenly, said, "Bowen, where did you get that pig?" Bowen, who stammers a little, was nonplussed. At last he blurted out. "Well, c-c-confound it, Colonel, I c-c-c-confiscated him." "Haven't you heard the orders about that?" "Well, Colonel, I haven't had a mouthful to eat except five crackers since yesterday, and I can't build corduroy on that." I need not say that Bowen was forgiven, and Colonel said yesterday he wished I could get him another turkey. The pig was pretty well disposed of during the day, but how do you think we cooked our chicken? We had used up every grain of salt on the pig. Our supply is very limited and we have had to lose some meat on account of having no salt. I went down to the bay and got a mucket of sea water and we boiled a piece in that to try it. It relished so well that the chicken was boiled in sea water, and, if it was not as well cooked as some have been, I assure you there was no meat left on the bones. I hardly know what you will think of this work. You may call it stealing to go prowling round nights snatching poultry and pigs, but my conscience is seared. I don't feel the least compunction. I am well satisfied that a man who has a farm and stock here where the rebels have had undisputed possession for months, is nothing else than a *secesh*, and when Uncle Sam can't furnish food, I see nothing wrong in acquiring it of our enemies. That is the general sentiment of the soldiers, and, if you think it is wrong you need not feel any delicacy in telling me so.

I suppose L. is married, though I have not heard from home since the wedding. I am looking anxiously for a letter. Our mails were very much interrupted for a while after our coming here, but now they are pretty regular.

I don't think you have anything to fear from the Merrimac. The Monitor is watching her as a cat does a mouse, and, if she should succeed in getting out, she would probably run up the York river to take part in the coming fight. She evidently fears the Monitor. We heard heavy firing near the fort yesterday and considerable excitement was caused in camp by the report that the Merrimac had taken the Monitor into Norfolk, but it was all a hoax. While I am writing this I hear the roar of cannon. Some of our gunboats are throwing shell from the river at the rebel batteries. Perhaps it is the commencement of the battle, and before this reaches you it may be fought and decided.

Camp near Yorktown, Va.,
Monday, April 21, 1862.

Dear Sister L.:—

Father writes encouragingly about the war; thinks it is progressing rapidly and hopes I will soon be on my way home. Home! What will that be to me, do you think Mr. P., now that you have taken away its greatest attraction? There was always a blank there when she was gone and now she has gone to return no more except as a transient visitor. Henceforth, it will be a home to me no more.

If I survive this war, do you know, C., that I've almost determined to quit roving, adopt farming as a business, and work steadily and perseveringly till I have a comfortable home for myself and the best woman I can find who will marry a soldier. I'm almost afraid that when we get home and the girls see what rough, sunburned and disgusting fellows we are—I'm afraid soldiers will be at a discount. Yes, my dreams of the pleasures of an exciting life are passing away and I have almost come to believe that the plain honest farmer who surrounds his home with comforts is the happiest man. How I wish I could live near you and that we could grow up into substantial, prosperous farmers together! But why be building castles in the air, when, perhaps, the bullet is even now rammed home to lay me under the sod on the field of Yorktown? I would not, if I could, unveil the future and see my fate. Still it has always seemed to me that I should escape death on the field. A wound has seemed more than probable. Indeed, I would not shun it, but it has ever seemed to me that I would not be called to sacrifice my life, yet such may be my fate. If so, I am content. Farewell, sweet dreams of life and love! Traitors are striking at the citadel of our beloved country. My life may check their murderous course and it must be given.

The papers are full of prophecies of the Waterloo that is to be fought here, the greatest battle of the war, and of course, a great Union victory. They don't tell the date of the coming battle, however. Now, if you ask what I think of it, I should answer, "It isn't coming off till after Richmond is taken." And then it will not be the great affair the New York papers are making out. I will give my reasons for thinking so. I judge from the present state of things and from McClellan's acknowledged skill in planning. He is a careful, cautious man and will not sacrifice lives in a fierce battle when time and skill will accomplish the same purpose. "Look at the situation," as the papers say. McClellan lands 150,000 men at Fortress Monroe and sets out for Richmond. At Yorktown the rebels have fortifications extending across the Peninsula to the James. Here is the only place they can hope to hold against our forces.

Here then they rally. All their forces are few enough to check such an army, and so they are all brought here. Manassas is deserted and now not 5,000 men are left between that and Richmond. All their army that lay along the Rappahannock was transferred to Yorktown, and they had scarcely gone when McDowell appeared at Fredericksburg with 40,000 men and Banks was following them down the Shenandoah valley with 70,000. An army of 100,000 is thus marching on Richmond, while we keep the rebel army here. It is, no doubt, repugnant to their feelings to see things go in this way, but what can they do? If they fall back to Richmond they will have a quarter of a million to fight without fortifications, for we shall certainly follow them up. If they grow desperate enough to come out from their forts and attack us, we outnumber them and they admit our courage, so they would inevitably be whipped at that. If they lie still awaiting an attack, they will lose Richmond, and wake some fine morning to find an army of 100,000 in their rear and McClellan at last ready to crush the rebellion.

April 22.

Your letters of the 13th and 14th came last night as I expected. I passed about as uncomfortable a night as I have seen lately. It had been raining all day, but at night it commenced to pour down, and the water ran through our tent, round it, and under it, and we just had to lie in a puddle of it all night. There was no dodging it; scarcely a dry spot in the tent. To-day I don't feel very keen, so, if my letter is not interesting, you will see my excuse. You certainly deserve credit for giving me a good long letter. I like to receive such, but, if I don't mention that I noticed such and such items, charge it to want of space, for this is my second sheet and I can't get in but three. One thing, however, you made a mistake in, and that was in giving me an inventory of your wardrobe. Haven't you known me long enough to know that I never can remember what color the ribbon on a bonnet is long enough to get out of church to talk about it? And all those details about the black broadcloth dress trimmed with traveling goods, the paramatta cloak, the black satin congress gaiters, the white bonnet with yellow crossbars and flowers and all those things—why, I can hardly remember them now long enough to write them. I have no doubt but you looked well in them though, for you always do.

Well, the Tribune said that Porter's division made the attack. Did they, and we have been in a battle, have we? To be sure, we led the column, and our brigade the division, but there was not much infantry fighting. Our batteries opened on them at long range and we came up in line of battle to support them. They replied with spirit from their forts and their first shell killed two brave fellows in Follett's battery, which was planted in the very spot where the rebels had been practicing at target. The firing was heavy on both sides till dark and we lost some eight or ten, and a good many horses. We all expected that Sunday would prove a bloody day, but it was very quiet and the great battle has not come off yet, though there is considerable firing every day and some skirmishes.

On picket, April 23, 1862.

I felt so unwell that I could not finish my letter yesterday, and I have resumed it this morning. Our regiment came out at 3 o'clock this morning for picket duty, and as I wanted to see the fun I came along. Now I wish I could tell you just how everything looks here, or better still, that you could just look in and see us. In a deep wooded hollow you might see seven or eight hundred men, their arms stacked in a glistening line down the middle, knapsacks and haversacks lying round and the men lounging in groups smoking, joking or telling stories. Little brush houses are scattered here and there and the sun is just coming up and making everything look so bright and pleasant that it seems more like some holiday gathering than it does like a gathering of men armed to the teeth and ready to engage in deadly conflict at a moment's notice. This is historical ground. As long ago as 1781 Yorktown was surrendered, and here is the very place it was done. Just back of me is a long bank of earth now overgrown with trees, a breastwork thrown up by Washington's men, and, if you could creep with me so as to just look over the top of it, and be out of range of *secesh* bullets, we could see more. Away across a level field three-quarters of a mile off, just in the edge of a wood, you might see a yellow line of earth. That is a rebel fort. Farther to the right is another, and still farther another and a larger one. A few rods from me are two large siege guns, and a little way on the other side a battery of Parrott guns. Now for a little amusement—a heavy report at the rebel fort, a wreath of white smoke curls gracefully up from the yellow bank and a ten-inch shell comes hissing and screaming through the air directly toward our siege guns. The gunners jump aside and fall flat on the ground; the shell strikes a dozen rods behind them and harmlessly explodes. Up they spring, with "All right, boys." "Give 'em two for that." They step to their loaded guns, step back a pace, pull a string, and, Boom! Boom! two reports that make the earth tremble and two shells go screaming back in reply to the rebel missile. They have kept up this cannonading ever since we came here on the 5th, and there is scarcely ten minutes in the day when we do not hear the report of cannon. We are getting used to it so we pay no more attention than to the birds singing, unless the firing is unusually sharp. They have tried several times to drive in our pickets, but they have not succeeded yet. I almost forgot to tell you about the posted men. Nine men are put on a post. They stay twelve hours, for they cannot be relieved oftener for fear of revealing their position. They are posted behind a clump of bushes or in a rifle pit in the open field. Three watch while the others rest, taking turns, and they watch every rod of ground in sight. If a rebel shows himself in range, they blaze away at him.

The guns are popping and cannon thundering away now, and I've got my foot on a six-inch shell that was thrown over here this morning and did not burst. I am glad there are no women here, for I am afraid they would make me nervous. Every time a shell exploded they would jump and think "there goes death and misery to some poor fellow," but we have grown so careless and hardened that we don't heed them. I have seen some fellows who had narrow escapes. One had his knapsack shot off his back by a solid shot and was not hurt. One had a ball through a cup that he was just about to drink from. One had a Minie ball pass through fifteen thicknesses of cloth (a knot in his cape) and lodge against a rib. Another had the tassel shot off his cap.

The boys have just captured something about a foot long that looks like an alligator.

Glad to hear of Daniel's success in raising stock. Mine is improving. Woke up the other morning and found a snake and a lizard in my bed.

Near Yorktown, Va.,
Sunday, April 27, 1862.

Dear Sister L.:—

I have nothing more to do to-day, but it is not so with all the regiment. I can hear them calling the roll in some of the other companies, and one company just passed armed with "Irish spoons," going out to work in the trenches. Six of our companies, including K, went out at daylight yesterday and worked all day in the rain. It was a very disagreeable day and we came back at night soaked through, cold and hungry, but as merry a lot of fellows as you ever saw. You won't understand the thing very well unless I describe it particularly. I think I told you about there being a large field in front of the forts. A trench four feet deep and twelve feet wide and over a mile long is to be dug on this side of the field just in front of the woods. We followed a road up one of the ravines till we came to our pickets and then one by one crept cautiously up into the ditch. A ditch two or three feet deep and wide enough to walk in had been dug during the night and dirt thrown up in front so that by stooping down we were concealed. One thousand men filed in there the whole length of the ditch and then each one laying his gun on the bank within reach, commenced picking or shoveling the dirt up on to the bank. The rebel forts were in plain sight and their sharpshooters were within thirty rods of us, hidden in rifle pits, so that, if a fellow got his head above the bank, he might get a bullet in his cap. We soon got a bank high enough to stand up behind and then it would have done you good to see the dirt go out of that ditch. Many hands make light work, and I tell you our regiment and the Sixty-second handled a pile of dirt. We had two reliefs—I went in at 6 o'clock and worked till noon and then the other relief worked till night. Last night there were 10,000 men at work all night and as many more to-day, so you may guess there is something going on here. George says that when he gets ready, he will throw one hundred and thirty shells per minute into each of those forts. I think there will be lively dodging there if nobody is hurt. Oh, we are gaining on them slowly but surely.

When I was out on picket I cut a hickory stick that grew on Washington's old breastwork. I picked up a *secesh* bullet there too and brought them into camp. I thought I would make something out of them to remember Yorktown by, so I whittled out a tatting needle and made a rivet of the bullet and I send it to you. It is a poor thing I know, but the stick was green and I had nothing but a knife to make it with. After it gets seasoned you can get C. to smooth and polish it up, but I can't get anything here to do it with.

There is not much firing lately and some deserters say that the rebels begin to think they will have to surrender at last. I guess they will think so when George gets ready to make them.

Camp Winfield Scott,
Thursday, May 1, 1862.

Dear Cousin L.:—

Your letter of the 26th arrived yesterday. We have a resting day to-day, as we were in the trench yesterday, so I will write to-day. To-morrow we go on picket, next day in the trenches, and so on. We received news day before yesterday of the capture of New Orleans and as it went from camp to camp it seemed to give the men a new start. There was no cheering. I have not heard a cheer or a drum since we came here except in the rebel forts. But men, when they get such news as that, must have some way of working off their excess of joy. If the orthodox way of allowing it to escape from the lungs in boisterous and prolonged cheers is not permitted, some other will be found. We worked ours off with the pick and shovel. The general in command of the trenches said we threw more dirt out of the ditch in three hours yesterday than the same number of men did in all day the day before. Men will work when there's a prospect ahead and there seems to be a determination on the part of this army, that, if it depends on us, the honor of restoring the Union shall not rest wholly on the army of the west. That portion of the army has done nobly. They have had the hardest fighting to do, but, if I do not mistake the character of the men I see in the army here, they only wait the opportunity to do as well. The Vermont troops at Lee's Mill the other day, walked, so to speak, into the very jaws of death without flinching. Not one-fourth of them live to tell the story. The sons of the "Green Mountain Boys" of the Revolution do not seem to have degenerated.

You think I make light of our annoyances and privations. Well, it may be so. There are a few who are constitutional grumblers. They never are satisfied with any treatment or any regulation. They find fault with everything. In fact, if they ever get to Heaven, they'll be finding fault with the music. Such fellows are the butt for all the ridicule their comrades can heap on them. No mercy is shown to them. A man must show himself a man to get along pleasantly with the company. In general it is so. "Come what will, we'll be gay and happy still," is the song and the sentiment of the greater part of the men. There seems to be a pride felt in enduring what at home we would consider hardships, without complaint. But the soldier's life is not all hardship. It is a pleasant sight to look on a group sitting round a fire in the evening, whiling away the time with stories of the past and speculations of the future. Then you would always see the pipes there. That you wouldn't like. But for some reason a soldier does enjoy his tobacco. A count was made the other day of the men in our company who use tobacco and of the eighty-seven present sixty-one fell under the ban. I think that a fair average of the regiment. Since we came here the boys have gone to making pipes of the laurel roots that grow on the old breastwork thrown up in the Revolution. I have one that I think a great deal of.

We were sitting round the fire the other night passing the time away when H. joined us. He is the life of the company, and always welcome anywhere. He was asked for a song and gave "Bingen on the Rhine," a song you have probably seen. As he sang one verse and another, "Tell my mother that her other sons shall comfort her old age, Tell my sister not to weep for me or sob with drooping head," and so on, I saw a good many faces that relaxed their look of firmness and I thought a good many in the circle were thinking of their friends. There are hours when the soldier "unbends his iron front" and allows the thoughts of home and its pleasant associations to occupy his mind, but it is only as a relief that this is done. You will generally find him apparently careless of the past or future, buoyant, self-reliant, and only mindful of the present.

L. was married the 2d of April at home. She is now Mrs. C. H. P. There, your nose is broke, as they tell the next older when the crisis or cribub arrives. You can't monopolize the marriage list any longer. Who would have believed though, that she would be married before I thought of such a thing? Oh well, there's time enough yet. If the young ladies think half as much of the soldiers as they pretend to, perhaps I may find one somewhere if I ever return. E., I believe, has given up his idea of going to West Point. He found that there was no vacancy from our district. He has hired out to farm it this summer.

I see that my correspondents intend to keep me supplied with stamps. I got a letter from home the other night with a number in it. Then Aunt A. sent me some, and now I have to thank you for a number more. They are really an accommodation here. I have seen a good many of the boys sell their rations for stamps because they could not get them in any other way. But the arrangements are better now and I don't think there will be much difficulty in procuring them hereafter.

*White House, Va.,
May 20, 1862.*

Dear Father:—

There are long rows of "quarters," log huts with no windows but holes in the walls and only a mud floor. The slaves were mostly born on the plantation, and, though many had been sold south, but few had been brought on. One old "Uncle Tom," over sixty years old, had worn his strength out in sight of the house—had never been five miles away. One man told me he was owned over on the State road six miles away. He married a woman on this plantation, had been married eight years and had six children. The only time he had ever been allowed to visit his wife was to come on Saturday night after dark and be back to his work in the field by daylight on Monday morning. He was a good looking, intelligent man and gave me much information about the modes of cultivation, the crops, etc., and about negro life in the system of slavery. He could hardly believe or realize that he and his family could never be slaves again. He said "if he was sartin of it, he would stay where he had always lived." He could find "right smart to do," and felt very confident he could support his family. There were all sorts of darkies there, stalwart field hands, and old worn-out men, laughing, careless "Topsies" carrying buckets of water on their heads, strong-limbed boys, and little toddlers running round with nothing to cover their ebony but a nether garment that looked as though it had been in contact with their master's character. They all appeared very healthy, except the very old men and women.

Well, if I don't stop running on so I shall have no time to answer any questions. About that Zouave cap, it is dark blue, and, of course, it has no front, that's Zouave style. The Duryea Zouaves wear a red cap, conical, with a white roll around it, and a very heavy, long tassel of yellow worsted, blue jacket (some like our three months'), red pants, very baggy, and yellow leggings. They are a dashing set of fellows.

I am very glad if the money I sent was of use. We expect another two months' pay in Richmond.

I saw Conway Ayres at White House. His regiment was to be mustered out of service in a few days, but he said he should not go home till we got to Richmond.

We have lately got a suit of government uniforms and the Zouaves are played out.

General Porter is raised to the command of a corps and the division is now Morell's division.

I hope you will reply as promptly as I have, and that our letters will be received a little more quickly hereafter.

Cold Harbor, Powhite Swamp, Va.,
Friday, May 23, 1862.

Dear Sister L.:—

I think I have not written to you since we left Yorktown. Doubtless you have plenty of papers and have heard all about that long ago. We went on board a steamer there and landed at West Point, the head of York river, the day after the battle and camped three days on the battlefield. We then followed the "river road" up the Pamunkey to Kent Court House, Cumberland and White House landing, Tunstall's, Hanover, etc., on the road to Richmond. We are now within ten miles of the rebel capital. What lies beyond I do not know, but suspect that the enemy is in considerable force not far off. General Butterfield sent me an order this morning not to give the reveille with the bugle, and the bugles and drums are as silent to-day as they were before Yorktown. We have had all the varied experiences of the soldier in the field since leaving Yorktown, marching through rain and shine, mud and dust, wading through creeks and drawing artillery and baggage wagons out of the sloughs. We make slow but sure progress.

The country is as beautiful a section as I ever saw. Lovely scenery, glorious landscapes, everything is beautiful and "only man is vile." Great clover fields in full bloom spreading away over gentle swells of ground and broad fields of wheat all headed out abound. We stopped three days at the "White House" on the Custis estate. This is a large plantation, seven thousand acres of very productive land on the Pamunkey river, late the property of the rebel General Lee. It is the old homestead of the Custis family and occupied by them in the days of Washington. Here Washington first met Martha Custis, and here, on the very spot where Lee's White House now stands, they were married. There are several hundreds of slaves on the estate and we had the opportunities we wanted to talk with them. Oh, they were a happy set of darkies when they learned that they were free. They were most of them born on the place. I saw one old Uncle Tom, over sixty years old, who had never been five miles from the place in all his life. He had worn his life away on these fields. Contrabands are pouring in on us every day. Almost every officer has one or two along now. They hardly know what to do with themselves on learning that they will never be returned to their masters.

The white inhabitants of the country are a miserable set. Every house exhibits the white flag as our troops pass. They are mean enough to take advantage of such protection and refuse a drink of water to our troops almost suffocated with heat. We have had some days when we could scarcely march half a mile without resting. Some of the boys went to fill their canteens at a well near the road. The woman of the house came out and stood by the well and told them they might go to the river to drink. She wasn't going to have the d—d Yankees drink out of her well. It was well for her she was a woman. Our boys would have knocked a man endways who would insult them in that way and perhaps put a bayonet through him. The men are just as mean as the women, but a little more discreet. I went to one of the white flag houses and said to the man who stood in the yard, "Where do you get water?" "No water here, sir, I have to tote all I use right smart o' two miles." "I couldn't see" any such yarn as that, so I made a reconnoissance and found a splendid spring not a dozen rods behind the house. I filled my canteen, and, when I went up showed it to him, with, "What do you call that but water?" "Oh," says he, "we don't never use that." Says I, "What kind of a flag do you call that?" "Flag— flag—Oh, that's a white flag." "What is that a sign of?" "It's a sign of truth." "Don't you think it would look better for a little more coloring?" "Well, I don't know but it would, but I hadn't anything handy to color it with." "Well, I think you better get it down as soon as possible and fix it over as near like that one as you can" (pointing to our regimental colors). "Well, I guess I will if I can find anything about the house to color it with." (Mem. I guess he won't.) I bought a *secesh* bill of him, and, thinking possibly you haven't seen any, I'll send it to you. It is a specimen of Confederate States art, beautiful to see but "not worth a red" to spend. Save it as a memento of the war.

Cold Harbor, Powhite Swamp, Va.,
Saturday, May 24, 1862.

Dear Brother and Sister:—

My duty as bugler exempts me from guard and picket duty. While at Yorktown bugles and drums were not used and I had nothing to do, so I went into the ranks again and volunteered to do picket duty and work in the trenches, and took my regular turn in all the work of the regiment except camp guard which I always had an aversion to and wouldn't do when I was not required to. We had a corps of twelve buglers when we left Fort Monroe and I was the leader, but, finding that a good many more than was necessary, the colonel dismissed all but two, Lederer and myself. Now, I'll just give you an idea of our duties. At sunrise buglers at brigade headquarters sound the "brigade call" and the "reveille" (rev-el-lee is camp pronunciation). The buglers of each regiment as quickly as possible assemble on the color line, give their regimental call and repeat the reveille. The fifes and drums follow and awake the men. This is the signal to rise and fall in for roll call.

You may guess that the buglers of an army of 30,000 men all within sound of each other, make some music. At sunset we have another call, "The Retreat." At half past eight the "Tattoo," at nine the "Extinguish Lights." Then there are calls "To Strike Tents," "To Assemble," "To the Color," "Sick Call," "Officers Call," "Church Call," etc. It is our duty to repeat all such calls that are first sounded at headquarters. On the march, the order to march, or halt, or lie down and rest, etc., in fact, all orders are given by the bugle.

New Bridge, Chickahominy River, Va.,
Monday, May 26, 1862.

Dear Friends at Home:—

It seems a long time since I received your last and a long time since I have written. In that time we have traveled over the country from Yorktown to within six or eight miles of the rebel capital. Half a day's march now without special delay would bring us to Richmond. And yet we've seen no rebels except prisoners and deserters, and they are but very poorly calculated to inspire a high opinion of their associates in arms. When we entered the rebel works at Yorktown and looked back at our own, we were surprised at their apparent nearness and at the little loss of life with which they were constructed. I begin to suspect it was the smell of fresh dirt which sickened them and made them leave their forts, for the last night of their stay our boys dug rifle pits under their very noses. At Yorktown, we took a steamer at dusk and the next morning found us in sight of West Point. We landed and camped on the field where the battle was fought the day before. The papers have given you much better accounts of it than I can, for I was a day too late to see anything, but some of the wounded and dead. In Captain Woodward's street considerable blood was still seen on the ground and the boys gathered around it with a curious interest and expressed all sorts of feelings at the novel sight. We stayed three or four days at West Point and then were on the road to Richmond. The time from that day to this has been passed in various camps and marches in the heat and dust and in the rain and mud. Slow and toilsome progress was made but it was sure. No going back. "On to Richmond" is the watchword in earnest now. Yorktown has taught me a lesson, however, and I would not dare to prophesy how soon we shall be there. I am well satisfied that, if fighting is necessary to get there, we are good for that. I think the battles of Lee's Mill, Williamsburg and West Point have amply demonstrated the fact that McClellan's army is not one drilled for grand reviews alone, but that the spirit of the men is just as impetuously brave as any found in the western troops.

Camp near New Bridge, Hanover Co., Va..
Friday P. M., May 30, 1862.

Dear Friends at Home:—

We have had our first battle. The accounts will reach you in the papers and I know you will be very anxious till you hear from me, so I embrace the earliest opportunity I have had of writing to give you some of the particulars, though I am so very tired that I am afraid I shall not make out much of a letter.

Last Tuesday morning we were called out at 3:30 o'clock and ordered into line without our knapsacks, taking one blanket and tent, three days' rations, and sixty rounds of cartridges. We had no time to make coffee, and had no breakfast but crackers and water. It was raining heavily and continued to do so till 10 o'clock and then cleared off very hot. The roads were horrible and the artillery was constantly getting stuck and causing delay. We took the road to Hanover Court House, twenty-four miles from camp, and traveled as fast as men could travel except when hindered by the artillery. The bridges were all destroyed but one, and the creeks had to be waded through. It was the severest march we ever had. Officers could not stand it any better than the men, for we had not very heavy loads, and officers and men gave out and lay by the roadside together, utterly unable to go any farther without rest. Captain Austin, Captain Carpenter, Captain Stowe and Captain Graham all gave out, and half the lieutenants in the regiment with scores of the men fell out and lay down to rest.

Saturday P. M., May 31.

A tremendous thunder storm came up yesterday and prevented my finishing my letter. The rain fell in torrents and the lighting was very sharp. A flash struck the quartermaster's tent in the Forty-fourth, about five rods from me, instantly killing him, and stunning twenty others. The bright steel bayonets made excellent lightning rods and a great many in all the camps around were sensibly affected by it.

To go on with my story about the battle. About two miles south of Hanover Court House the Seventeenth New York, which was in front, came upon a North Carolina regiment in the woods. They immediately formed in line of battle in a wheat field and the battery just behind came up and commenced throwing grape into the woods. We followed the battery into the field and took position in time to support it. The rebels retreated and Companies A and B were thrown out as skirmishers and we followed them half a mile through the woods and halted just in the further edge with our skirmishers in front in the field. This was a large clover field three-quarters of a mile across and on the further side we saw two regiments of rebels with three pieces of artillery. They shelled us as well as they could, but only one man was hurt. Our skirmishers kept picking off the stragglers and our battery soon came out and drove them again. We came out and followed across the field (or fields, for it was cut up by numerous gullies) and in them we took several prisoners. Company K took the first two. They were skirmishing under the bushes, and, as I jumped over the fence, I almost stumbled on them. They were instantly disarmed.

Camp near New Bridge, Hanover Co., Va.,
Monday, June 2, 1862.

Dear Brother and Sister :—

Before this reaches you, you will have heard of the battle of Hanover Court House, and I know you will be very anxious to hear from me. I should have written before, but my time has been so taken up and I have been so worn out by the extraordinary exertions of the past week that really I could not. In fact, I can scarcely write to-day.

Last Tuesday morning at 3:30 o'clock we were called out and formed in line without time to get breakfast. It was raining great guns and continued to rain till 10 o'clock and the rest of the day was intensely hot. We took a blanket and tent, three days' rations and sixty rounds of cartridges and started, we knew not where, and cared not, only that we went toward *secesh*. We had the hardest march we have ever had yet, over twenty miles through mud, swamp and cornfield, fording creeks and climbing hills. Officers and men gave out, unable to go further. Four captains, ours included, and a half a score of lieutenants, gave up and still we kept on at a killing pace. At last we came up to them. The Twenty-fifth New York was ahead and was the first fired on, which they returned with interest. Then our brigade and a battery. The rebels, of course, were in the woods and we in the field, but they were driven out and we drove them over two miles to the north and then turned, supposing the fighting was all over. In this we were mistaken. A train of cars from the south brought reinforcements to the enemy, and, when our boys were half way back, the rebels, six regiments strong, attacked the Forty-fourth and Twenty-fifth, which had not joined in the chase. They stood their ground well, though they were terribly cut up, but Butterfield came to the rescue. On came the brigade and poured in a fire that quickly caused the discomfited *secesh* to beat a retreat. They were totally routed. Here then is the amount of the day's work—a forced march, three separate fights and three victories, with a loss on our side of three hundred and seventy-nine in killed, wounded and prisoners—fifty-three killed, over one thousand rebels ditto, and over two thousand prisoners, North Carolina and Georgia troops. The Eighty-third lost two killed and thirteen wounded. Sergeant Hulbert and Frank McBride in Company K were both shot in the foot. Sergeant H. loses his foot and Frank his toes, the only casualties in our company.

I cannot tell you how I felt that day. As long as there was any prospect of a fight I kept my place in the ranks, but when we gave up the chase and turned back to where our blankets were left, I fell out to get some water and bathe my head. My tongue was swollen with the heat and thirst, and I so faint I could hardly stand. I followed on, however, but the regiment was some distance ahead. I came up to Denny and Henry. Henry could not walk but a little way without stopping, and Denny and I waited for him and helped him along, but soon we heard the sharp rattle of musketry ahead and the third fight had commenced. We tried to get Henry along, but finally left him and he came on slowly while Denny and I pushed on as fast as we could, but the firing was done when we caught up. The regiment was in line in a very large wheat field and the rebels in the woods beyond. The balls whistled round us, but none touched me, so I am perfectly safe, but I was so worn out that I have not felt right since. Night closed in and we went back to our blankets and, wrapping up, lay down between the rows of corn to sleep. Generals and privates alike spent the night on the ground. Morning came, and stiff and sore we rose. The work of collecting and burying the dead was soon commenced. The woods were full of dead rebels who lay, as they fell, in all shapes. They were carried out and laid in a ghastly row on the grass. One fine looking young man was shot through the heart as he was loading his gun. His hands had not changed their position, one extended above his head drawing his rammer and the other grasping his gun by his side. His eyes were open and the expression of his countenance as calm as though he was sleeping, but the fearful wound in his breast told that he would never wake on earth again. We buried over one hundred of them. We spent the day in recruiting our exhausted soldiers. General Porter gave permission to slay and eat, and, if an army ever made havoc with an enemy's provisions, we did. We killed all the beef, pork, veal, mutton and poultry we could eat and carry away. We captured a train of cars loaded with supplies for the rebels, and our regiment got over fifteen hundred pounds of sugar and nearly a ton of splendid tobacco, which will all be given to the men. *Secesh* knapsacks were scattered everywhere, and our boys, if they could have carried away the things, would have got a good many comforts, but we could not. We got a good many love letters, etc., bowie knives and pistols, and I got a great bowie but I threw it away, I couldn't carry it. I send you a letter that I got in a knapsack, and a *secesh* stamp. The letter is an excellent specimen of *secesh* literature and love. I almost wish I had as fond a sweetheart. We retraced that long weary march on Thursday night, arriving in camp at 3 o'clock in the morning. On Saturday night we were ordered out at midnight and went out to the Chickahominy. We came back yesterday afternoon. Lowe's balloon is up in our camp watching the rebels and the report is that they are all leaving Richmond. I have heard no firing to-day and we are expecting orders to follow them every minute. I must close. Goodbye. Write very soon to your brother Oliver. Direct Company K, Eighty-third Pennsylvania Volunteers, Morell's Division, Porter's Corps, Army before Richmond, Va.

Camp near New Bridge, Va.,
Tuesday, June 10, 1862.

Dear Sister L.:—

The last week or so has been very dull here. Nothing to break the monotony but an occasional artillery duel across the Chickahominy, in which the rebels are always worsted. Sunday, the day you wrote your letter, was a pretty big day on the lines further to the left (Battle of Fair Oaks). We lay in our tents and heard the constant war of artillery and the rattle of musketry, and, as the sound retreated, we knew our boys were driving them. Lowe was up in his balloon right beside our camp, watching them and telegraphing to McClellan just what they were doing. You wanted me to tell you something about the large guns. I don't know much about artillery myself, still I might tell you something new perhaps. "Parrott guns" are not all of the same size. In Battery No. 1 at Yorktown we had one hundred pound

Parrotts and Griffin's battery of light artillery has Parrott guns of three-inch bore. The peculiarity of this gun is in the construction. It is very long and slim and is noted for the strength and accuracy of its range. Those guns at Yorktown would throw a one hundred-pound shell two miles with great accuracy. I saw them drop just inside the rebel fort time and again. And these field pieces will throw a shell eight inches long and three inches in diameter as accurately three miles as they will half a mile. Our artillery and our artillerists are vastly superior to the rebels, and they are well aware of it. But of all the artillery, we have the greatest one yet in our regiment. We have a cannon drawn by one horse that one man can fire two hundred times a minute by merely turning a crank. Every revolution fires one ball. It is a curious Yankee contrivance. The cartridges are put in a hopper, carried one by one round in a cylinder, shoved into the barrel and fired. It makes a noise like the dogs of war let loose. The balls are only a size larger than our musket balls, a regular "Minie ball." Don't you think one of those coffee mills would "weed out" a *secesh* regiment about as quickly as any tools they have? I understand that every Pennsylvania regiment in the service is to have them. All the Pennsylvania regiments near here have them.

I have been quite unwell ever since the battle. I got overdone. Friday is the first day that I have felt at all like myself these two weeks. I think I shall be all right again soon.

Yesterday we had a grand review in honor of the Spanish General Prim. You have seen his name in the papers lately, I presume, in connection with the tripartite intervention in Mexico. He presented quite a contrast to the plain dress of "our George," as he rode by in his gold lace and trimmings. Well, every nation likes its own style. There are many men even in McClellan's staff who dress more showily than he does, but they don't command the respect. There is hardly a man in the army who does not know George by sight and not a man but likes him.

I had more fun with some of the darkies at Hanover the day after the battle, more than a little. One old fellow told me how he acted when our shells began to come where he was. Says he, "Dere was 'bout twenty of us plowin' and I hearn sumfin' go pop-pop-p-p-pop, and pretty soon sumfin' crash, bizz-z-z, right ober my head. I luff dat plow right dar and I went in dem woods quicker dan I went so far afore. I got down behind a log and I thought you gemmen was a makin' our people run, and I jumped up and cried, 'Glory to God!' and just den 'long comes 'nudder of dem t'ings, bizz-z-z-z. Golly! I was down on my belly agin mi'ty quick. De oberseer run as if de debil was after him, but I larfed."

A man named George Taylor who had inhumanly whipped a slave, came into our camp after him and he came near losing his life by the operation. He escaped by taking the oath of allegiance, but he lost his nigger. Peter is now with the colonel of the Twelfth regiment. Our camps are full of niggers. They are rapidly taking the place of white men as teamsters. They seem well adapted to that.

Richmond is not taken, but we could have taken it two week ago if George had wanted it. He wants to end the war here and he has not got everything ready yet. There is a good time coming yet, boys.

Camp at Gaines' Mill, Va.,
Monday, June 16, 1862.

Dear Mother:—

I received your letter of the 10th yesterday. I was writing at the time and intended to answer yours as soon as I finished the one I was writing, but a thunder storm came up and prevented me. I suppose you would think at home that was a singular excuse, but anyone who has lived in these shelter tents any length of time can appreciate the difficulties of writing in a heavy shower, perfectly. The wind blows and the rain comes down in great drops that spatter right through our light canvas tents. It whirls round and comes driving in the door, and by the time we have something hung up to stop that fun, there is a pretty large creek running right through where we want to sleep, and as that won't do, why that must be attended to also, and so it goes. This is a great country for rain. It rains for two days and the next day it rains, and then we have some rain and wet weather. For a wonder we had three or four very hot days last week, but the rain yesterday afternoon was cold and last night we slept cold. Night before was very hot and we could not sleep for the heat.

I feel better this morning than I have in some time before. I have been quite unwell since the fight. I got very weak and couldn't eat, but I'm just about all right again now. It seems wonderful that I have stood it so well.

With regard to Captain Austin's complimentary remarks, I presume he was conscientious in what he said, but I must say if that was a specimen of his judgment, he is a very poor judge of military matters. I think, however, that I have done tolerably well in some things. I've been in the service over a year now and I've never been "pricked" (marked absent without leave) or had any extra duty imposed on me for misconduct. I've never been in the guardhouse or had any serious difficulties with officers or men. The nearest I have come to that was two or three days ago when I turned around and struck a fellow a tolerable crack in the face for his extra exertions to get his feet entangled with mine in the ranks. It made some little stir for the time being, but the captain did not say a word. I know he did not blame me much, but it would not do to say anything in defense of such conduct in the ranks, and so he said nothing. I feel well enough satisfied myself and I have an idea that the fellow, who is the veriest bloat and bully in the company, will conclude to let me alone. I suppose he thought as some others did, because I never wrestle or scuffle or box, that I hadn't much spunk, and could be snubbed round by a bigger fellow with impunity. I don't know as my temper is any better than it used to be, but I control it rather more. I suppose you won't think the above is evidence of the fact, but my ideas of non-resistance are different from Father's and, perhaps, from yours.

Camp near James River,
July 4, 1862.

Dear Friends at Home:—

I sent a few words to you yesterday just to relieve your suspense, and to-day I will write a little more, though, in the present condition of my mind and body, worn out by fatigue and exposure, you cannot expect much but a disconnected letter. The papers will have told you of the strategic movement of McClellan's army, its causes and its complete success. All that remains for me to write, and all that I can be expected to know is where the Eighty-third went and what it did. The fight on the right began on Thursday, the 26th of June, and we took all on our backs and went out that afternoon but did no fighting. Friday morning at daylight we fell back to a position on a stream near Gaines' Mill. The rebels soon followed, feeling their way along, and at about 2 o'clock the fighting became general along the whole line. Our brigade formed the left flank of the line and lay nearest the river. The Eighty-third was posted in a deep gully, wooded, and with the stream I mentioned running in front of us. We built a little breastwork of logs and had a good position. On the hill behind us the Forty-fourth and Twelfth New York and the Sixteenth Michigan were posted. When the rebels made the first attack, we could not fire a shot, the hill concealing them from us, and so we lay still while the bullets of two opposing lines whistled over our heads. They were repulsed, but only to pour in new troops with greater vigor than before. Suddenly I saw two men on the bank in front of us gesticulating violently and pointing to our rear, but the roar of battle drowned their voices. The order was given to face about. We did so and tried to form in line, but while the line was forming, a bullet laid low the head, the stay, the trust of our regiment—our brave colonel, and before we knew what had happened the major shared his fate. We were then without a field officer, but the boys bore up bravely. They rallied round the flag and we advanced up the hill to find ourselves alone. It appears that the enemy broke through our lines off on our right, and word was sent to us on the left to fall back. Those in the rear of us received the order but the aide sent to us was shot before he reached us and so we got no orders. Henry and Denison were shot about the same time as the colonel. I left them together under a tree. I returned to the fight, and our boys were dropping on all sides of me. I was blazing away at the rascals not ten rods off when a ball struck my gun just above the lower band as I was capping it, and cut it in two. The ball flew in pieces and part went by my head to the right and three pieces struck just below my left collar bone. The deepest one was not over half an inch, and stopping to open my coat I pulled them out and snatched a gun from Ames in Company H as he fell dead. Before I had fired this at all a ball clipped off a piece of the stock, and an instant after, another struck the seam of my canteen and entered my left groin. I pulled it out, and, more maddened than ever. I rushed in again. A few minutes after, another ball took six inches off the muzzle of this gun. I snatched another from a wounded man under a tree, and, as I was loading kneeling by the side of the road, a ball cut my rammer in two as I was turning it over my head. Another gun was easier got than a rammer so I threw that away and picked up a fourth one. Here in the road a buckshot struck me in the left eyebrow, making the third slight scratch I received in the action. It exceeded all I ever dreamed of, it was almost a miracle. Then came the retreat across the river; rebels on three sides of us left no choice but to run or be killed or be taken prisoners. We left our all in the hollow by the creek and crossed the river to Smith's division. The bridge was torn up and when I came to the river I threw my cartridge box on my shoulder and waded through. It was a little more than waist deep. I stayed that night with some Sherman boys in Elder Drake's company in the Forty-ninth New York.

Sunday night we lay in a cornfield in the rain, without tent or blanket. Monday we went down on the James river, lying behind batteries to support them. Tuesday the same—six days exposed to a constant fire of shot and shell, till almost night, when we went to the front and engaged in another fierce conflict with the enemy. Going on to the field, I picked up a tent and slung it across my shoulder. The folds of that stopped a ball that would have passed through me. I picked it out, put it in my pocket, and, after firing sixty rounds of my own and a number of a wounded comrade's cartridges. I came off the field unhurt, and ready, but not anxious, for another fight.

Camp near James River,
July 5, 1862.

Dear Cousin L.:—

The past ten days seem to me more like some fearful dream than anything else, and I shall not be able to give an intelligent account of what has passed in that time.

For two weeks previous to the 26th of June I had been unfit for duty. On that day the fighting began on the right wing. We were marched from place to place, but did not fire a gun. We slept in an open field till 3 o'clock a. m., Friday, when we fell back with the rest of the right wing to a position along the stream at Gaines' Mill. The enemy followed soon after daylight and the fight recommenced. Butterfield's brigade formed the left flank of our line. We were told that the retreat was a feint to draw the enemy into a trap and that we were to hold our present position. The Eighty-third was posted in a gully on this stream, and on the hill behind us the Forty-fourth and Twelfth New York and Sixteenth Michigan formed the second line, in position to fire over our heads. The enemy came up and were twice repulsed with terrible loss, but only to return with renewed vigor. It was a singular situation of ours—lying in the hollow with the balls of two opposing lines flying over our heads, but we were cool, and confident of victory. Suddenly we found out that the enemy was firing on us from the rear, and instantly all was confusion, but only for a moment. Our men faced about, formed, and advanced on them, and then commenced a scene such as I hope never to see again. It appears that the enemy broke through the line somewhere on our right. The order was sent for our brigade to fall back across the river, but the aide sent to our regiment was shot and we did not receive the order. The rest of the brigade was gone and we left alone to fight a brigade of the enemy. Our colonel fell dead at the first fire and the major immediately after. Our senior captain was shot and we were almost without officers. My two tent mates were wounded, and after that, they tell me, I acted like a madman. God only knows why or how I came out alive. I had three guns shot to pieces in my hands, a rammer shot in two, and I was struck in three places by balls. One that cut my gun in two lodged in my left shoulder, one went through my canteen and struck my left leg, and one just grazed my left eyebrow. The deepest was not over half an inch and is almost well now.

We were surrounded on three sides and at last we retreated and crossed the river. The bridge was torn up, and when I got to the river I threw my cartridge box on my shoulder and waded through the water up to my armpits. We left our knapsacks and our all in the hollow where we first formed line, and everything was lost. Blankets, tents and everything, fell into the enemy's hands. I had $1.50 in stamps, a lot of paper and envelopes, gold pen, ink, $5 in money (all I had, except a little change) and other articles that money could not buy, but all are gone now. We have only such things as we could pick up here and there to keep us from the storms. Our regiment lost in that bloody field two hundred and thirty-six killed, wounded and prisoners, and our colonel and major. The papers have told you about the falling back of the army to the James river, and you know more of this probably than I do. I only know where we went and what we did, and not much about that. The fight reached us again on Monday. We were ordered out to support our batteries, and through Monday and Tuesday we were constantly exposed to the shells and grape of the enemy.* About sundown Tuesday night the remnant of our brigade went out again to the front.† Here the rebels swarmed out of the woods, seemingly without end, and though again and again repulsed, and the field piled

---

Note.—Battles of White Oak Swamp and Glendale.
†*Note.*—Battle of Malvern Hill.

with their dead by the deadly fire of our rifles and showers of grape, they still came on, determined to drive us from our position, but they could not do it. Night finally put an end to the roar of the musketry and artillery, and we still held our position. Our regiment, after firing an hour and using all their ammunition, was relieved by a regiment of the Irish brigade (God bless them!) and we fell back. Sergeant Wittich of Company I went out twenty rods in front of our line and brought off a stand of rebel colors. Our last corporal, Walter Ames, who brought the colors safely off the bloody field of Gaines' Mill, was shot through the heart while waving them in front of our lines in this last fight.

As we were going on to the field Tuesday night I picked up a tent that had been dropped and slung it across my shoulder. That tent stopped a ball that otherwise would have entered my heart, and after firing seventy rounds I came out still unhurt. It seems to me almost a miracle that I am yet alive and able to write. But we have had hard times. We were marched off at midnight, where, we knew not or cared not, but we took the road down the river and marched some ten miles. It commenced raining hard at daylight and continued all day, and now, here we are, somewhere on the James river, just where I don't know, but where I hope we will rest a little.

It is again clear and warm, and our little regiment numbering one hundred and ten men is beginning to feel a little refreshed. We have not had half rations for some time, but now they begin to come more regularly. The box you were so kind as to send me I never expect to see. I am afraid it was destroyed at White House. I am sorry for your sake that you could not have the satisfaction of knowing that it reached its destination, and I do not doubt that I should have done full justice to your bounty if I could have received it, but such are the fortunes of war; and, if I can only get plenty of hard tack, I believe I shall come out all right yet. I appreciate your kindness as much as if I had received it.

I received a letter from Father yesterday. Our folks were all in good health and thankful for my escape at

Hanover Court House. I thought that was a battle, but now it seems like a mere skirmish.

I received your letter last Sunday, but you will readily see why I could not answer it before. Yesterday was the first that we could write at all, and I thought I must write home first and to the parents of my two tent mates, who have no other acquaintance in the regiment. I hope you will write again as soon as you can. I love to get your letters always and particularly at such a time as this. Address as before, "Army before Richmond."

Camp near Harrison's Bar, James River,
Monday, July 7, 1862.

Dear Sister L.:—

I have missed your letters very much, especially for the last two weeks, and I have thought that you might write oftener. I am very lonely now. My two most intimate friends, Henry and Denison, were both wounded on the bloody field of Gaines' Mill on the 27th of June, and left on the field to the tender mercies of the rebels. Henry, I fear, I never shall see again. He was badly wounded, and everyone in the company except myself thinks he is dead, and I am hoping against hope. Denny was shot through the left hand, and I left them under a tree together. If I should tell you of the narrow escapes I had, you, who know so little of the dangers of the battle, would hardly be able to believe me. Three guns, one after another, were shot to pieces in my hands, and one of these was struck twice before I threw it away. My canteen was shot through, and I was struck in three places by balls, one over the left eye, one in the left shoulder, and one in the left leg, and the deepest wound was not over half an inch, and I came off the field unhurt. God only knows how or why I escaped, but so it was, and though I lost my knapsack containing my little all, I lived "to fight another day." Saturday night I slept in a corn field in a rain storm with no shelter but the clouds and no bed but the furrow. Sunday night what little sleep I got was on a log in the White Oak Swamp. Monday afternoon I was with the regiment supporting a battery on a hill near the James river, and exposed to a heavy fire of shot and shell. Tuesday forenoon we lay in the woods till the rebels made it so hot it was safer in the open field, and towards night we again went to the front and had another terrible fight. A tent over my shoulder stopped a ball that was speeding straight for my heart, and thus again my life was saved. But I am now alone and the next fight may lay me low with my comrades.

The report sent in from our regiment yesterday gives the names of four hundred and fifty-two killed, wounded and missing in our regiment. Think of that for one regiment! Four hundred and fifty-two out of less than six hundred that went into the fight on Friday. Colonel McLane was shot at almost the first fire, and died without a struggle or a word. Major Naghel followed him an instant after, and our two senior captains were shot during the action. The third one who then took command was wounded, and can only get round now by the help of a horse. I have nothing to say of how the regiment fought. It is not my place, but I am not ashamed yet of the Eighty-third.

What the result of all this fighting will be, I cannot say. The rebels undoubtedly will claim a great victory, as they always do, generally with far less foundation than they now have. McClellan has succeeded in withdrawing his army from a position they could not hold to one that they can hold where his flanks are protected by gunboats and his supplies cannot be cut off. What the rebels have gained I cannot see, except the ability to boast that they have driven McClellan's army. Their loss is certainly much greater than ours and includes their best General "Stonewall" Jackson.* They have but little to boast of.

Harrison's Landing, James River, Va.,
Wednesday, July 9, 1862.

Dear Father:—

Having leisure to-day and knowing that you are glad to hear from me often in these troublous times, I will

---

*Note.—This is an error. Jackson was killed at Chancellorsville.

write a little, though there is nothing of much interest to write.

As for myself, I have great reason to be thankful that it is as well with me as it is. The final report of our loss gives the names of four hundred and fifty-two killed, wounded and missing in our regiment. This seems like a fearful loss, as we went into the fight on the 27th with less than six hundred men. Of the small number who remain, not half are strong enough to stand a march of ten miles. A great many are sick, not very sick, but worn out, weak, and unable to endure full duty. Last night the President was here, and our brigade was out in full strength for a review. Every man who could carry his gun one hundred rods was out, and while we were waiting we stacked arms, and our regiment had thirty-two stacks, or one hundred and twenty-eight men out. If ordered out for a march not more than one hundred of these could go. This will give you an idea of how we are reduced. I am as well off, I think, as any one in the regiment. I am not as strong as I might be, but I charge it to the weakening effect of the hot weather as much as anything. I am entirely free from that bane of the soldier, diarrhea, etc., from which so many suffer. Hundreds of our soldiers have not seen a day in six months when they were what I should consider well. My weight is only 117 pounds, but what there is of me is bone and muscle. I attribute my good health in part to my constant use of woolen drawers and shirts. I never have gone without them a day since I have been in the service. I have now but one pair of drawers; one pair and one of the shirts you got for me when I first enlisted were left in my knapsack. They wore like iron. Another cause of sickness among our men is spending too much on the sutler. His wares are generally of a kind that do more harm than good. I have spent but very little with him for eatables, and though our diet is a constant succession of the same articles, and these not very tempting, I believe it is the best plan to live on our rations alone. The climate and exposure, with the bad water, are enough to contend against. Sometimes we have excellent water, and again we can get nothing but roily swamp water. I have drunk a good deal of water that at home would have turned my stomach, but in such circumstances I drink as little as possible, and make it into coffee. We usually have plenty of coffee and sugar when we can get our rations.

I am very anxious to know how the call for more troops will be responded to. It seems to me all important that the people should rise immediately. A week's hesitancy may bring results terrible to contemplate. It seems to me that nothing but such a show of our power and purpose to put a speedy end to the rebellion as will awe the European powers and force them to respect us can save us from foreign intervention and a war that no one can see the end of. There is no use in grumbling at this secretary and that general while we let things take the course they are now taking. McClellan should have been reinforced when he called for more troops. If he had been listened to and supported, Richmond would have been ours before this, and the backbone of the rebellion broken. There is a fearful responsibility on the shoulders of the men who have denied his requests and forced him to his present position. I don't pretend to know who is to blame about the matter, but someone is. No one in the army thinks of blaming McClellan. His men have the fullest confidence in his ability to do all that any living man can do with the force at his disposal, but anyone who saw how the rebels fought at Malvern Hill on Tuesday, and saw them pour five different lines of fresh troops against our one, can tell why he does not take Richmond. We are not whipped and cannot be, but we are obliged to take the defensive instead of the offensive in our fighting. The rebels are before us in such overwhelming numbers that I cannot see how it is possible for us to take Richmond without a great increase of our present force. We must have it or give up all.

I understand that an effort is being made to have us sent to Erie to recruit. I see but one objection and that is this—there are a great many regiments as badly or nearly as badly cut up as ours. To send them away will weaken our force here, already far too small. But we are not in condition to be effective at present and I am not sure but it would be best under the circumstances. Men who enlist would much rather enlist in a regiment that has been tried and earned a name than in a new regiment, and, if we were in Erie, had a camp and were drilling so that men could see the regiment and knew what they were going into, we would get ten men where we could one by staying here and sending out recruiting officers. I don't know, I am sure, what is best, but I hope something will be done soon.

I have not heard anything from E. in a long time. I expect that when the call is made and recruiting commences in your vicinity, he will want to enlist, but don't let him. I am convinced he never would stand it. His looks may be stouter than mine, but he has not the endurance, and if he should enlist he would be sorry for it afterwards. One representative from the family will do. It is more than probable that I shall not outlive the war, and you will want him left. Now that sounds selfish, I know, but I cannot help it. I don't want him in the army. If I could just have taken him for one hour from home and put him on the field at Gaines' Mill on Friday, it would have banished all thoughts of enlisting from his mind instanter. Let him see a ditch half full of dead and wounded men piled on each other; let him see men fall all round him and hear them beg for water; let him see one-quarter of the awful sights of the battlefield, and he would be content to keep away. This may be a weak spot in me, but I cannot help it. I feel as though I could not have him enlist. I presume he thinks he has a hard time where he is, but if he only knew the truth he would never want to leave.

It is past time for me to get dinner, and still I am writing. I only thought of writing a short letter, but this would hardly be called very short.

We are getting some new things in place of those we lost—new blankets, pants, shirts, socks, blouses, haversacks, etc., are furnished as fast as possible.

I hope we shall get our pay soon. Two months pay is

due and I have not a dollar left. A dollar here is not more than twenty-five cents at home. Write to me as soon as you can.

P. S.—Wicks is well. Not a word from Henry or Denny yet.

Harrison's Landing, James River, Va.,
Sunday, July 13, 1862.

Dear Brother and Sister:—

The morning inspection is over, and as I have not much to do for the rest of the day I will spend a portion of the time in writing to you, though I have no letter to answer.

We have no preaching to-day. Our chaplain (Elder Flower) has resigned and gone home, and I don't think the most pious man in the regiment is at all sorry. The great thunderer who was so conspicuous at all the war meetings, and who "expected" to go with us "to pray for us, to preach to us, and to fight with us," has proved a miserable failure. He has not preached one-fourth of the time when he might just as well as not, and as to fighting with us, when the shells began to fly and the balls to hiss around, he always concluded that fighting was not in his line of business. I don't say it was, but one would naturally expect a little show of pluck from a minister of the gospel who was so wonderfully courageous and war-like way up in Erie. He might at least have been round with some cheering word for a mortally wounded or dying soldier; but, ah no, such men are always lying too close to bursting shells and such things, for a chaplain to risk his precious life for his country. I may be severe, but it is just as I feel, and I am glad he is gone, for we may in time get a live man for a chaplain. I warrant you, when he gets home he will have some big stories to tell about the Eighty-third fighting, but if you see or hear him, just ask him how much he saw of it. Ask him where he was at the battle of Malvern Hill.

A short distance from where I am writing was where President Harrison was born. His father and mother are buried here, and all this section was once his estate. It is now owned by a man in Richmond by the name of Carter, I believe. He left the house in charge of the darkies, with orders to burn it if the Yankees came, but they didn't obey orders, and in and around the old mansion some eighteen hundred sick and wounded soldiers are now quartered.

We had a review by moonlight a few nights ago. "Old Abe" was down here to see the army, and he did not get round to us till 9 o'clock at night, but it was beautiful moonlight, and as he went galloping past, riding beside "Little Mac," everyone could tell him by his "stovepipe hat" and his unmilitary acknowledgment of the cheers which everywhere greeted him. His riding I can compare to nothing else than a pair of tongs on a chair back, but notwithstanding his grotesque appearance, he has the respect of the army. But the man in the army is "Little Mac." No general could ask for greater love and more unbounded confidence than he receives from his men, and the confidence is mutual. He feels that he has an army he can depend on to do all that the same number of men can do anywhere. He is everywhere among "his boys," as he calls them, and everywhere he is received with the most unbounded enthusiasm. He was here yesterday about noon. The boys were getting dinner or lounging about under the trees, smoking, reading or writing, when we heard a roar of distant cheers away down the road a mile or more. "Little Mac's a-coming" was on every tongue. "Turn out the guard —General McClellan," called the sentry on the road. The guard paraded and the men flocked to the roadside. He came riding along on his "Dan Webster," by the way as splendid a horse as you ever saw. He rode slowly, looking as jovial and hearty as if he could not be more happy. Up go the caps, and three rousing cheers that make the old woods ring, greet the beloved leader of the Army of the Potomac. He raises his cap in graceful acknowledgement of the compliment, and so he passes along. Those cheers always give notice of his approach. He speaks an occasional encouraging word, and the men return to their occupations more and more devoted to the flag and their leader. But what have they to say to the men who have been using their influence to prevent his being reinforced, to secure his defeat, and in some way to so prolong the war as to make the abolition of slavery a military necessity? Curses loud and deep are heaped on such men. Old Greeley would not live twenty-four hours if he should come here among the army. I used to be something of an abolitionist myself, but I've got so lately that I don't believe it is policy to sacrifice everything to the nigger. Such a policy as Greeley advocates, of letting this army be defeated for the purpose of making the people see that slavery must be abolished before we could end the war, I tell you is "played out." Ten thousand men have been sacrificed to that idea now, and the remainder demand that some other policy be adopted henceforth. We want that three hundred thousand men raised and sent down here immediately. We want them drafted if they won't volunteer. We want the men who have property to furnish the government with the means to carry on the war. We want such a force sent here that the whole thing can be finished up by fall. We've been fooling about this thing long enough, and now we want a change. No more playing at cross purposes by jealous generals, no more incompetent or traitorous officials. The army demands and the people demand such a vigorous prosecution of the war as shall give some hope of ending it some time or other. McClellan must be reinforced sufficiently to enable him to do something more than keep at bay three times his force. That will never conquer the South. We must take the offensive and destroy their army and take their capital. When this is done, the clouds will begin to break.

We are doing nothing but lying still now. The weather is so warm that nothing can be done in the middle of the day.

We get plenty of hard tack, bacon, salt pork and coffee and sugar, and we have learned to be content with that. Some new troops (Thirty-second Massachusetts) that arrived here a few days ago, thought they had pretty hard fare—"they hadn't seen any soft bread for three days."

We are getting some new things in place of those we lost at Gaines' Mill. We have got new blankets, haversacks, blouses, pants, shoes, socks and shirts, and requisitions are sent in for tents, knapsacks, canteens, etc., in fact, everything we need. But we never will get what we lost in our knapsacks.

I received a letter from Uncle Newell a few days ago and he said the story was circulated in Sherman some time ago that I was to be shot for deserting. What do you think of that? Had you heard much about it? I hadn't. I didn't even know that I had been courtmartialed.

There has been some talk lately of the possibility of our being sent to Erie to fill up our regiment and reorganize. The officers got up a request to that effect, and it was signed by Generals Butterfield, Morell, Porter and McClellan, and sent to the Secretary of War and Governor Curtin, but I have not much of an idea that it will be granted. We may be sent somewhere to guard prisoners or something of that sort, till recruits are raised to fill up our regiment again, but I don't believe we will see Erie till the war is over. The bands are to be discharged and I presume Alfred Ayres will be home soon.

Harrison's Landing, James River, Va.,
Friday, July 18, 1862.

Dear Cousin L.:—

I never was much of a believer in signs and wonders, lucky and unlucky days and things of that kind, but you know what a bad reputation Friday has, and how many there are ready to believe all that is said of it. Well, just see what an unlucky day it has been for me. The first note of the reveille this morning started me to my feet (for I'm a bugler, you know, and have to give the regimental calls) feeling better than I have for a week before. The mail came after breakfast and three letters for me, yours, one from my comrade Bushnell's mother, and one from Father. I had not heard from him since he got my first letter after the battle. I sat down to answer my letters and had just finished one to Father, when one of the boys came along saying—"Norton, you're always in luck. I just brought up a box from the landing with something on the cover that looked like your name." "Where is it?" "Major's tent—came by express." Well, it was not in the major's tent long, and it would have made you laugh to hear the remarks made from the time I came into the street with it till we found what was in the bottom. I was as much astonished as any of them, for I never expected to see it, and now let no one after this say anything to me about unlucky Fridays. If they do, you know how I can stop them. Contrary to your expectation, everything in the box was in good condition. Your judgment was admirably shown in the selection of articles—just such as were of real utility and would not spoil by a little delay. With all respect for your husband and Aunt A.'s, I believe the ladies of the family had just as much to do about it as they had, though you labored so hard to make me think it was some "strangers" I had never seen. The pineapple cheese was the great curiosity though. Many of the boys brought up in a dairy country had never seen one. They are not made so extensively of late except in large dairies. "Don't drop that percussion shell or you'll blow your box and contents into the river," said one fellow, and another was going to report me for "leaving fixed ammunition exposed." I'm not sure but it is a good thing, or rather I am sure it is, that I did not get it while I was at Gaines' Mill. If I had, I should have lost the most of it, but if the rebels get any share of it now, I shall miss my guess entirely. Please return my thanks to those who united with you in conferring so acceptable a present on me and my comrades (for you know I can't sit down and eat a meal with the embellishments, as the boys say, and not share with them).

It seems strange how much the rest of our company has become united since the battles. They are almost like brothers in one family now. We used to have the "aristocratic tent" and "tent of the upper ten," and so on, but there is nothing of that kind now. We have all lost dear friends and common sorrow makes us all equal.

Your account of the interest that is taken in reading my letters is beginning to scare me. Young ladies from Boston must see them, and others that I don't know, beside the whole circle of relatives. Don't you think I had better put at the top as the Herald does—"Daily circulation, ... thousand?" You can fill up the blank. You know how many better than I do. Really, I am getting to be a celebrity. But I have about made up my mind that I shan't risk my reputation by coming to New York after the war. Down on the Peninsula here I excite quite a sensation in Gotham just by writing letters, but one day's personal acquaintance would dispel the illusion, and I would be nothing but a common "soger," and a very rough specimen at that. If I only had shoulder straps, now, with an eagle or a star on, why, it might be worth while to be talked about, but do these young ladies know that all there is on the shoulders of my blouse is a threadbare spot where the musket rubs? But really, if anyone wants to read my letters, and you are willing to have it known that you have such a rattle-brained correspondent, I have no objections. I can understand how my own relatives should take an interest in me for my mother's sake, but how strangers should want to see my next letter, I can't see. How much longer do you think I could draw out a thread on that subject without breaking it? I think I'll drop it before it gets any finer.

The stamps you sent were another most acceptable gift just at this time. I had been studying for some days to contrive some way to get along till pay day. But our boys are all in the same fix as myself—terribly short. I thought I should have to stop writing or send home for some money, and I did not want to do either, but "unlucky Friday" settles it. I find paper and envelopes in the box, and stamps in the letter. No one who has not been in the situation knows how relieved I felt.

Well, I must bring my letter to a close. I have got to go half a mile for water and by the time I get back it will be time for dress parade. "All is quiet on the James," very quiet. Please write soon.

Harrison's Landing, James River, Va.,
Saturday, July 26, 1862.

Dear Brother and Sister:—

General Porter's corps, which is quite an army of itself, is now encamped on the large wheat field of the Westover estate. The Pennsylvania Reserve of thirteen regiments, three batteries and a regiment of cavalry lies next to us on the north. Morell's division of fifteen regiments, three batteries and two regiments of cavalry lies next to them, and between us and the river is the camp of the regulars under Sykes. All these troops belong to General Porter's corps. You may guess that with their tents and all the baggage wagons and horses, cannon and ammunition wagons, this field is pretty well filled up. Through all the camps there is constant activity. The men are cleaning up their arms or cooking round the fire, sitting on the ground eating their hard tack and sipping their black coffee. Little squads are marching about drilling or going through their inspection, which takes place twice a day. Every thing is kept in tip top order, ready for a fight at a moment's notice. And then, if you could see the road—it looks like the road near a county fair ground, full of teams from morning till night, long trains of wagons that are a curiosity in themselves, great covered wagons as large as two of our lumber wagons, with six mules, and a driver riding the near pole mule and guiding his team with one line. These things would all amuse you, but I have seen so many of them that they have lost their interest.

I suppose this is the height of the haying season at home. Mowing machines are rattling over the meadows, and the barns are filling up, but I see nothing like that here. Grain fields are turned into camping grounds and the cavalry horses harvest the wheat. War makes sad work with the country it passes over.

You ask me how I felt when the battle commenced, if I feared I should fall, etc. That is a very hard question to answer. In the fight at Gaines' Mill I had lain in the woods almost all day waiting for them before I saw a rebel. They had been shelling us all the time, and occasionally a shell would burst within a few feet of me and startle me a little, but we had so strong a position and felt so certain of driving the rebels off that I was anxious to have them come on. The last words I heard Colonel McLane say were, "You'll see enough of them before night, boys." His words proved too true. We had but little to do with repulsing them, for they did not come within range of our guns either time, but we could hear the firing, and, when the cheers of our men announced their victory, a feeling of exultation ran through our minds. "Come on," we thought, "we'll show you how freemen fight," but when they attacked us so unexpectedly in the rear, my feelings changed. Surprise at first and a wonder how they could get there, and then, when the truth flashed through my mind that they had broken through our lines, a feeling of shame and indignation against the men who would retreat before the enemy. Then, when the colonel was killed and Henry and Denny wounded, I felt some excited. I was stronger than I had been before in a month and a kind of desperation seized me. Scenes that would have unnerved me at other times had no effect. I snatched a gun from the hands of a man who was shot through the head, as he staggered and fell. At other times I would have been horror-struck and could not have moved, but then I jumped over dead men with as little feeling as I would over a log. The feeling that was uppermost in my mind was a desire to kill as many rebels as I could. The loss of comrades maddened me, the balls flew past me hissing in the air, they knocked my guns to splinters, but the closer they came they seemed to make me more insensible to fear. I had no time to think of anything but my duty to do all I could to drive back the enemy, and it was not duty that kept me there either, but a feeling that I had a chance then to help put down secession and a determination to do my best. My heart was in the fight, and I couldn't be anywhere else. I told you it was hard to describe one's feeling in a battle, and it is. No one can ever know exactly till he has been through it. In the fight at Malvern Hill my feelings were a little different. The memory of the scenes of the past few days was fresh in my mind, and as I marched up the hill that concealed us from the enemy, I must admit I felt a reluctance, rather a fear of going in. We were so worn out by excitement, fatigue, and want of sleep, that there was not the spirit in the movement of the men that usually characterized them, but there was the bitter determination to do or die. We would not falter, let the consequences be what they might. Butterfield and Griffin dashed here and there, cheering on the men—"Go in, my gallant Eighty-third, and give 'em h—l," yelled Butterfield as he dashed along the line, and his inspiring manner cheered the men up. We rushed over the hill on the double quick and there were the rebels. Column behind column was swarming out of the woods and advancing on us. Ten times our number were opposed to us. There were so many that they had not room to deploy, but came up in close column. Their intention evidently was to send such an overwhelming force against us, that, if we killed twice our number, there would be enough left to drive us from the field and capture our batteries. They were perfectly reckless of life and bent on driving us off, cost what it might. We went part way down the hill to meet them, so that our artillery could fire over us, then we waited for them. The hill behind us was covered with cannon in two rows and as they advanced our artillerists poured in such deadly charges of grape that it was more than any troops could stand. Each discharge would mow a swath through their lines, from five to eight feet wide. Still they closed up their ranks and came on till they met our fire, and then they wavered. We poured it into them as fast as we could load and fire, and I tell you my fear was gone then. I felt exultant. We cheered and cheered and shouted our watchword—"Remember McLane," and the rebels, disheartened, fell back. Butterfield's expression of "give 'em hell" was not inapt. It was more like the work of fiends than that of human beings. The roar of the artillery, the rattling of musketry and the unearthly screaming of the great two-foot shells from the gunboats made such music as is only fit for demons, and the appearance of the men was scarcely human. The sweat rolled in streams, for there is nothing like fighting to heat a man's blood, and as the men wiped their faces with powder-grimed or bloody hands, they left the most horrible looking countenances you ever saw. But no one cared for looks or sound. That roar of artillery was the sweetest music I ever heard, for it carried death and terror to the enemies of our country and our flag. I said the rebels retreated—they fell back out of range of our infantry, formed again and again came up. Fiercer grew the conflict and our excitement rose with it. Our men fell thick and fast, and wounded men were all the time crawling to the rear, but we did not heed them. We sat there and fought till our ammunition was gone and we had to fill up from the boxes of our dead and wounded comrades, and still we had no thought of leaving, but another brigade relieved us and we retired. Then came the reaction. I must say that the time when one feels the horrors of war most keenly is after the battle, not before it or in it.

Camp at Harrison's Landing, Va.,
Thursday, July 31, 1862.

Dear Cousin L.:—

Though everything in the box was very acceptable and we enjoyed it all so much, still I do not want to have you send another. If my health continues as good as it has been almost all the time I have been in the service, I can get along first-rate on Uncle Sam's rations. Almost everything we get is of good quality, and though there is nothing very nice or tempting to the appetite in the whole list, still it is good and wholesome food, and I do not wish to put you to the trouble or expense of sending me anything more when I can do very well without it, especially after all you have done for me now. There are so many poor fellows sick and wounded who are suffering in our hospitals, to whom such delicacies would be so acceptable, that I should feel guilty, feel as though I was receiving what they needed more than I, if I should allow you to send so much to me when I am sound and well, and very well able to get along on what the government furnishes. I know the ladies of New York and Brooklyn are doing all they can for the soldiers and I have no doubt that you are doing much that I never hear of, but I would rather you would give them what you would otherwise send to me than to receive it myself under the circumstances. They may be all strangers to you, but they are Uncle Sam's boys, and so cousins, are they not? —and they are brave and gallant boys that the fortunes of war have brought to suffering. The ladies are doing all they can for them, but there are more coming every day, and when you have done, isn't there always room for something more? Please, then, don't send another box, not because I do not appreciate your kind intentions in doing so much to make the hardships of camp life easier for me, but because I do not really need it.

In regard to money, too; when we are paid off I generally send most of my wages home, reserving what I think I shall need to last till we are paid again. Sometimes it happens that it don't hold out, the paymaster don't come at the expected time, and I get short and have to do without. I could get money by sending to Erie for it, but it seems just about like throwing it away to take it out of the bank and give it to those army sharks, the sutlers. It is so now. Our pay has been due a month, but it does not come yet. We are expecting it, and so I don't send for any. Money is well enough off at home, but it isn't of much account here. I must and will have enough to write all the letters I want; that is something I will not deny myself. I would rather receive a good letter any time than anything else I get here, and they don't come unless I write. And then I spend considerable time in writing that I should not know what else to do with. So, as to the money that Aunt Buckingham sent, if that must come, I would like to have you send me a gold pen. Ask Ollie, when he is over some time, to get as good a one of Morton's as he can for $1.25 or $1.50 and send the rest in stamps. That will be just what I want most for writing. I lost a good pen in my knapsack, and since that I have had to get along as I could.

Won't you send me Aunt B.'s address when you write next time? I think I had it once, but I have forgotten, and I would like to write one letter to her.

It is no use for me to try to pick those bones with you, for I would have to give up before I was half convinced. I can dispute and "argufy" with a man and "hoe my row," but I never quarrelled with a woman yet but I got the worst of it. I have almost a mind to pick up the second bone, though. It is a misfortune of mine to know no better than to write sometimes just as though I meant it and then expect that people will know that I don't mean any such thing. L. says she never knows, when I am talking, whether I am in earnest or not, and I suppose it's just so with my writing. But I would not insult you by writing, for anything more than a little pleasantry, such absurd ideas. I have always thought, since I had any ideas about it, that money or rank could not make a man of the person who would not be a man without either, and that, if I was just as much of a man as another would be stripped of his wealth and titles, I was just as much of a man anyway, but don't you believe the money was to me as the "sour grapes" were to the fox. Paper is full and I must stop. Write soon as you can.

Harrison's Landing, Va.,
Friday, August 1, 1862.

Dear Father:—

I was very glad to learn that there is some prospect of your being appointed chaplain for our regiment. I suppose the appointments are made by the Governor on the recommendation of the officers of the regiment. If Colonel C. favors your appointment, I think there will be no difficulty about the other officers. My opinion is that the majority of them care but little who is chaplain, or whether there is any or not. Unless some of them have some other person in view, I have no doubt they will all sign the recommendation. You will find the duties of chaplain very different from that of pastor of a church. There will be no deacons or active sympathizing brethren to "hold up your hands." You will have the whole management of the spiritual concerns of the regiment. The officers will neither aid nor oppose you, but expect you to attend to your duties while they do theirs. I do not know that there is a professor of religion among them, unless I except Lieutenant Colonel Campbell, who I have heard is a Presbyterian. Your charge will be a hard one, a motley assemblage of all sorts of characters, among whom the name of God is used much oftener than he is thought of. One thing I have noticed, however, and that is that profane swearing and card playing are not near so prevalent lately. I do not attribute this to any thought of the sin of these practices. There were many when we first entered the service, who, when they found themselves away from the restraints of society and home, let loose their tongues and indulged in swearing till they could scarcely utter a sentence without an oath. One night when we lay at Hampton, I listened to a couple of fellows in our company awhile, and finally spoke. "Boys," said I, "I think if you keep on you will make first-rate swearers. I've heard you use fifty-nine oaths in about ten minutes." "Is that so?" said one. "Yes," said I, and they stopped talking at once. One of them told me since we came here, that he had broken himself of the habit entirely. He was getting ashamed of it.

I am glad Horatio is doing so well. Poor fellow, I pity him. I think of him very often, and hope you will keep me informed how he gets along.

My health continues first-rate yet. If we march I shall stand it as well as any, I think. I shall have no gun to carry. I have no use for one now, and mine was given to a man who came back from the hospital. I have made up my mind that I shall not carry one while I am not required to, for if we get in any place where I need one there is never any difficulty in getting one.

Harrison's Landing, James River, Va.,
Saturday, August 2, 1862.

Dear Sister L.:—

We have had very dull times for a long while, at least dull to us. Very little drill or other duty, no picket duty or trenching, and not much of anything doing to create any excitement at all. Night before last, however, we had a little bit of an entertainment, just by way of variety, that stirred us up a little for the time being.

We are lying on a point of land formed by a bend in the river, and this point is just as thickly studded with camps as it can be, clear to the river's edge. The river is full of transports, steamers, tugs and all kinds of craft, and beyond them, in a long black line, the gunboats usually lie guarding the other craft and acting as pickets, but with steam up and ready to move to any other place ordered. Thursday was a rainy, muggy sort of a day, and the night cloudy and very dark. The gunboats had all but one gone to some point up the river, and the army had gone to bed and to sleep, little dreaming of an attack. I was sound asleep in my tent, when, just after midnight, the report of a dozen pieces of artillery and the screaming of as many shells over and through the camp awoke me very suddenly. It seems that the rebels had brought some eighteen pieces of artillery right down to the bank of the river opposite to our camp, taking advantage of the darkness and the absence of the gunboats, and, when they had everything ready, opened on us all at once, and if you don't believe they sent their shot and shell over here pretty rapidly for a while, I only wish you could have been here to see, that's all. I bounced out of my tent to see what was going on. It was very cloudy and dark, and looking down towards the river, I could see the flash of the guns' streams of fire, and the little spark in the air that marked the course of the shells. They came in all directions and it made a pretty lively stir through the camps. "Where are the gunboats?" was in everybody's mouth. "Are we going to lie here and be shelled out?" But the answer soon came. Screaming along the river, whistling and snorting their impatience to "get into posish," came the Monitor, the Galena and others, and the one down the river came quickly back and "opened on 'em." I tell you the thunder of those ponderous guns is music to us, but I fancy the rebs don't like it. It did not take many of her two-foot shells to scatter their batteries of light artillery, though it was so dark that there was nothing to aim at but the flash of their guns. They were silenced and they skedaddled. They did not do much damage—killed a few men and some horses, but it made quite a little episode. It showed us that we were closely watched.

Yesterday the Michigan regiment in our brigade and some other troops went over to a large house that stands in plain sight of camp, and burnt it with all the barns and other buildings. It was said to be the residence of an intense rebel, Edmund Ruffin, father of the man who fired the first gun at Fort Sumter, and was a magnificent residence, and used by the rebels as a lookout on our movements. Ruffin has met a just retribution.*

Harrison's Landing, James River, Va.,
Monday, August 11, 1862.

Dear Brother and Sister:—

I received your letters of the 1st and 4th last night. I do not know how long I shall be permitted to write, as everything is packed up and we have marching orders. As usual, we know nothing about our destination, but I think a general movement of the army is contemplated.

Last week we spent over the river. We crossed Tuesday morning and we had a splendid time. I was mistaken in the ownership of the house that was burnt over there, of which I spoke in my last letter. It was not Edmund Ruffin's, but belonged to another man. Ruffin's plantation is next above the burned house. We spent most of the week on it or in the vicinity. He had a beautiful situation and an excellent farm. There are acres of corn there eighteen feet high—the largest corn I ever saw. Apple and peach orchards breaking down with their loads of fruit stand ripening in the southern sun, and southern sun means something, too. The thermometer was up to 109 last Friday, and Thursday was hotter still. We lived while we were over there. Guarding *secesh* property is played out and we had full liberty to "acquire" anything we could find to eat. Pigs and poultry were plenty and we

---

*Note.—This statement, founded on camp rumor, was an error. The home of Edmund Ruffin, the man who fired the first gun at Fort Sumter, is mentioned in letter of August 11.

could have lived on them if we had taken salt with us, but salt could not be found. Flour and meal were found, though, and if we didn't have pancakes and hoecakes and apple sass, peaches and plums, and new potatoes and green corn, it was because we were too lazy to get them. We slept in the woods. It would have been a novel sight to you to have passed through the woods at midnight and to have seen how soldiers sleep. Lying on the ground with no covering, heads pillowed on the roots of oaks and beeches, faces upturned in the moonlight, they might have looked like inanimate objects, but the sharp note of a bugle, or the "Fall in Eighty-third" would have started them to their feet in an instant.

I wish I had the ability to describe the home of the Ruffins to you. It is the only place I have yet seen that gave much evidence that the owner is anything more than in name and pretension an F. F. V. The house itself is not very large or pretentious, but it shows that it was the abode of wealth and taste. There is an air of aristocracy and luxury about these old southern mansions that time alone can give. We never see it in the north. The grounds about this place are the most beautifully laid out of any I have ever seen. It is the realization of the imaginary residences of the heroines we read of in romance. Before the house is a beautiful clean-swept lawn, shaded by magnificent oaks and tulip trees that look as though they had seen a century's growth at least. And then, the winding walks and avenues, shady bowers and summer houses covered with roses and drooping with graceful festoons of flowers, whose names are unknown to me, but whose beauty and fragrance I can appreciate——you must see them to know their beauty. The "servants' quarters" are not the miserable log huts with mud floors like those at the White House, but clean painted frame buildings tastefully arranged in the shade of those old trees. A little apart from the main building is a smaller one, where I imagine the master spent much of his time. It was his library, study and office. He is evidently a scholar and a writer of no mean ability. He was the editor of an agricultural periodical and had held many offices of public trust and confidence. His library was very large and valuable, mostly of agricultural works, but containing a great number of scientific and classical books. Thousands of books were carried off by our men.

Harrison's Landing, James River, Va.,
Thursday, August 14, 1862.

Dear Father :—

I received your letter of the 9th and Mother's last night. It is gratifying to know that the 300,000 men first called for will probably be raised without a draft. I have thought for a long time that the cheapest way, in fact the only way, to end the war in a reasonable time is to raise such an overwhelming force that the rebels will be dismayed and feel that it is useless to continue the contest longer. It will save time, it will save lives, it will save money, to come down upon the rebels in our strength. I am glad that the government is acting at last on this principle, and I am in hopes that the effort will not be fruitless, as some have been.

We have heard of a desperate fight that occurred last Saturday between Pope and Stonewall Jackson. It does not seem to have been decisive in anything except bloodshed. Jackson evidently had a superior force, but a dispatch from Culpeper Court House on Sunday says that he sent in a flag of truce asking permission to bury his dead on the field of battle, so I think Pope is not badly beaten. Burnside is up that way with his forces, and my private opinion publicly expressed is that McClellan's army is going there too. In my last letter I mentioned that we had "marching orders." We have not gone yet, but troops have been going down the river as fast as they could for a week past. Artillery is being loaded up every night, commissary stores are going, and everything looks to me like preparations to abandon the Peninsula. The heavy guns mounted on the works lately thrown up in front, it is said, are being removed, and the rebel device of wooden ones substituted. The letter from the Herald's correspondent in last night's paper says: "If these 'forbidden-to-previously-notice' movements should not prove entirely successful, we may have something startling to send you, but if they do, the event will doubtless be highly satisfactory." This is rather unintelligible language, but I think it means nothing more or less than this: If McClellan succeeds in evacuating this position without exciting the suspicion of the rebels, all will be well, but if they get wind of what he is doing too soon, they may attack him after part of his force is gone, and make a big thing of it. I confess I am a little fearful that this will be the result, but I have confidence yet in "Little Mac," though it seems many have not.

I do not see how it is possible to move this army with all its stores and equipment and not have the rebels informed of it. They have their agents all along the river who watch everything that passes, and send instant information to Richmond. But I think "Little Mac" is enough for them. He commenced by sifting out every man not able for full duty and sending them away first. Then the knapsacks containing everything but a tent and blanket were sent off. The cartridges, all but forty rounds per man, were returned to the quartermaster, and the men were then lightened of everything that would impede a rapid march. If the rebels attack us, we can move as fast or faster than they can. We can follow down the Peninsula, if necessary, to Fortress Monroe, or when we get out of their reach, get aboard the boats at any convenient place. Our gunboats will protect the shipping, and render material aid to us in case of attack. Thus, I apprehend, ends the campaign on the Peninsula. By some it may be considered a failure, but whatever may be thought or said of McClellan by others, I still have confidence in him, and consider its failure attributable to causes for which he is not responsible. He may do better another time. I sincerely hope it may be so. If we can succeed in uniting our forces with Pope's and Burnside's and together fall on Jackson with overwhelming numbers, we may strike a blow that will tell, but I do not have any great hopes of achieving much in that way. Jackson is wary. He will get news of the movement, retire before superior numbers, fall back on Richmond and laugh in his sleeve, or perhaps more openly at his success in getting our army off the Peninsula by head work when he could not do it by force. Ah, well, time will tell.

Camp near Alexandria, Va.,
Monday, September 8, 1862.

Dear Sister L.:—

For over three weeks we have been constantly on the move, not sleeping in the same place two nights in that time.

We marched down the Peninsula, camping at Chickahominy, twenty-seven miles; Williamsburg, sixteen miles; Yorktown, fifteen miles, and Fortress Monroe, twenty-eight miles; eighty-six miles in four days. Next day embarked at Newport News, and next day landed at Aquia Creek; thence sixteen miles by railroad to Fredericksburg, then following the north fork of the Rappahannock, we went out in the direction of Culpeper and after scouting round that country a few days, took the back track and followed alongside the railroad to Manassas Junction. We left the railroad there and marched back and forth near the old Bull Run battlefield, and on Saturday week we were engaged in the second Bull Run fight on the same ground as the other, a fight that throws the first one into the shade. If I had time and felt able, I would like to describe the battle to you and our retreat to Centreville. But I don't know as you would like to hear such terrible details. Suffice it to say it was another of McDowell's victories—a fearful scene of bloody carnage.

We stopped at Centreville one day and then made a long round-about march to Hall's Hill, stopped there one day, and then a march of sixteen miles brought us here.

I would not, if I could, tell you how we have suffered on this march. Eating raw beef without salt, and drinking water from mud holes, were done more than once. I have marched forty-six miles on nothing but raw beef and ditch water, and yet I held out to the end. Now I am worn out, and can neither write nor do anything else till I am some rested.

I had to smile a little at your questions about the battle

smoke. I think it more probable somebody was burning the brush in his pasture that week.

Bivouac south of Sharpsburg, Va.,
Tuesday, September 23, 1862.

Dear Sister L.:—

I think I wrote to you last from Hall's Hill. Our stay there was short. We spent several days in marching about between Hall's Hill, Washington and Alexandria, and then crossed over into Maryland. There, that reminds me that I have dated my letter in Virginia, a habit I have fallen into from being so long in that accursed state, but this time my habit led me astray and I am still in Maryland, and so is Sharpsburg, or what is left of it. It is a village about the size of Panama, and in passing through I could scarcely see a house that was not riddled by musketry or pierced by cannon balls. That town has had a taste of war it will not soon forget.

We have had quite a march in Maryland from Washington up through Frederick City, across the two ranges of the Blue Ridge mountains and the Cumberland valley between, and then down on the west side of the mountains to the Potomac above Harper's Ferry, where we are now. I shall always remember the march through Maryland as among the most pleasant of my experiences as a soldier. The roads were splendid and the country as beautiful a country as I ever saw. It has but little of the desolate appearance of the devastated Old Dominion, but everywhere landscapes of exquisite beauty meet the eye. Pretty villages are frequent, and pretty girls more so, and instead of gazing at passing soldiers with scorn and contempt, they were always ready with a pleasant word and a glass of water. I almost forgot the war and the fact that I was a soldier as I gained the summit of the first range of mountains, and the Cumberland valley was spread out before me. I was in love with the "Sunny South." The brightest, warmest, richest landscape I ever saw lay sleeping in the mellow sunlight of a September afternoon. Oh, how I did enjoy the pure sparkling cold water gushing from the rocks after drinking so long from the swamps of the Chickahominy and puddles by the roadside in Virginia! I did think when I saw the luxury in which the aristocratic Ruffin lived, the beauty and elegance of his country villa, that a man might be happy there, but when I reflect that it is a palace in the desert and that but few can live as he did, I say, give me the humbler dwellings but better farms of Maryland, where one man does not own all that joins him, but his neighbors can live comfortably, too. It don't take ten thousand acres here to support one family. Maryland will yet be free and then she will be a noble state. One thing I noticed so different from what we see in the north. There, in the vicinity of cities and large towns, the land is always more carefully tilled and more productive than it is farther from the markets. Here, just the opposite is the case. As we receded from Washington and approached the mountains, the country increased in richness and in beauty. Maybe you think I am getting too warm in my praises of a southern state. Perhaps I am, but it seemed such a relief to get into a civilized country after a year's sojourn in the deserts of Virginia, among the few Arabs left of the original population, that I grew enthusiastic at once. But I have seen war in Maryland, too. I was a spectator, though not a participant, in the greatest battle ever fought on this continent—the battle of Antietam. I stood on a hill where a battery of twenty-pounders was dealing death to the enemies of our country, and there, stretched out before me, was a rough, rolling valley sloping away to the Potomac. The mountains do not rise abruptly out of a level country, but for several miles on either side the ground gradually rises. The country is broken and hilly, affording strong positions for defense, and on the western slope of the mountains along the Antietam river, the battle was fought. Our division was held in reserve near the center of the line, and from where I stood I could trace our lines extending in a semi-circle for several miles. The valley was wrapped in smoke, but the white wreaths curling from the cannon's mouth, the boom of the report and the scream of the shell showed the position of the batteries, and the sharp rattle of musketry deepening to a roar told where the most desperate fighting was going on.

I felt proud, exultant, that night when I knew the enemy had been driven from two to three miles at every point. Many, many were the homes made desolate that day, but it is not to us as though we had lost as many and yet gained nothing. The victory is ours, and the enemy took advantage of an armistice granted them to bury the dead and care for the wounded, to ingloriously retreat across the river.

Colonel (late Captain) H. L. Brown's new Erie regiment arrived here lately and one of our boys who was over to see them told me that he saw a young man there who inquired for me and said he was my brother. Can it be possible that E. has enlisted? The last I heard from him was at Hall's Hill. He wrote that he would take my advice and stay at home; he had given up the idea. I cannot understand why, if he has enlisted, he did not come and enlist with me.

I am waiting news from home with anxiety. I have had but few letters lately. Our mail comes very seldom. In fact, we are constantly on the move. I have not pitched a tent but once since I left Virginia, sleeping every night on the ground, rolled up in a blanket.

I hope you will write often whether you hear from me or not. I will write as often as I can.

*Camp near Sharpsburg, Md.,
Friday, September 26, 1862.*

Dear Brother and Sister:—

Nothing of interest has occurred since I wrote. We are guarding this ford and "All is quiet along the Potomac." The impression prevails that the rebel army is not far off on the other side of the river, and some morning you may hear of another great battle.

I must answer some of your questions. On the march from the Rappahannock to Manassas, we were surrounded by the rebels most of the time. They got in Pope's rear at Culpeper and then they kept there, going back between him and Washington as far as Centreville and Fairfax. They followed up in our rear and cut off our supply train, and were continually hovering round our left, waiting an opportunity to attack us. If a fire was kindled, the smoke in the day or the light at night would reveal our position and invite a shell, and we were not allowed to make any. Do you see? But I guess "nobody was hurt."

You ask what good McClellan accomplished by his campaign on the Peninsula, and add that he has but few friends in your neighborhood. Now I might ask you, what has anyone done on our side towards crushing the rebellion? Is the end of the war apparently any nearer than it was last spring? Have not the rebels a larger army to-day than they had last spring? And are they any less determined to continue the war?

In its leading object, the capture of Richmond, the campaign was a failure. Such men as Greeley instantly pounce upon McClellan and blame him for the fact, when, in my humble judgment, the blame belongs on other shoulders. At Yorktown, he first met the enemy intrenched in one of the strongest positions in the country. When he arrived there, if he had had fresh men, artillery and ammunition, provisions, etc., he might have taken the works by assault, but he had not. His artillery and ammunition trains were stuck in the mud that was almost impassable, and by the time they could be got up, Yorktown was defended by twice our number of troops. Then Greeley and his party sneered because McClellan went to digging. He did dig, and compelled a superior force to evacuate their fortifications. Now, I say, he showed consummate skill in driving them from such a place with scarcely the loss of a single life. He followed the army to their new defenses on the Chickahominy. We all hoped he would take Richmond. We were disappointed, and Greeley sneered again. Of course he blamed McClellan, and thousands who swallow every word the Tribune utters as gospel truth believed him. Well, you ask, if he was not to blame, who was? I blame McDowell. I have hardly patience to call him a general. Great events sometimes spring from slight causes. If you have read the history of the war closely, you will remember the quarrel between McDowell and Sigel, when the latter asked permission to burn a certain bridge to cut off Jackson's retreat up the Shenandoah, and the refusal of the former.

See the result—the bridge was left unburnt and Jackson crossed in safety and hurled his command of forty thousand on McClellan's right wing. That sudden reinforcement of the enemy compelled McClellan to withdraw his right wing, leaving the White House unprotected, and consequently, to change his base of operations to the James. His success in doing this won for him the admiration of every military man in this country and Europe. Napoleon said that he who could whip the enemy while he himself retreated, was a better general than one who achieved a victory under the prestige of past success. McClellan retreated fifteen miles and fought the enemy every day for seven days, whipping superior forces every day, winding up with the victory at Malvern Hill. There we learned that he is a general. Those who have seen what he had to contend with have confidence in him, and although his campaign was a failure, we see that the blame rests not on him, but on those who failed him just on the eve of success. Had McDowell allowed Sigel to burn that bridge, Fremont could have come up with him, and uniting his forces with those of McDowell, Sigel and Banks, they could have annihilated Jackson's army, or at least beaten it so it never could have troubled us, and then following up, united all their force with us and swept on into Richmond. When you wrote, you had not heard of McClellan's victory at Antietam. If you had, I think you would not have asked the question. Public confidence, led by Greeley, and ever hasty to condemn, was severely shaken when he left the Peninsula. I think he has regained at least a part of it by that hard earned victory. If I were at home nothing would make me ready to fight sooner than to hear some home guard abuse McClellan. I am afraid I should lay myself liable to indictments for assault and battery pretty often, if public opinion is as you say. Don't swallow every word old Greeley says as the pure truth. A man will do a great deal for party and call it country. McClellan is a Democrat, though not a politician. Fremont is a Republican. Now, see if Greeley don't join in the popular outcry against McClellan and want Fremont to take his place. Compare what you know of the generalship of the two men, and ask yourself if Greeley's spirit is party or country.

I got started so about McClellan that I almost forgot the one-fingered mittens and everything else in both letters. I will answer that by informing you that my whole wardrobe consists of what I wear at one time. I have not even one extra pair of socks or a shirt. When I get a chance to wash I hang my shirt up and go without till it gets dry. I should not wonder if another year's soldiering would enable me to do without clothing altogether, and save my $42 for postage and tobacco money. I suppose Almon thinks his mittens and his oil-cloth fixings "big things," but I wouldn't give a snap of the finger for them now. They are very well in winter quarters, but I would not carry them ten miles on a march for them.

I suppose that two thousand soldiers looked as big to you as our regiment did to me when I first enlisted at Erie. I would not consider that much of a crowd now. I can see the camp of ten thousand from where I am writing. The greatest show of troops I have seen was at the review near Washington last fall. Old Abe and Little Mac had eighty thousand there on parade and that was a show. I have seen the most of McClellan's, McDowell's, Pope's, Banks', and Sigel's armies, but I would rather see two or three pretty girls and a glee-book this afternoon than the whole of them. Write soon as you can.

Sharpsburg Ferry, Md.,
Monday, Sept. 29, 1862.

Dear Sister L. :—

Dennison T. has got home discharged. I wish I could have seen his mother's greeting. I warrant you it was a joyful meeting. But Mrs. B. writes her sorrow. She cannot forget that though he went from home with a companion, he returned alone. Henry, I am afraid, will never return to receive such a greeting. They have never heard a word from him since the news of his arrival in Richmond severely wounded. I think he must be dead. Still they have no direct intelligence of his death, nothing but dreadful uncertainty.

If I should come home and call to see you I don't believe you would be very sleepy for one hour or two, but I have no such expectations for the present at least. I have often told you that I was in for the war, and I never suffer myself to think for a moment of any going home till I go home honorably discharged, either unfit for service or at the close of the war. That day may be a good way off, but still I do not get homesick in the least. I know I never could feel easy to remain at home in full health while the war continued. No one would be more happy to see the war come to a close, the troubles settled, and the Union restored, than I, but few perhaps think less of military life than I, or would be more glad to leave it than I, if the cause were removed, but principle is at stake. I have cast my lot here from choice, and I'm not the one to back out because it's hard.

I don't just know about Almon's garrison duty at Fortress Monroe. I rather guess they have garrison enough there. He may go to Yorktown or some of the other places in the vicinity, but I miss my guess if he stays long in the Fortress. I hope he will not be homesick, for of all the forlorn objects I ever saw a homesick soldier is the most pitiable. If he gets along the first month or so he will stand it afterwards.

So Uncle Joseph's folks are down on McClellan, are they? Well, you know they are strong abolitionists and get most of their ideas on national affairs from Greeley and Beecher. Now McClellan is a more moderate man and deals with things as he finds them. He is no pro-slavery man, no more than Beecher, but I think he is a more practical man. He will do his duty just as well, now the "proclamation" is out, as he would before Greeley said the war would end in thirty days after the issue of the proclamation. It was done September 22d, so I suppose the war will end by October 22d, and some time in November I shall be home. Pleasant prospect, but I "don't see it." I approve of the proclamation, but I don't think it is going to scare the South into submission. I think it will result in the total overthrow of slavery, but next winter will witness scenes so bloody that the horrors of the French Revolution will be peace in comparison to it. If the South will have it so, the blood be on her own head. Seward was right—the "irrepressible conflict" will continue till freedom or slavery rules the nation. I can't see through the mist that clouds the future, but I'll hope.

So you will allow me to laugh at you for thinking the smoke of battle reached old Chautauqua. Well, you are good humored about it to say the least, especially as you are not in a situation to help yourself very well. I do not say it didn't come there, but did you see any repetition of the performance after the battle of Antietam on the 17th? There was more smoke there than I have seen at any other battle. It was a hundred miles or so nearer, too.

Sharpsburg, Md., October, 1862.

Dear Sister L.:—

I always liked Steve. We tented together ever since we left Erie, and he was sensible. He is a queer, eccentric genius like his relatives, but he did not stay long. He was just out of the hospital and he fell out on the march. I've heard nothing of him since, so I went on alone again.

At Hall's Hill our Tommy came back. Tommy Hopkins is an Irishman. He is now nineteen years old. At sixteen he came over alone, and now he has not a relative this side of the ocean. He came into our company a total stranger. Now no man in the company has more friends than Tommy. There is something so manly about him that no one can help liking him. No one could be more obliging, and now no one could receive a favor more easily than little Tommy Hopkins. At Malvern Hill he was terribly wounded. Dauntlessly he faced the foes of his adopted country, but a stern trial was in store for him. While loading he was struck by a Minie ball which cut off the forefinger of his left hand, went through the ball of his thumb and out at his wrist then in at his breast, and only stopped when it struck his shoulder blade. He refused all assistance and went a mile to the hospital alone. His wound was dressed. Next day, in all the rain and mud, he walked to Harrison's Landing, ten miles. A brave young heart is Tommy's. With no kind friends to write and soothe his pain while in the hospital, he still kept his spirits, and finally ran away from the hospital and came to us. Of course I welcomed him back with his stump of a hand and the great red scar on his breast. There is no other man in the regiment I like as I do Tommy. But he couldn't handle a gun, so the colonel took him to headquarters for an orderly.

Well, then I got in with T. H., a bilious, crotchety, quarrelsome old bach. He is terribly profane, boasts of being selfish and everything else that is disagreeable. I tented with him till we came here and then I changed. My chum now is a quiet, inoffensive, obliging fellow, a new recruit by the name of Palmer. He sings, reads and talks through his nose like a U. P. preacher, loves everything good and hates evil, especially tobacco, which I don't, you know. I am very well contented, however, with him. I was with H. In fact, I am tolerably contented with everything. Dennison taught me to philosophize and take things easy.

Camp three miles north of Fredericksburg,
Saturday, Dec. 6, 1862.

Dear Sister L.:—

We have been here a couple of weeks now, and things begin to look some like winter quarters. The papers still keep up the hue and cry of "on to Richmond," but we don't go on to Richmond, and my "opg." is we won't this winter. The fact is, winter is upon us, and winter in Virginia, though very different from northern winters, is just as fatal to a campaign as frost is to cucumbers, or arsenic to rats. The moving of an army implies more than the marching of the men that compose it. Long trains of wagons, heavier wagons, too, than you ever saw, must accompany each division. Batteries of artillery, too, and when a few of these have passed along a road after one or two days' rain or snow, the following teams are floundering belly deep in mud, and everything must stop. Now, notwithstanding what the papers say, I believe they know it is not the intention to advance on Richmond this winter. My own opinion is (you may have it for its worth) that we will stay here a month or so till the mud will prevent the rebs from moving north, and then if Congress has not done anything in the way of settling the matter, we will be sent south where winter will not hinder our fighting.

I have been much interested in the President's message. I presume you have read it, at least that part relating to emancipation. It meets my views exactly. It is broad and deep, but yet so simple a child can understand it. Nothing he has ever said or done pleased me so much as his reasons for his policy, and his earnest appeal to Congress and the people to support it. "We say we are for the Union," he says, "but while we say so the world does not forget we do know how to save the Union. . . . We shall nobly save or meanly lose the last best hope of earth."

I do hope that Congress will heartily support his plan, and remembering that "the dogmas of the quiet past are inadequate to the stormy present" will "rise to the occasion."

I think I wrote to you at Warrenton what I thought of McClellan's removal, but if you did not receive my letter I will tell you in a few words. I think the whole army thinks as much of McClellan to-day as they ever did. We ask no better leader. I believe, too, that the President had as much confidence in his loyalty and ability the day he removed him as he ever had. "Why did he remove him then?" you will ask. On account of pressure of public opinion. There was a strong feeling among the people that he was not the right man, and they had lost confidence in him. They could not understand the difficulties of his position, and chafed at his delays. Time will show if they were right. The President saw that the people did not like him, would not enlist, would not come forward with their money, and thought best, though against his better judgment, to yield. Now, that is my opinion. It is not what the public press says, but merely what I think, and as I said before, you may have it for what it is worth. Burnside was a good man in his place, but not equal to "Little Mac." His race is almost run.

I sympathize with you in your sorrow at the loss of one of your household band. Though I never knew her, I can almost read your hearts, as I fancy you gathering round the fireside or the table and missing her from the circle. The blow will be sudden and severe on Albert. I have often thought how I should feel if news should reach me of the death or dangerous illness of any of my dear friends while I was kept away from them. So far I have been spared the trial.

I am still established at brigade headquarters and very comfortably fixed, too. I am in a tent with two orderlies. We have built a log house just about seven by nine, five logs high, and covered it with ponchos. We have our bed in one end and a fireplace in the other, so we are quite comfortable. We need it, too, for yesterday it snowed and was bitter cold, and to-day it just thawed enough to be sloppy and nasty.

We have not been paid since we left the Peninsula, and money is scarce, I tell you. I don't know but I shall have to stop writing for want of stamps. I must close this letter any way, for it is getting so dark I can't see to write.

Falmouth, Va., Dec. 20, 1862.

Dear Sister L.:—

I have not heard from you since I wrote last, but you will want to hear from me now, so I will write a little if nothing more than to tell you of my safety. We have had a terrible fight, but you have heard of that, and I need not give particulars. I don't feel like it, for it was nothing but humiliating defeat. I suppose the radicals have got enough of Burnside now and will want another change. I have nothing to say—of course it makes no difference to the country how many of her sons are offered on the altar of this incapacity. Oh, no. If it was Little Mac, thunders would be hurled against him, but no. We have got a man now who will move, no matter what reason he has for standing still. You may think I am talking bitterly. Well, I feel so. I'm sick of such useless slaughter. McClellan never made an attack and failed, and never showed stupidity as Burnside has.

But enough of that. You'll want to know what "hairbreadth escapes" I had. I always expect you to want a string of them after every battle. I shall not gratify you this time. I think it humors a bad taste, but I'll merely say I had enough of them, such as a rap on the head with a board thrown by an exploding shell, a mouthful of gravel raised by a ploughing grape shot, running the gauntlet of rebel sharpshooters in carrying a dispatch to General Griffin. I'll tell you about them some time if I ever get home.

It would have done a person good, or at least given him an idea of war, to have walked through the town of Fredericksburg on Monday last. It was a place about the size of Erie, perhaps larger. On Thursday one hundred and fifty pieces of our artillery played on it, and after we had done all the damage we could the rebs played on it with their "brass bands" and "bass horns" from the other side. Between them both there was not much of it left untouched. It was battered and burnt, the streets were filled with a confusion of all things, splendid furniture and carpets, provisions, bottles, knapsacks, dead men and horses, blankets, muskets, the pomp of war and paraphernalia of peace mingled together. Men were ransacking every house, taking everything they wanted, and baking pancakes in the kitchens. Slapjacks were plenty while we stayed at Fredericksburg. I have heard from Alf. since the fight. He is safe and sound. My orderly sergeant was killed in the charge. That was all the loss in our company. Some few received slight wounds. Captain A. led his company like an officer.

Stoneman Station, Va.,
Tuesday, Dec. 30, 1862.

Dear Brother and Sister:—

I have been hard up for stationery and stamps lately, more so than ever before. This month nearly gone makes six months for which we have not received a cent of pay, consequently there is very little money in camp. The sutler won't come where there is no money, and of course we can't buy anything. You don't know anything about it at home. All you want is a little money, and paper, ink, pen and postage is forthcoming. But I couldn't get it now if I had $26, unless the regiments had money, too, for there is none to buy—no sutlers. Postage stamps we have to send home for. Sutlers won't sell them; there's no profit. I got half a quire of paper—this is the last sheet—out of a knapsack on the battlefield, and it has lasted me till now, and I just found a man who has a bottle of ink, so I'm all right for this letter, but the next, ah, me, the next!

I see plainly that I have not kept you posted in regard to my own affairs. I have taken it for granted that you understood more than you do, so I must answer some of your questions. I have acted as chief bugler since we left the Peninsula, but I did not stay at brigade headquarters till we left Antietam. My duties are to give the signals for morning and evening roll calls, guard mounting, drills, dress parade, etc. I have a programme furnished by the assistant adjutant general and keep my own time, so that I may say as long as I attend to my duties strictly I am my own master. For instance, the time arrives for "tattoo" in the evening. I take my bugle, sound the brigade call, "Dan, Dan, Dan, Butterfield, Butterfield, Dan, Dan, Dan, Butterfield, Butterfield," and the tattoo. After I finish, the regimental buglers in each regiment sound their regimental call, and the tattoo. Whatever call is sounded from headquarters they repeat. When I first came the adjutant general used to tell me when to sound, but finding I attended to my business, he left it all to me, so I am giving good satisfaction and like my place well.

Ollie M. thought I was a sergeant, and congratulated me on my promotion. According to the regulations I should be, but I did not enlist as a musician and so I do not expect promotion as such. I should receive $20 per month, but doubt my getting over $13.

Three of us, two orderlies and myself, have put up a log building five logs high, and covered it with ponchos, got a fireplace and everything comfortable, and now we've got orders to march.

LETTERS OF 1863

Friday, Jan. 2, 1863.

We did march in about thirty minutes after I wrote that last line, and I have not had a minute's time to write since. We went off on a reconnoissance, or "reek-o-nuisance," as the boys call it. We went about fifteen or twenty miles up the river to Richard's Ford and came back yesterday. We had a tough march—such a march always is, for we don't wait for trains, and when we got into camp we were all tired, I assure you.

You were asking me if my present position entitled me to more privileges than a private—the privates seem to think it does. It entitles me to have my knapsack carried on a march, and—to go without my blankets if the trains don't come up. It entitles me to a horse if I want it, but I don't want it, so I am dubbed "dam phool" by said privates. But all in all, I guess I'd rather be chief bugler than private.

I saw Alf a few days ago. He was looking well, and this morning I had a good long chat with Mrs. A. She arrived last night. It was the first time I had spoken to a civilized woman in six months, and you may imagine my "phelinks."

Stoneman Station, A. C. & F. R. R., Va.,
Sunday, Jan. 25, 1863.

Dear Sister L.:—

I thought the subject of bugler was exhausted, but I see you want to know more about it. I am chief bugler of the brigade. My duties are, in camp, to sound the calls for roll calls, drills, inspections, guard mounting, etc., at regular hours each day; on the march, to attend on the general in command and sound the calls to march or halt and rest, strike tents and form in line, etc. In short, to act as mouthpiece for the general. So much for duties. As to privileges

—one, I've nothing to do but bugle; two, my luggage is carried in the headquarters wagons; three, I get better rations than in the regiment, and more of them; four, I get my wood hauled, and in the regiment the men have to carry all they burn a long distance. Well, there are four, perhaps that's enough, but I might add others. As to the horse, I have one now, and a splendid one, too. He would be worth $175 at home. Colonel Vincent, acting as Brigadier General, went to the brigade quartermaster and told him to furnish me a horse that I could carry the brigade colors on and keep up with him. He is a dashing rider, and no raw head and bloody bones could keep up with him, so he gave me a beautiful black horse, and I am now the brigade color-bearer and bugler. My pay should be $21 per month, but I don't think I shall get now more than $13. They have commenced to-day paying our brigade four months' pay. Nearly seven months are due.

Well, Burnside has moved again, and got stuck in the mud. That is the short of it. The long of it was the five days it took us to get six miles and back to camp. It beat all the Peninsula mud I ever saw, and demonstrated the falsity of Burnside's theory that if twelve horses couldn't draw a cannon twenty-four could. The more horses the worse it was.

We got back to our old camps yesterday, and I apprehend we shall stay a while. The army cannot move in this climate in the winter, and perhaps the people will believe now that "Little Mac" was right in not moving last winter.

Stoneman Station, Va.,
Friday, Jan. 30, 1863.

Dear Sister L.:—

Last Friday an agent of our benevolent but dilatory Uncle Sam paid us a visit and four months of greenbacked promises. He was an oily tongued fellow, and just euchred me out of $2.00 and over. The government owed me $6.41 on clothing account, and he paid me $4.25 and put the rest in his own pocket.

There were some rich scenes during his visit. One fellow

in the Forty-fourth New York had been paid twice in hospital on his "descriptive list." The first time he drew $52, the next by some oversight he drew $78, when but $26 was due him. He returned to his regiment and chuckled over his smartness in cheating Uncle Sam out of $52. He told it to everybody he knew, and when the pay-day came they were all on the lookout to see how he would come out of it. When his name was called he stepped to the table and Mr. Oily Tongue commenced: "You owe the United States $52, the United States owes you $48; $48 from $52 leaves you just $4 in debt to the government. Got the money?" He rattled it off like an auctioneer, and the tricky Ellsworth was non-plussed. He finally stammered out that he had not. "Oh, well, never mind, we'll wait till next time, but don't forget that $4." Oh, you ought to have heard the smile that rose in the crowd! The poor fellow can't stir out of his tent but somebody puts out his hand with—"Got the money?"

We have been having a big touch of winter for this country. Yesterday morning we had snow a foot deep, the most I've seen in Virginia. It was not very cold, but it is melting off now and it will make terrible roads when it is gone. Snow is twice as bad as rain for that. To-day is clear and warm, that is, thawing.

There is an order out to allow three men in each company to go home on furlough. This and other orders intimate to me that we are to stay where we are some time, or that we will not attempt another movement till the winter is over enough to make it safe.

Stoneman Station, Va.,
Friday, Feb. 6, 1863.

Dear E.:—

Wicks' golden opinions of "Little Norton" may do very well to repeat at home. Perhaps he thinks, as he has said so much for me, I should return the compliment and praise him up to the skies. I can't see the point. I don't thank anybody to say that I have done more than I agreed to do, more than a soldier's duty, and if any one says I have not done my duty, send him to me to say it. I don't know what Wicks saw me do at Malvern Hill. I didn't see him at all in the fight. I was under the impression that he was "taken with a sunstroke" just before the fight commenced. At Bull Run the boys say he did "fight like the devil."

I don't care anything about what he told you of my smoking. I could have told you that long ago if I had thought you cared anything about it. You all knew when I left home that I used tobacco some, and Mother and L. particularly urged me to quit it. I wouldn't make any promises about it and continued to smoke, but a year ago last Christmas I did quit, and then I wrote home and told all about it. Well, not the first one said so much as "I'm glad," or advised me to stick to it. I waited a month or so and heard nothing, and then I thought if that was all you cared about it, if it made no difference to any of you, it didn't to me, so I went at it again. If Wicks had told you that I chewed two pounds of plug a week and a pound of opium, drank gin and gambled, would you have believed him? Well, if it makes any difference to you I will just say for your comfort that I don't.

I am glad to hear that Wicks is looking so well. The boys who saw him in Alexandria said there was nothing left of him but his mustache. If I get down so low as that, I would not be much to load down an ambulance or a hog-car, would I?

No, siree, I wouldn't take a discharge now if I could get it. You need not trouble yourself about that. If I did want one, I fancy (pardon my vanity) I could play off on the doctors and get it, but I don't want it, and I would kick a man that would offer me one. As to being the "captain's friend" I don't see the point. I despise him too much for that. Personally I have no fault to find. He has always treated me well, perhaps favored me some, but I am not the friend of the man who always has the piles or something of the sort when a fight is coming off. At Hanover Court House he couldn't keep up, at Gaines' Mill he lay behind a tree and laughed while the men fell all round him. At Malvern he shouted retreat and ran like a greyhound, and got shot in the back with a three-cornered something. Last summer at Fredericksburg when we expected a fight he was too weak to march, and we didn't see him again till after Antietam. At this last at Fredericksburg he did go in and acted something like a man, the first and last time he has done so. When we moved last, expecting another battle, he couldn't go, he had the piles. Should I be the "captain's friend"? I don't know that he has but one in the company, and he is a sort of sucker. Mrs. A. is a woman, a true woman. I respect her very much, and so does every man in the company. Nothing but that respect for her feelings prevents the company from complaining of him and having him cashiered for cowardice.

I think some of my letters must have been lost. Did you never get the one that told of Henry's watch being lost? I felt so bad about that. I would have bought a dozen rather than lost that. I kept it till we got to Antietam, waiting for a chance to send it by express, but finally after getting Mary's permission, sent it by mail, and it was never heard from. I took all the precautions I could to make it safe, did it up in a little box like an ambrotype, but the last I heard it had not arrived, and if it had, they would have told me.

I wrote you in my last how our march terminated. Did Wicks tell you anything about camp lice? I do not know that I have ever said a word about them in all my letters, but they are so plenty here that they are the subject of half the standing jokes and *bons mots* in camp. I presume you never saw one. They are the soldier's pest. I never saw one till we got to Yorktown. They resemble head lice in appearance, but not in habits. They don't go near the hair, but stay in the clothes, shirt and drawers. There is no way to get rid of them, but to scald them out. They will hide in the seams and nit in every hiding place possible. Cold water won't faze them. They multiply like locusts and they will fat on "onguentum." At the time we left the Peninsula they were plenty, and until we got to Antietam, more than a month, no one had a chance to wash his clothes in hot water. I do not believe there was a man in our brigade, officer, private or nigger, but was lousy. They grow to enormous size and are the most cunning and most impudent of all things that live. During the late snow storm the boys, for want of something else to do, made sleds of their jaw bones, and slid down the bank of the railroad. The other night after supper I was sitting by the fire smoking a cigar, when I felt something twitch at my pants' leg. I looked down and there was one of the "crumbs" with a straw in his mouth, standing on his hind legs and working his claws round like a crab on a fish line. I gave a kick at him, but he dodged it and sticking up his cigar squeaked out, "Give me a light."

I woke up the other night and found a regiment of them going through the manual of arms on my back. Just as I woke the colonel gave the command "charge bayonets," and the way they let drive at my sirloin was a proof of their capacity. Any one of them can throw himself into a hollow square and bite at the four corners. I would be willing to let them have what blood and meat they wanted to eat, but the devils amuse themselves nights by biting out chunks and throwing them away. Well, this is a pretty lousy leaf, ain't it? Most likely the next one will be something different if it is not.

Joe (my housemaid) is sitting by the fire picking his teeth with a bayonet and swearing at the beef. He says it is a pity it was killed, it was tough enough to stand many a long march yet. Well, it is tough. When Burnside got stuck in the mud, the artillery harness all broke, and the only way they could get the guns out was for the men to cut their rations of beef into strips, and make tugs out of them.

Stoneman Station, Va.,
Sunday, Feb. 8, 1863.

Dear Sister L.:—

I send you a Harper's, thinking you do not often see them. It is one of the choicest numbers I have ever seen. "The Picket" is a gem for a wood cut. It is lifelike and true. The officer's uniform is an exact copy. Don't it strike your fancy there is a bit of romance in the midnight—

"Who goes there?" There is, and much matter of fact, too. You see a good portrait of our "Little Dan" (General Butterfield), too. If I ever get home I'll show you the bugle he took out of my hand to "sound the charge" at Bull Run. I'm proud to see him now Chief of Hooker's Staff.

"The army stuck in the mud" is just as good as illustrated papers can make it. The road that looks like a river is mud, not water. In front of the barn you see a "caisson," or ammunition wagon. The officers on the jaded horses, the coffee pots and pails on the muskets, in fact the *tout ensemble* of the picture is first rate. The literary part of the paper I don't think so much of, but the pictures are good. Keep it to show me when I come home. "Ould Graaly" is a decided hit.

Stoneman Station, Va.,
Sunday, Feb. 15, 1863.

Dear Brother and Sister:

I received your letter last night, and, as you say my letters don't come too often, here goes for the answer in hopes to get another soon.

Really you have been having a time visiting. Hope you don't go as some folks I have heard of, just to get something to eat. "Go it while you're young," or while the year is, and the sleighing lasts. By George, but I would like just one spanking sleigh ride this winter! Nothing but a 2:40 horse, drifted roads, a duck of a cutter, and a little ducksie with a duck of a bonnet would do me, though. I wouldn't be worth a cent without a lively "schoolmarm" to help do it. Do they have any such in your part of Chautauqua? But talk of sleigh rides for me—it's all bosh.

You need not look for me to be "one of the three." I wouldn't go if they should offer me a furlough. No doubt you want to see me, but won't you want to see me more after three years? Such a coming home then will be worth talking about.

The winter is passing away rapidly. About three weeks more will bring us round to the same time we left Hall's Hill last winter. Ah, then for another summer of fighting!

Captain C. W. Ayres, Ninth New York Cavalry, called to see me the other day. Con is a first-rate fellow. Straps on his shoulders add no "style" to his character. Perhaps now you don't understand the military significance of that word. It is the same as "airs," "putting on airs." Charlie will remember him as we saw him soon after the first Bull Run. He says he is coming home on leave soon. He bought that farm Uncle Joseph is to live on.

I went over to see Alf day before yesterday. You may believe I have attended to my business pretty closely, when I tell you that is the second time I have ever had a "pass" to go visiting since I've been in the service. I found Alf well, enjoying himself like an oyster in the mud.

You may be surprised to hear that half this army is gone, because you see nothing of it in the papers. At least, I do, but it is a fact. The Pennsylvania Reserves, Ninth, Sixth and Second corps, are all gone. I don't know where, and more are going every day. There was a rumor that the center Grand Division was to be withdrawn to the defenses of Washington and the rest of the army sent to reinforce our armies in the south and west. In my opinion that would be a good plan. We can do nothing here this winter, and if the war is to be fought out there is poor policy in keeping this army idle. Even if it is to be settled by writing, an overwhelming force at Vicksburg and New Orleans would be a good basis for negotiation.

So the cares of life have begun to fasten on you so soon! Don't know what to do with yourselves, eh? Oh, don't you wish you were soldiers, and then you wouldn't have to know. All you would have to do would be to do as you were told.

I should think if the Adkins place was for sale it would be cheap. Some of the Virginia farms remind me of that. A house in the middle of a goose pasture. Well, now, how do I know but you have bought it, and here I am ridiculing your homestead? Well, I stop it. "Nuff ce'd."

Falmouth, Va., Feb. 25, 1863.

Dear Cousin L.:—

Though I receive a good many from here and there, your

letters have had a charm for me I found in no others, and I have felt uneasy and restless when the mail has come night after night and no letter from you. I don't know but I am babyish to think so much of my letters, but it is almost all I have to do now, to read letters and write and think, think. I get tired of this thinking, too, so don't blame me if I write the second time in return for yours.

I received a letter a few nights ago that interested me very much. When I left home there was a young lady teaching in the village academy. She called the day I left to bid me good-bye and godspeed, and remarked that "she could not shoulder the musket but she was going to the war, not as *la fille du regiment,* but as nurse." I am afraid I smiled a little incredulously. I did not think she was really in earnest, but was only saying something to express her sympathy for the soldiers, and every one had plenty of that. Before I left Erie, however, she had gone—tendered her services, been accepted and sent to St. Louis. I heard no more from her till I received that letter, and supposed she had long ago returned to her friends in Indianapolis, but all this time she had been in the army wherever she could soothe the pain or add to the comfort of the sick and wounded soldiers. Six months she was a prisoner among the chivalrous butternuts, much of the time in Corinth. I must confess I admire her spirit, don't you? She was not bound, as our volunteers are, for any length of time, still she has not deserted yet. "Weary often, but never tired," she writes.*

One of my tent mates left me yesterday morning to report in New York. He goes to receive a commission in one of the black regiments. He has been in the service three months, has never seen a fight except from a distance, and cannot tell to-day whether to hold his gun at shoulder arms with the barrel or rammer to the front. He has been a bugler, an orderly, and the brigade postmaster since he came out, and has never drilled at all. Friends got him the commission. If our negro soldiers are officered by such men, I'm afraid they won't amount to much.

---
*Note.—Her name was Ada Johnson.

Whenever you have leisure, remember that I would be very thankful for a letter. Do not think me too much a reprobate. I have made a discovery—there are some in the army who try to live Christians. The other night I stumbled on a little prayer-meeting. The gathering was small, only seven, but it did me more good than many a sermon has.

Stoneman, March 3, 1863.

Dear Cousin L. :—

I can never forgive myself for writing such a letter to you as I did last week. How it must have jarred on your already overwrought feelings, but, L., I did not, I could not, have guessed that the reason I did not receive my usual letter was that your baby's cradle was empty. It grieves me beyond measure to think that I should have written anything that would add a sorrow by my thoughtlessness, when you had already all you could bear. I can only ask you to forgive my haste. If I caused you pain, believe me it was unintentionally done. I have read your letter again and again, and every time I have laid it down feeling that I could not understand it. Something of that feeling of loneliness I can understand. I know how ten thousand times in the day something reminds you of the lost, and how, as you move about the house lost in thought, your mother's chair might almost seem to be occupied again, or you would listen as though you heard the little cry that told you baby's awake, and then, as you felt the delusion and knew it never more could be, it seems to me I know something of that desolation that would creep into your heart, but that does not seem to be the main thought in your letter. There is a sweet and quiet joy, I might almost say, that I cannot understand. I can sympathize with you in your double bereavement, but in that consolation so precious to you I have no share.

I have asked myself again and again what is this mysterious power of religion that so wonderfully supports its possessor in times like this? How can she, while the earth is yet fresh above the coffin of her only child, and before the first blade of grass has sprung on her mother's grave, so far forget her own sorrow and bereavement as to feel such an interest in me, a person almost a stranger in comparison with these? Oh, L., I believe I need your sympathy more than you mine. I cannot tell you just how I feel. I would be a Christian but I cannot. I mean there is a vague longing for that happiness I know must be there, but an unwillingness to do my part to secure it. I cannot even yet desire to be a Christian so much that I am willing to try. I wonder at myself and you will wonder, too, but that is only too true.

You say "we all have idols." What is mine? If God should take my sister or my brother or my father I could not bear it as you have borne your loss, but I do not think they are idols. I hope I shall not wait to be driven home, but I'm afraid I shall.

If you cannot understand this confusion of ideas, this mixture of regret and stubbornness, you are no worse off than myself. I cannot understand my own heart. Your letters have aroused some latent sparks of tenderness, but I cannot see that that stubborn unconcern is gone—I only wish I could.

As yet all is quiet here in the army. It is just one week earlier than the time we started last year, but I hardly think we can move so early this spring. In fact it has seemed to me that no attempt would be made to take Richmond with this army. Two of the six corps have been entirely removed, and what remains is not strong enough to gain much except by strategy. Ah, well, I cannot see what we are coming to. If I had your faith I should be a better soldier.

Remember me in kindness to your husband, and, if I did not know you would do so unasked, I would say—remember me in your prayers.

Stoneman Station, Va.,
Dear Cousin L.:— *March 16, 1863.*

I received a letter from O. M. last week. He appeared to be enjoying himself well. The weather was June-like, and the boys went round in their shirt sleeves when off duty.

He says there is a nigger regiment near him with black commissioned officers. What do you think of that idea? Contact with the contraband has so modified his ideas already that he don't like to see them in the same uniform he wears, and woolly headed captains are a step in advance of his ideas. Ain't you glad you wasn't born in the South where such ideas originate?

Just as you say, there is nothing to write about the war. "Pugnacious Joseph" still maintains a state of masterly inactivity.

We had a thunderstorm last night, but the storm was snow. Robins were singing in the morning. That was spring-like, but this morning is winter again.

Of course I cannot move till we get the command, so I am waiting the progress of events. A constant indulgence of my Kendallistic propensities enables me to keep a stiff upper lip.

From home I hear that father expects to move to Michigan in April. I shall have no home to go to now, will I? L. is gone and it never did seem like home when she wasn't there. I shall have to look out for myself if I ever do get through the war.

E. writes me that he don't want to go west, but if I will only say the word he will be down here in the Eighty-third as soon as steam can carry him. He is not eighteen yet, but will be to-morrow, and I think he better wait, don't you? I have had all I could do to keep him at home. He promised me once that he would not enlist without my consent, and the next letter I received from him he was in a company in Harrisburg. He excused himself on the plea of extraordinary circumstances (Stuart's raid into Pennsylvania), and I couldn't blame him much, as he went home again soon. Perhaps you will think I do wrong to discourage him, but I cannot bear the thought of his coming. It seems to me one in our family is enough, but I am afraid that, just so sure as there is another excitement, he will come. He will never go home if he does, at least so it seems.

Stoneman Station, Va.,
Tuesday, March 24, 1863.

Dear Brother and Sister:—

Well, now about those officers. "Commencing with the

Corporal" Imprimis (seems to me that's commencing at the little end of the horn, though): A Corporal (there are eight of them in a full company) occupies about as responsible a position as a printer's devil. As "Corporal of the Guard" it is his duty to post and relieve the guards and keep an open ear for the call of the sentry, "korboral of de gart, last number"—when that individual may have discovered a "mare's nest" or wants to be relieved to attend to his Virginia quickstep. He is considered of little account, and his privileges are immunity from standing guard and all fatigue duty. He is distinguished by two stripes on the sleeve

The Sergeants come next (in your order), five in number. The fifth or lowest in rank is the Commissary Sergeant. He draws and distributes the company's rations. The Fourth Sergeant superintends the details of guards and fatigue parties. The Third Sergeant and the Second in turn act as "Sergeants of the Guard." As such his duty is to keep the names of the daily guards, form all reliefs and turn them over to the Corporal, turn out the guard on the approach of an officer entitled to the compliment. The First, or Orderly Sergeant, is the most important of any of the non-commissioned officers. He has more to do than any other officer in the regiment, except perhaps the Adjutant. He calls every roll, always forms the company, makes the reports, and does all the business of the company. His pay is $20, other Sergeants $17 per month. They are distinguished by three stripes on the sleeves, and the Orderly by the addition of a diamond. These marks are called chevrons. Of the commissioned officers I need say but little. The Captain's duty is to command the company. You know what that is well enough. The First Lieutenant takes command in the absence of the Captain, and the next the Second Lieutenant. These officers are distinguished by their shoulder straps. A Captain's has two bars at each end. A First Lieutenant's has one bar at each end, and a Second Lieutenant's plain strap without bars. A Major has a gilt leaf on each end of his straps, a Lieutenant Colonel silver leaves. A Colonel has a silver eagle in the middle of each strap. Now, could you tell a man's rank by his marks? If we go further up, I might say that a Brigadier General is distinguished by a silver star in the place of the eagle, and a Major General by two stars. Officers are also distinguished by the buttons on their coats. A line or company officer and a staff officer (Adjutants, Surgeons, Chaplains and Quartermasters) wear only a single-breasted coat. A field officer (Colonel, Lieutenant Colonel and Major) wears two rows of buttons at regular spaces. A Brigadier General wears three in a group, and a Major General two.

The meeting of the debating club last night was a feast for a hungry mind. The scene reminded me much of some exhibition at home. The building is a log one covered with canvas, and the seats mere logs, but a big fire was blazing in the fireplace, and the room was warm and comfortable. It was decorated with pendant wreaths and loops of evergreen, and two tasty chandeliers lit up the hall cheerfully. It was filled with well dressed, gentlemanly soldiers, and the exercises, a paper, a poem, and a debate, were so interesting I had hard work to tear myself away before it broke up, but duty first and pleasure afterwards is military style.

Stoneman, April 2, 1863.

Dear Cousin L.:—

You come out so hard on O. M. I've a good mind to side with him just because he is the weaker party. Perhaps, too, I did him injustice in representing that his opinions had changed. I supposed that, from his education, he would think very much as you do, but if he left home with such opinions I shouldn't wonder if he came back with a couple of contraband servants, his own property, so much does contact with the system change northern minds. I am changed, too. I used to be quite an abolitionist, as you know, but see how hard-hearted I've become. I had been chopping wood enough to last me two or three days and left it to help the postmaster (my tent mate) tie up the letters for the mail. A great lazy nigger whom the general had sent to cut wood for his cook, took advantage of my absence, and instead of cutting any wood, carried all mine into the cook's tent. Now I suppose you, out of sympathy for the oppressed, would have said nothing about it, but cut some more wood. I couldn't see it in that light. I persuaded the darkey to correct his mistake and pile the wood under my bed, and I fear I chuckled some over my good fortune in getting my wood in for nothing. If it had been a white man now, larger than myself, I should have forgiven him, but not a "nigger."

The question for discussion at the club to-night is, "Which is the more consistent editor, Horace Greeley or James Gordon Bennett?" Which side do you think will (not should) gain the decision?

Nothing will do, I see, but to tell you all about my office. I haven't got any office and don't expect to have. The nearest approach to it is being my own hostler, for I have a horse, and my principal business now is petting and taking care of him. I wrote a pass once for Private Norton and took it to the general to sign. He wrote at the bottom with an "N. B.", "Private Norton is my Brigade Bugler." He seemed to think there might be a difference, but I am a color bearer, too. I carry the brigade colors on my horse with the staff in my stirrup, *a la* Lancers. Perhaps this is the change I may have hinted, for I've only had the colors since the battle of Fredericksburg. I have a splendid horse. His only fault is that he can only keep two feet on the ground at a time.

Don't be in a hurry about our moving. We shall go when Joseph "gets a good ready."

We had a snow storm on the 31st of March and it will take a few days to dry that off. To-day is a glorious day for that purpose, though, the wind blows almost a hurricane. It has taken half the roof off my house since I commenced writing. If such a thing should happen to your house, I suppose you wouldn't write any more that day. However, it did not disturb me much. It only took about five minutes to fix it.

I've half a mind to denounce you as a dangerous person, and have you sent to Fort Lafayette. "You don't want to see the Union on its old basis." Well, I do; that's just what I came here for. My word for it, you are quite a secessionist. You are very frank about it—why didn't you "define your position" with an *if* some way? You don't want the Union *if* slavery is not abolished. Candidly, now, I don't like slavery a bit better than you do, but I think it is done for by this war, and I want the Union and the old Constitution.

Yesterday was "All Fools'" day, and it was generally observed in the army. Our camp was in a roar from sunrise till "tattoo" with the cracking of practical jokes. One of the tallest was perpetrated by our adjutant general. A captain in the Twelfth New York has been trying to secure the colonelcy of a negro regiment, and Captain Estes (adjutant aforesaid) made out an order purporting to come from the Secretary of War, discharging him from service and tendering him the commission. It was done up in good style, red inked in the right places and regularly signed, all right. He was overjoyed, bought several bottles "elixir vitae" to treat his brother officers and wet his promotion. He then went to Corps Headquarters to get his transportation ticket, and there the officers who had been posted by Captain Estes let grimalkin out of the reticule. Captain E. sent another order to a thick-headed lieutenant, the butt of the regiment, to report to Colonel Stockton as Aide-de-Camp in the absence of Lieutenant Jewett. He reported, and was coolly informed that Lieutenant J. was not absent, and when his services were required the colonel would send him a mule.

Stoneman Station, Va.,
Wednesday, April 8, 1863.

Dear Sister L.:—

Your long letter of March 31st reached me in due time. For once I have not been very prompt, but you will have to excuse me. I have been moving. Yes, moving, for I am returned to the regiment. Colonel Vincent could not be satisfied to let me stay when I had a good berth, but insisted on my coming back. My reward for strict attention to duty is this, retrograde promotion. The colonel's reason for promoting me was to put me in charge of the bugle corps here to play for dress parade in the place of a band. You may believe I was some vexed about it, and if it were not that I hope to get back to headquarters, I would smash my bugle over a stump and take a musket again. Some one else will ride my horse now (you know how I have always loved a horse and can guess how I shall miss him), and some one else will carry my colors. Perhaps you will be glad of that. I come back to the original position of a private. Though I was nominally only a private there, I had really the privileges of a commissioned officer, some of them, at least, and the advantage of line officers, in that I had a horse to ride. My pay, too, by the next muster would have been twenty-one dollars per month. If I had been thrown out of this place for any fault of my own, I would have said nothing about it, but I did squirm some to find that I was only recalled because Colonel Vincent wanted a good bugler in the regiment, and cared nothing about what they had at headquarters. Coming back to the regiment seems almost like leaving the comforts of a home and enlisting again. I did not half realize the privileges I did enjoy till I came to be deprived of them.

If you don't have better weather than we have had for a week past you will not make much sugar. It is cold for April. Cold north winds blowing all the time, most. I cannot stand round without my overcoat, without shivering like a man with the ague.

Yesterday Abraham paid us a visit, or rather he didn't. He reviewed all the other regiments in the brigade, but by some blunder of Colonel Stockton's he made a bridge of our nose. It was rather provoking to see him pass within ten rods of us and not so much as nod to us. We had made great preparations and expected a speech. Our old Peninsula flag, tattered and blood-stained, was brought out and put beside the new one, but it was no go. Abraham didn't see it.

To-day there is a big review. Our brigade has gone on picket, so I didn't go out, but I saw the most of our corps go by. The regulars (Sykes' division) don't begin to come up to the volunteers in soldierly bearing and appearance.

They seem to have no pride about it and only do what they are forced to do.

Stoneman Station, Va.,
Friday, May 8, 1863.

Dear Sister L.:—

Well, now to dash right into it, for I have something to write this time. We left camp Monday, April 27th, with eight days' rations, and night found us at Hartwood Church, ten miles up the river. Here our corps (Fifth) joined the Eleventh and Twelfth corps, and next day we all marched to Kelly's Ford. Wednesday morning early we crossed the river, and after marching hard all day forded the Rapidan, water waist deep, and the Eighty-third was sent to the front on picket. Next day we marched on again, and noon found us at Chancellorsville, a big brick house in a field surrounded by a wilderness of woods. Here we halted and spent the night, and here the great battle of the war was fought.

Friday morning our brigade made a reconnoissance towards the Rappahannock. On the road we found a newly deserted camp with tents all standing, and in it some of the French knapsacks and muskets we lost at Gaines' Mill. We returned in the afternoon and there was some skirmishing with the enemy. Saturday was spent in building breastworks, and in the afternoon the rebels arrived. They attacked our lines furiously in the center, but were repulsed. At first the Eleventh Corps (Sigel's Dutchmen) gave way, and Sickles' division (the one Alf is in) was sent in. They drove the rebs back and held them. At night we lay on our arms behind our works. The moon was full and it was almost as light as day. Six or seven times the attack was made in the same place and every time repulsed. It was an anxious night, for the morrow all felt sure would be a bloody Sunday, and so it was. We were up at light and moved off to the right of the center, and immediately went to work building breastworks. Just as the sun came up the enemy came on. Their whole army was massed on half a mile of our center, and Jackson told his men "they must break our line if it killed every man they had," but we were prepared for them. Our first line in front of the works was overpowered and driven in, and they rushed on. Artillery and infantry met them. Protected by their breastworks, our men poured it into them. Grape and canister swept through their columns, mowing them down. Still, on they came, like a vast herd of buffaloes, struggling over the trees and brush, dashing, brave, impetuous, but doomed to destruction. Thousands of them charged right up to our works, but, the line shattered, comrades killed, they could do nothing but throw down their arms, retreat being impossible. For six hours they persevered and then withdrew. You must imagine the scene—I cannot describe it. The roar was unearthly; there is no better word for it. I shudder at the slaughter. Ours was fearful enough, but a drop in the bucket to theirs. In it all our brigade did not fire a shot. Right in sight of the fighting, expecting to be attacked, they spent the day and night, and next day and night. Monday and Tuesday we were waiting for them, confident of victory. While we were busy there, Sedgwick with his corps crossed the river and took the heights of Fredericksburg, capturing their big guns, but I learn that he was afterwards driven back.*

Wednesday, to our great surprise, we recrossed the river and returned to our old camps. No one seems to understand the move, but I have no doubt it is all right. It rained all day and it was the toughest march we've had in many a day. Tramp, tramp, through the mud. I was almost ready to drop when I got in, but I did not fall out, though half the regiment did when they found we were coming to camp.

So here we are with eight days' rations and orders to be ready to march again. I don't know anything about the meaning of it. I would give half a dollar for to-day's Herald.

*Stoneman Station, Va.,
Sunday, May 10, 1863.*

Dear Mother:—

I wrote to E. on Monday. Perhaps I better continue

---

*Note.—Error—Sedgwick was not driven back, but recrossed the river at Banks' Ford.

my journal. We were then lying in line of battle, and soon after my letter was off, our Second brigade went out to feel of the rebels, and stirred up a muss that we expected would result in a general engagement. The firing was sharp for half an hour, our men retreating till the rebels had followed into range of the artillery, which opened on them, and they soon fell back. That was the last of the fighting. During the night the pickets had a sharp skirmish and we were called to our guns, but it soon died away and we slept again. We, I say, for I counted myself in. I do not carry a gun, and in battle as a musician I am in charge of the surgeons to carry off the wounded. This did not suit me at all. It involved the necessity of going on the field, and I am too much of a coward to walk quietly where bullets whistle and have nothing to say myself. When I can return ball for ball, cheer, and shout defiance to the enemy, my courage is as good as anybody's, but not to walk through them with my hands full. So, on the first appearance of fight, I picked up a rifle and cartridge box and joined Company K. Our good fortune kept us out of the fight, but I felt much better with the company than anywhere else. But this is a digression. Tuesday was very quiet. In the afternoon a tremendous thunder shower burst upon us. Our trenches in an hour's time were full of water. The rain continued all night, yes, for three days.

About 2 o'clock Wednesday morning we were ordered to pack up silently, and in a few minutes we were on the retreat. To say we were surprised would give but a feeble idea of our feelings. We felt more confident than ever that we could repulse all that could be brought against us. But for some reason, satisfactory to General Hooker no doubt, we did recross the river, and night saw us in our old camps. The Eighty-third had the post of honor, the last regiment to cross, and our brigade was the rear guard, but we were not molested. It was one of the hardest marches we ever had, and I am stiff and sore from the effects of it. Most of the way the mud was over shoe, in some places knee deep, and the rain made our loads terrible to tired shoulders, but it is all over now.

We have eight days' rations again, and orders to be ready to move at any time.

Headquarters Third Brigade,
May 20, 1863.

GENERAL ORDERS NO. 3.

I. The hours for service and parades of ceremony will be the same throughout the brigade.

II. Each duty will be ordered by its proper call, sounded first by the bugler at these headquarters, and the call at its close will be immediately taken up and repeated by the buglers at Regimental Headquarters.

III. Reveille .... 5:00 a. m.
Breakfast call .... 5:30 a. m.
Sick call .... 6:00 a. m.
Drill call (by company)............. 6:30 a. m.
Recall .... 8:00 a. m.
Assembly of the guard............. 8:30 a. m.
(The proper Troop will be sounded by the drums of the guard before beating off.)
Dinner call .... 12:00 m.
Drill call (by regiment or brigade)... 4:00 p. m.
Assembly (for dress parade)........ 6:45 p. m.
To the color .... 7:00 p. m.
(The proper Retreat will be sounded by the drum corps of each regiment before beating off.)
Tattoo .... 8:30 p. m.
Extinguish lights (taps with drums). 9:00 p. m.

IV. Brigade drills will be had on Tuesdays and Thursdays.

V. Saturdays will be given to the men as heretofore for purpose of bathing and washing clothes.

VI. The usual Sunday morning inspection will be by regiment at 10 a. m.

BRIGADE HEADQUARTERS FLAG.
THIRD BRIGADE, FIRST DIVISION, FIFTH ARMY CORPS
ARMY OF THE POTOMAC.

VII. Guard will hereafter be mounted by brigade according to the form indicated in General Butterfield's "Standing Orders", with such alterations as will be verbally communicated by the A. A. A. G.

The detail from each regiment will be one commissioned officer, one sergeant, two corporals and twenty-six men.

VIII. Dress Parade will, on Sundays, be held by brigade according to a form to be hereafter designated.

By command of
STRONG VINCENT,
Colonel Commanding Brigade.

Headquarters, Third Brigade,
First Division, Fifth A. C.,
Wednesday, May 27, 1863.

Dear Sister L.:—

The concluding portion of your letter is already answered. I have a very good prospect of getting back to headquarters, inasmuch as I am here now. My horse is fat as a cub and sleek as a mole, and my flag—oh, I must tell you about the new flag; it is a quaint concern. This is the shape of it: triangular, six feet on a side. The border is blue, the middle white, and the Maltese cross is red. The red cross is the badge by which our division is known. Red, white and blue crosses, First, Second and Third Divisions of Fifth Corps.

We have moved camp about two miles northwest of the railroad station. The brigade is camped in line on a big hill, and headquarters are in a large orchard overlooking the line. It is a splendid place. I have pitched my tent under an apple tree that shades me all day long, and a mocking-bird sings to me the sweetest song ever heard. He combines in one the song of every bird I ever heard and many I haven't. One minute he's a bobolink, the next a lark or a robin, and he's never tired of singing.

Benson's Mill, Va.,
June 1, 1863.

Dear Cousin L.:—

You see by the dating of my letter that we have moved again. Benson's Mill is the most appropriate name of this village. I wonder they didn't call it a city or at least a "ville." It is a larger place than Charles City or Chancellorsville, as it contains two buildings, and those places only one each. Perhaps I am wrong about Charles City and it ought to be called the city of magnificent distances, for there is a jail about half a mile from the court house, and a tavern of "ye olden time" the same distance the other way, probably all within the limits of the corporation.

But about our moving. Our brigade had just got comfortably settled in the nicest place for a camp I have seen yet, when at 10 o'clock one morning the order came, "Break camp and prepare to march immediately," and by noon we were on the road. We found that we were to relieve cavalry pickets on the river and at the fords beyond the infantry lines of the army. The brigade is scattered along the river for six or eight miles. The Eighty-third is on the right at Richards Ford, the Twentieth Maine next at United States Ford, the Sixteenth Michigan next at Benson's Mill and the Forty-fourth New York (Ellsworth's Avengers) at Banks Ford on the left. The camps are near the fords, and the pickets extend right and left to connect with each other and watch every point. The rebel pickets are in plain sight on the other side of the river, not over ten rods apart, and though no communication is allowed, there is some talking across the water. One of the rebs called out yesterday at United States Ford: "I say, you Yanks, why didn't you shoot General Hill? He stood right here half an hour ago." Our boys had seen a man pass along their lines, but supposed he was the officer of the guard. There is a good understanding between them, and neither side will fire unless an attempt to cross is made. The rebs go in bathing on their side the river, and our boys do the same on ours. Colonel Vincent and his staff rode along the lines in plain sight and I followed carrying the flag, but they did not fire. I thought it was a risky piece of business, but I think I can go where he can. I am afraid he is a little too rash sometimes. We were riding along the bank last night just about sunset. Suddenly he stopped, and taking a map from his pocket, commenced to examine it. Just in the edge of the wood on the other side I saw the glistening of a rifle barrel, and I uttered some exclamation of surprise. "What is it, Norton?" said he. "Nothing," I replied, "only I was thinking if I was a picket here, and should see a rebel general across there, I couldn't resist the temptation to draw a bead on him." "Well, it is a little risky to stop, that's a fact," said he, "we'll get out of this," and I was glad when he got out of range. Confound 'em! I don't think it's safe to trust them. I wouldn't be afraid of their firing at me, but I'm afraid to trust their promises with a Union officer within range of their guns.

I don't remember whether I told you that I had returned to my old place at headquarters or not. I came back on the 22d of May. Colonel Vincent took command of the brigade then and took me with him. Headquarters are located near the center of the brigade, and of course I have no bugling to do. In fact I have just nothing to do. The Colonel says he shall find me some work in the office, copying orders, probably.

We are pleasantly situated, though it seems rather lonely to see none of the regiments about.

Strawberries are beginning to ripen, and I presume we shall have them quite plenty, as there are so few to pick them.

I am much obliged for your description of the house and its inmates. I think I have a pretty good idea of it now. I had no idea till lately that you had so large a family. That young man—well, I suppose he is like most young men in that respect. No doubt he did not intend to do any such thing, but was betrayed into it.

And now I've got a "bone to pick" with you. "It seems much more terrible" to enslave a white child than it does to enslave a black one. You "suppose it is no worse," but "it seems to be." Then you have some of the prejudice of color? You must be more guarded. Don't let such expressions drop in your letters to me, for I may make capital of them to oppose your "radicalism."

June 6, 1863.

Dear Sister L.:—

Headquarters are at Crittenden's Mill, twenty miles above Fredericksburg. The Eighty-third guards Kempel's Ford. The Sixteenth Michigan and Twentieth Maine guard Ellis' Ford. The Forty-fourth New York is in reserve at the Mill. Franklin has crossed below Fredericksburg and is fighting this morning. I can hear the cannon.

Headquarters, Third Brigade, First Division,
Fifth Army Corps,
Crittenden's Mill, Va., June 8, 1863.

Dear Sister L.:—

I have no letter of yours to answer, but having nothing to do and knowing that you are always glad to hear from me, perhaps I can't do better than to spend an hour jotting down for your amusement a few incidents by the way. Life at headquarters is pleasant on one account—it gives me a better opportunity to see and talk with the people of the country than I had in the regiment.

You will see by this that we have again moved. Since the 27th ult. we have been engaged in guarding the river at different points above Fredericksburg. Crittenden's Mill is some twenty miles above town and two miles back of the river. Ellis' Ford and Kempel's Ford are near, and our brigade is ordered to guard these crossings and watch the enemy on the other side. Reports of the observations have to be sent to Division headquarters every four hours of the day and night. Headquarters are at the house of a certain widow James. She has three sons in the rebel army and is a pretty loud *secesh* herself. My bivouac is in one of the old lady's tobacco houses, and there I am writing this at present, so if it smells of tobacco don't charge it to my habits. On the road up here we stopped one night at the house of a Mr. Imbray. He was a cripple and at home, but made no secret of his being *sccesh* to the backbone. "I belong to the South," said he, "and my heart is with the South. If I was with the army I should shoot at you with all the power I had, but, meeting as we do, I shall not allow any difference of opinion to influence my treatment of you." (Very considerate, wasn't he, when we had the force there to enforce respect?) But it wasn't of him I meant to speak, but of his daughters. There were two, one a lady of "uncertain age," and the other not. The "not" was about eighteen, and the bitterest, rabidest, outspokenest, cantankerous-est specimen of *secesh* femininity I've come across yet. She had no objection to talk, and she commenced at me when she saw my flag, with, "Is that a Yankee flag?" "Well, the Yankees use it," said I, "but here's the Yankee flag," and I unrolled a new silk "star spangled" and waved it over her head. "Don't you think," said I, "that that's a prettier flag than the 'stars and bars?'" "No, indeed! I can't see it, sir—no, sir—give me the Confederate flag. I don't want none o' yer gridirons about me." Finally after some bantering we dropped the subject and I induced her after a chaffer to sell me two quarts of milk for half a dollar, and she offered me half a loaf of rye bread for the same price, but I preferred hard tack. "We're no way particular about prices with you all," she said. "So I see," meekly replied I. Next morning we were going, and I was bound to have some fun first, so I opened by asking her if she didn't sometimes feel lonesome with none of the young men about. "Well, sir, not lonesome enough to care to see you Yankees about." (Repulse.) "Have you any relatives in the rebel army?" "I have two brothers and a lover in the Confederate army." (Cool—that about the lover.) "Then Yankee boys stand no chance in your good graces?" "No, sir, I hate the sight of them." (Cooler yet.) "Why, I don't think you are a secessionist." (Tactics.) "Well, I am, sir, I am true to the South." (I wish I could write their pronunciation of South; it beats all the down-east you ever heard of.) "No, you are a Yankee, at least a Yankee *secesh*." "No, indeed, sir, nary drop o'

Yankee blood in my veins, I tell you, sir." "Oh, but you are, begging your pardon, and I'll prove it to you." "No, sir, you can't do that, sir; better tell that to some one else. If I had any Yankee blood in me I'd let it out. Yes, indeed, I would." "Well, you acknowledge that a Yankee thinks more of property and money than anything else, don't you?" "Yes, sir, I've heard they do, and I believe it." "Yes, well, you're a Yankee then. If you were a *secesh* you would go with the South and help them. True *secesh* women do that, but your family have some property here and you stay to take care of it and let the South get along the best she can. You are a genuine Yankee, say what you please. You wouldn't go and share the fortunes of your 'Sunny South,' but you must stay to keep the Yankees from destroying the property." Oh, how she did sputter! "To think that she should be called a Yankee!" I guess she'll get over it.

Down on the bank of the river I went into a house and met a young married woman with a baby in her arms. She had been pretty once and it was not age that spoiled her beauty, but care. "Can you sell me a pie, or something good for my dinner?" said I. "A pie! sir," said she. "Well, now, sir, if I was to tell you that I have not tasted or seen a piece of pie for more than a year, would you believe me?" "I certainly should if you said so. Of course I couldn't doubt a lady's word." "Sir, 'fore God it is the truth. I have only been married 'bout a year, and my husband, who was an overseer, came on to this place after the fruit was all gone, and I've had no fruit. I haven't seen a bit of sugar, nor coffee, nor tea for nigh eight months, I reckon," and she went on and gave me such a story of struggles to keep alive, to get enough to keep from starving, as made all the hard times I have ever seen seem like a life of luxury. I did pity her. On such as she, the poor whites of the South, the burden of this war is heaviest. She had but little sympathy for the South or North either. She cared but little how the war ended, so it ended soon. Poor woman, she understood but little of the nature of the contest. She sent a little darky girl to bring in a pan of milk.

The girl came with it balanced on her head, not touching her hands. I remarked how strange it seemed to me to see everybody in the south carry pails on their heads. "Why," said she, "how do you-all carry 'em?" "In our hands." She laughed. "I have to tote all my water up a steep bank, and, if I toted it in my hand, it would pull me over." She gave me some milk, and by the time I had eaten my dinner the colonel came back from the lines, and I mounted my horse and came back to camp.

Strawberries are ripe and I get a few. No more news from Fredericksburg.

Gettysburg, Penn.,
July 4, 1863, 10 A. M.

Dear Father:—

I am safe and well. We have met the enemy and given them hell. Colonel Vincent is mortally wounded. Alf Ayres is safe; so is Conway. No time for more.

Line of Battle,
Three miles southeast of Hagerstown, Md.,
Sunday, July 12, 1863.

Dear Sister L.:—

All my writing material is in my knapsack and I have had no chance to write since the 4th, when I sent you a line to say I was safe. Now I have begged a scrap of paper just to relieve your impatience for news, but I can't write much more now.

Since the great victory at Gettysburg we have been straining every nerve to overtake and strike the enemy before he leaves Maryland. Thousands of the men are barefoot, and officers, too, but they are bravely struggling on, footsore and hungry, enduring everything without a murmur, so we may finish the war now.

We had one of the greatest battles of the war, and a great victory, too. The old Third Brigade fought like demons, took four hundred prisoners, and laid the rebels in heaps before them. We were splendidly posted behind rocks and trees, and you may judge of the fight when I tell you that of thirteen hundred men in such a position we lost three hundred and fifty-nine and no prisoners. Colonel Vincent was mortally wounded, and died on the 7th. That was a loss to our brigade that cannot be replaced. The night he was wounded I went in to see him. He was very weak, but he held out his cold hand to me and asked "if I had just come from the front." When I told him yes, and how well the boys had fought, his eye brightened, but he was too weak to talk much. His commission as Brigadier General was read to him on his death-bed.

There are thousands of things I could tell you that I cannot write. The main thing is to tell you that I am still safe and well, doing my duty the best I can, never shunning danger when it calls, but ever coming out safe. With that for the present you must be content. I am tired, almost worn out, haven't had my shoes off for a week, lying sometimes in the heaviest rain without a shelter, not allowed a minute of my own, and you can see I have but little time to write.

Edwin Willcox has been within ten minutes' ride of me for a week, and yet I have not and cannot go to see him.

Last night there was one of the grandest sights ever seen. The whole Army of the Potomac advanced two miles in line of battle, column by division, ten lines deep. As far as the eye could reach through fields of wheat, corn and clover that grand line was moving on.

I have no time for more. Write to me (at headquarters) as soon as you can. Alf is well.

Headquarters Third Brigade, Berlin, Md.,
Friday, July 17, 1863.

Dear Friends at Home :—

I have received several letters from you lately, but have had no opportunity of answering them till now. I sent you a leaf from my memorandum book from the field of Gettysburg on the 4th, just to say I was safe, and I hope you received it. A citizen said he would take it to York. Since then we have been on the move constantly. I have not seen my portfolio till this morning, and had nothing to write on if I had had time.

STRONG VINCENT.
Colonel Eighty-third Pennsylvania Volunteers.
Brigadier General U. S. Volunteers.

The past three have been eventful weeks and I begin to hope the back of the rebellion is broken. If the Mississippi had any special relation to the monster, it certainly is, for yesterday we received official information that the river was open. At Gettysburg I think we broke the ribs on one side. At all events we came nearer to it than we ever did before. Oh, that was a terrible fight! I rode over a great part of the ground on the left, on the 5th, and of all the carnage I ever saw that was the most horrible. All over the field were scattered black and bloated corpses of men, and dead horses, wrecks of caissons and gun carriages. I was galloping along the road when all at once my horse sprang to one side, and looking to see what started him, I saw the bodies of thirteen rebels lying in the mud with the pitiless rain beating on their ghastly faces. That would have been a horror at home; there it was only a glimpse of what might be seen. The rebels seemed to have left all their dead, while ours were buried immediately, and the wounded all removed that could be, by the night of the 4th. Colonel Vincent died on the 7th, as brave and gallant a soldier as ever fell. His commission as Brigadier General was read to him on his death-bed. His loss is felt deeply by the brigade. There is no one to fill his place. No one here can march a brigade as he could. He had less straggling, less of everything evil and more of everything good than any other brigade in the division. Oh, how we loved him! But he is gone.

Colonel Rice, now in command, is known as "Old Crazy," as Colonel Stockton was "Jack o' Clubs." He is brave enough, but in a fight too excitable to do anything right.

We followed the rebs as fast as possible to Williamsport, but while we thought they were fastened, they again got away from us, and now we cannot catch them this side of Richmond. We are on the Potomac four miles below Harper's Ferry, and here we must rest a few days.

The men have pressed on since the fight, barefooted, hungry, lousy and faint, animated by the hope of giving Lee his finishing blow. The horses are worn out, every day's march killing from five to twenty in each battery. They must rest and be shod up before we can go on. I said the men were lousy. You hardly know what that means, but if you were in the ranks you would, not head lice, but body lice, that crawl all over shirts and pants. Nothing but boiling will kill them, and for three weeks no one has had a chance to boil a shirt. For eleven days and nights I did not take off my shoes to sleep.

Well, I must close. I have a dozen letters to write and my clothes to wash. If we stay here long enough I will write again, but whether you hear from me or not, write as often as you can. I saw Conway Ayres yesterday and Alf the day before, both well. Love to all.

Headquarters Third Brigade, Loudon Co., Va.,
Tuesday, July 21, 1863.

Dear Sister L.:—

When I wrote before, if I remember rightly, we were in line of battle near Hagerstown and Williamsport, expecting another fight, but again the wary Lee escaped. We stopped at Williamsport the night after he crossed, and next day moved on after him, marching twenty-five miles and crossing the famous South Mountain. Next day we moved on again twelve miles to Berlin on the Potomac, four miles south, and in sight of Harper's Ferry. Here we hoped to rest a little. We had reached a railroad and a good place for getting supplies, and men and horses needed rest. Thousands of men were barefoot, officers, too, and all were dirty and lousy. I believe I state a fact when I say that not twenty men (who carried their clothing) in any regiment but were swarming with vermin. They are the pest of the army, and though you hear but little about it, they are always here. More clothing is thrown away on that very account than is worn out.

I say we hoped to rest and get new clothes and shoes and boil up the old ones, but the pontoons were already laid and next day saw us in Virginia. We have been slowly moving down the Loudon Valley since. The weather is very hot, and eight or ten miles is all the artillery can march in a day, so that is all we move. We have got about down to the scene of our fight with the cavalry on the 21st of June. I must always think of the gallant Colonel Vincent in connection with that, but his sword is sheathed forever, and glorious "old Jim," who carried Colonel McLane at Gaines' Mill and the commandant of the Eighty-third, whoever he might be, ever since, has served his time and gone home to Erie. My horse is all right yet. He is a warhorse every inch. He will stand by a cannon while it is fired, without flinching, and I can ride him over all the dead and mangled horses that can be piled in his road. He don't like the shells too near his ears, but I can manage him then. While our line was forming on the hill at Gettysburg I came out with him in full view of the rebel lines. They opened two batteries on us instantly, firing at the colors. Colonel Vincent looked to see what was drawing the fire and yelled at me: "Down with that flag, Norton! D—n it, go behind the rocks with it!" I obeyed, of course. I did not see him again until he was brought back wounded. When the rebels charged our line I left my horse and flag with the mounted orderlies, and getting a gun went in on the right of the Forty-fourth New York, just in front of where we dismounted. In the cavalry fight I followed Colonel Vincent everywhere with the flag, most of the time right up to the skirmishers, but there he thought I had better keep it out of sight.

I am nearer sick than I have been for a year. I couldn't walk a mile, and if there was a hospital within reach I am afraid I should give up. As it is, I could only ride along in an ambulance, and as long as I can stand it I shall ride my horse. I manage to attend to my duties yet. I have never been excused a day, and if possible never will.

What glorious news of victory we are receiving! It looks as though we could see the beginning of the end. I wish the end were nearer.

Camp near Warrenton, Va.,
July 28, 1863.

Dear Parents :—

It is seldom that I have written so few letters after a

great battle as I have since the battle of Gettysburg. I have had two good reasons, one that we have been almost constantly on the move since, and the other that I have not been able to write. I have said but little about it, not wishing to cause you anxiety, but for three weeks I have had all I could do to keep along in my place. The night of the 4th of July it rained tremendously, and I had little shelter and lay in water half an inch deep all night. I was too much exhausted to stand up or even to keep awake. I was wet through most of the time for a week after, and a very bad diarrhea set in which destroyed my appetite and made me very weak. I would not take doctor's stuff, thinking I could wear it off as I always have done, but it held on well this time. At last I did take a physic, and when we got into Manassas Gap the blackberries cured me up. I feel more like myself to-day than I have for almost a month. Nothing but my horse and a firm resolve to hold out to the last has kept me out of the hospital this time. I could not have walked half a mile a good many days that I have rode fifteen. I could have found time to write a good many more letters if I had been well, but as it was, as soon as we stopped I could do nothing more than lie down and rest.

I received your letters of the 10th at Rectortown, on the Gap railroad. I was very glad to see them, the first I had heard from you since you received news of my safety. Two things in it surprised me—one was the direction—that letter was two days in the regiment before I got it because it was directed to the regiment. Always direct, "Headquarters Third Brigade, First Division, Fifth Army Corps, Washington, D. C." Don't put on regiment or company. Headquarters mail is pushed right through, when the large bags don't come, and very often I don't go to the regiment for three or four days, and any mail sent there waits till I come.

The other surprising thing was—"do come home." As many soldiers have been spoiled by just such letters from anxious parents as any other way. Mother writes, "Come home; I do so want to see my boy if only for a little while." Soldier writes that he would come if he could, and begins to think about it and chafe and fret at his bonds till he worries himself homesick and isn't worth a row of pins. You have never said much to me of that sort, but it would not make much difference if you did. I made up my mind when I enlisted to stay till the matter was settled or my three years served out. As long as I am well I wouldn't come home if I had a furlough in my hand, which, I might remark, is a place very difficult to get a furlough in nowadays. If I were sick and in a hospital, I should perhaps try to get home, but not while I stay in the field. This off and on soldiering is hard on a person's nerves. You will be the more glad to see me when I have been gone three long years.

I am very glad, Mother, that you like your new home so well. Aristocracy in these days ought to be at a discount. Shoddycracy is pretty large in New York, they say, the hideous offspring of the monster war. I am afraid the army would not suit you very well on that very account, supposing you could be in it. One of the officers of my own company can write no more than his own name, and that scarcely legible, yet military rules require me always to touch my cap when I speak to him, as an acknowledgment of his superiority.

You ask if I have any fruit. I have had but little. Cherries have been plenty in the country we passed through, but I have had little chance to get them. We never know at what minute we shall move. Orders come at daylight, at sunset, at noon, at midnight, "Prepare to march immediately," and the first thing is—"Bugler sound the general" (the call to strike tents), so that I am obliged to be always at my post. The men in the regiments scatter out in the country, get fruit and buy bread and pies, but I can't leave and so don't get much. Blackberries I have had a better chance at, for they are everywhere. You may know how close I am kept when I tell you that I have been trying for a month to see Edwin Willcox, and, though he has slept within half or a quarter of a mile from me a good many nights, I have never seen him yet.

I wish you would put up two or three cans of fruit for

me, so that, if we go into winter quarters again, you can send them to me. Fruit is something I miss as much as anything in the army. The sutler makes no bones of charging seventy-five cents for a tumblerful of jelly.

I wish you would send me, if you can get it, next time you write, a little camphor gum and assafœtida. If you cannot get the latter send the camphor alone, just a little, what you can put in a letter. I want it to drive away lice.

In regard to that expression that shocked you so much. I am sure I meant nothing irreverent, and, as Father remarked, it is a common expression in the army for a hot reception of the enemy. Used in that sense, it does not seem so inappropriate, for such fighting, such bloody carnage belongs more to demons than to this fair earth. No reference to anything in their condition after death was intended. That is not for us to judge.

I had intended to write more, but a heavy shower is coming up for which I must prepare, and I shall have no more time before the mail closes.

We expect to rest here a little while, hope to, at least.

Headquarters Third Brigade, Bealeton, Va.,
Wednesday, August 5, 1863.

Dear Sister L.:—

Your letter of Tuesday evening a week ago reached me last evening, just a week on the way. I answer to-day, for here in the army more than anywhere else it is not safe to boast of to-morrow, for we know not what a day may bring forth. We lay at Warrenton a week. At W. I said, we were three miles south of town.

Last Monday morning four hundred men left the brigade to go somewhere for "fatigue duty." I suppose you know that "fatigue" is duty where spades (or axes) are trumps. As soon as they were gone the remainder commenced laying out the ground for a permanent camp in accordance with orders. Well, at 4 p. m. came the order "Strike tents and prepare to march immediately." Such contradictory orders used to excite a deal of wrath among the men, but I have noticed that lately nothing is said. The men are ready at the minute and march off willingly.

We started about dark and marched about five or six miles south to near Bealeton. You may have heard of that city, situated on the Orange & Alexandria railroad, and comprising one small building (railroad station), and one water tank.

We are in almost a desert. There are some trees and a little grass and weeds, but of all the poor soils I ever saw, this strip for six or eight miles each side of the railroad beats all.

I heard General Griffin (commanding corps) say yesterday that we would stay here till September and he ordered the camps laid out accordingly. This intention is evidently to be taken without reference to rebel movements. Should they make another invasion or that sort of thing, of course it would change our program. If they keep quiet I think there is a fair prospect of our lying still through the hottest weather. In the meantime our drafted men will be coming in, our decimated regiments filled up, and by the time cooler weather comes we will be in splendid condition. I do not think we will lie six weeks of the best part of the year as we did at Antietam last fall. General Meade don't seem to be that sort of a man. But rest now is necessary, not so much for the men as for the horses. A week's rest will do for the men, but the horses must have time to get a little more flesh on and to regain their lost strength. Why, every day since we returned to Virginia, every day we have marched, Battery D. Fifth United States, has turned out to die from four to ten horses. Many of these will recover and make good farm horses (the farmers pick them all up) but some are so far gone that they die in the road. Everywhere we march there is a dead horse or mule on the road every bad place we come to, and often there are three or four. I tell you hot weather and heavy guns use up artillery horses. My horse stands it just first-rate. He is as fat as he ought to be to travel and always feels well. All the grain he gets is about a peck per day. I kept him on hard tack for nearly a week in Pennsylvania. Our teams were twenty-five miles off and no grain to be had.

I think the last I wrote to you I told you that I had been sick. Lest you should worry about me I will say this time that I am well, as well as ever. My bowel complaint is entirely gone and I feel like myself again. I lost considerable flesh while I was so weak, but that will soon come again. Hard tack is good to fat a man that likes it, and, without butter, I prefer it to soft bread. Soft bread and the paymaster are both reported to be on their way here.

My letters have been very scarce lately. One reason, I suppose, is that I have written very few myself. I do hope they will begin to come again now. Soldiering without letters is hard work. I don't blame you any for not writing. I know you have little spare time, but write just as often as you can.

Go in on the fruit and save all you can. Ain't you going to save a little to send me next winter when we get settled? I think I could dispose of a little Chatauqua County fruit with the greatest pleasure.

I am very glad to hear that you have such good health, and I think you enjoy yourself well too, if your letters are any evidence. It does me good to know that your life is happy.

Tell Mercy Clark, if you write to her, that I am as much in favor of a vigorous prosecution of the war as when I first enlisted. I have just administered a filial rebuke to my parents for asking me to get a furlough because they wanted to see me. This war must be fought out, and while I have health and strength I shall not so much as think of leaving the field till it is done. If I am sick or wounded and sent to a hospital, it will be a different thing, but I don't want to hear any whimpering from those I left behind. The only thing that I care to come home for is to make some of those copperheads hunt their holes. General Logan's speech at Cairo the other day just expressed my sentiments. Every copperhead, peaceman, anti-draft man, every cursed mother's son of them that does not support the war by word and deed ought to be hung or sent to the south where they belong. There is no middle ground. Every man who is not for us is against us, and I would just as soon fight a cursed copperhead as a southern rebel. Yes, rather, for they have means of knowing the truth and most rebels have not. If a man or a boy comes into your house and talks peace, or complains about the draft, tell him he is a traitor and you won't listen to him. Drive him out as Orpha Dart did with a broomstick. I tell you when the old soldiers get home, such cowards and sneaks, traitors and rebels in disguise, will have an account to settle. It won't be a pleasant neighborhood for them. The scorn and disgust the revolutionary tories met won't be a circumstance to what is waiting for them. Maybe you think I am excited. I mean what I say at all events, and I have been so provoked and disgusted that I, like every loyal soldier, am down on every opposer of the war "like a thousand of brick." I have no patience with them at all. I know that if I was home, I should have trouble with the first man that talked a word of such stuff to me.

*Beverly Ford, Va.,
Sunday, August 9, 1863.*

Dear Sister L.:—

A new date tells you that we have moved. We moved once before since I wrote to you and had orders to make a "permanent camp," but just as we got things nicely fixed for a comfortable stay during the heated term, somebody discovered that there was not water enough, so we pulled up stakes and moved to the river. Beverly Ford is a little way above where the railroad crosses the Rappahannock, so if you have a map you can see nearly where our present permanent camp is.

*Beverly Ford, Va.,
Thursday, August 13, 1863.*

Dear Mother:—

I received your letter of the 5th night before last. Yesterday it was so hot that I could not write or do anything else but lie in the shade and sweat. I don't know where the mercury stood, but I think it must have been above 100. It was as hot as any day we had on the Peninsula except one. Last night we had a furious thunder storm. The ground was completely soaked and I had fun enough this morning to last me a week.

Yesterday Colonel Rice had a large force of men putting up booths or shades of poles and brush over the tents. This morning they all fell down one after another and smashed down the tents. The colonel's was the first, just about daylight. He came crawling out under the edge *sans* everything but shirt. He came in such a hurry that he could not keep his perpendicular and went sprawling in the mud. Then Lieutenant Grannis' tent came down and he came out in the same cool dress like a mouse from a shock of corn.

We have just been paid $52. I'm going to send $50 home. Father inquired once what I did with my money lately. I don't remember whether I explained about that or not, but I have not wasted a great deal of it. Since I have been at headquarters, I have had to keep a good watch. The time of everything is left to me. Well, last fall I had a watch stolen from me that cost me $18, I think, and then I bought another, and both had to be paid for out of the next pay. This last watch kept time splendidly all winter, but when we forded the Rapidan, it got wet inside and stopped entirely. I sent it to Erie for Captain Austin to clean. When I went back to headquarters I bought a watch for $10 which turned out to be good for nothing. I bought another for $15 which is a good one. Last Monday my watch came back from Erie, so now I have three. That is where my money has gone to, part of it at least. I am going to keep my old watch and sell the other two.

I dare not risk sending much money in a letter, so I am going to send $10 at a time. Let Father do what he thinks best with it.

I am very glad you are having so much fruit and such a variety too. I should like it very much if I could have some too, but you are so far away and everything sent by express is so uncertain of reaching its destination that I don't think it would be best to try to send me any. Next winter there may be a good chance. There would be now if there was any certainty of our staying here any length of time. We have laid out three "permanent camps" this side of Warrenton. This is the best place we have found yet and I think we will stay here through the hot weather.

I have no correspondents in Springfield now.

Beverly Ford, Va.,
August 22, 1863.

Dear Parents:—

I received a piece of paper from E. a few days since, saying that he had received my letter and would answer it soon. The answer has not come yet. The envelope contained the perfumery I sent for, and, if it is not effectual, I don't know of anything that would be. Fortunately, I am not troubled with the "crumbs" now. All the men who ever are rid of them are so now. A good boiling does the business, but there are some who would be lousy if they had every convenience and a year's time, and just as soon as we start on a march again they will be all over. "All is quiet on the Rappahannock" yet. The hot weather paralyzes both armies, but lying still they are gaining. The flies are so troublesome that horses do not gain so fast as they would in cooler weather, but they still improve some. Many of the cavalry regiments and batteries are getting new horses.

The commissary is issuing soft bread two days out of three, nice fresh bread, too, and, oh, if we had some butter! He issues small rations of potatoes and dried apples occasionally, and dessicated vegetables. I presume you have never seen any of this last. It is in square cakes an inch thick and seems to consist of potato, carrot, turnip, onion, cabbage, red pepper, etc., scalded and then pressed and dried. I am confident that if we could learn how to cook it we should like it. We are all hungry for vegetables, but I cannot cook it nor have I seen any one who could so that it will be good. We have put in fresh beef and made soup of it, and we have boiled it down dry and tried it every way we can think of, and don't succeed yet. The fault seems to be that each vegetable loses its individual flavor in the cooking and all blend together in a nondescript sort of a dish that isn't good a bit.

The principal topics of news in camp are the arrival of the conscripts and the departure of Colonel Rice. Captain Judson came down from Philadelphia this week with two hundred men for the Eighty-third, and he has gone back for more. Of the two hundred but three men, so they say, were drafted. All the rest are substitutes, and most of them two years and nine months men. They seem to be pretty hard nuts. They are very quiet here, but Captain Judson says they had quite a tendency to get lost on their way down.

Colonel Rice's "eagles" have been setting a good while, and the other morning on waking he found they had hatched a pair of "stars" and "marching orders" to report in Baltimore, and with many thanks to the eagles he proceeded to obey immediately. The senior officer of the brigade now is Colonel Chamberlain of the Twentieth Maine, a former professor in a college and a very fine man, though but little posted in military matters. He is absent now on sick leave, though about to return, I hear.

Beverly Ford, Va.,
Aug. 26, 1863.

Dear Sister L.:—

My memory for dates is not very good, but it seems to me the 26th of August must be your birthday. Twenty-two years old to-day, and married almost a year and a half, and when I left home you were only my sister of twenty with the alliance in prospect. How the time rolls away! Why, I begin to look for twenty-four. I have thought every day lately that I would write to you, but then I thought if I did that the mail at night would bring me your letter to answer, so I have waited, but to-day being your birthday, I must write a little at all events. I wish I had some present to send you, but I cannot think of anything now. Stay —I will send you my "Maltese cross." It is a very simple thing, only a red cloth badge, but it may interest you from its associations, especially if anything should happen to me. I have seen letters addressed to our own boys begging them to send a badge that they had worn in some battle, and perhaps you may value even such a trifle, as something. I have worn mine through Chancellorsville, Loudon Valley and Gettysburg. It has lain between my head and a stone many a night since March. If it seems to you too trivial, you may give it to Sereno and tell him to put it on his cap. He don't write any more. I don't know what has "riled" him. Give him this *secesh* envelope and tell him I took it out of the pocket of a dead rebel away up on the top of a Blue Ridge mountain in Manassas Gap. He has been teasing me for something *secesh* this long time, and that is the "genewine article."

We are living "just old gay" now. The commissary issues soft bread enough to keep us all the time, and potatoes, turnips, onions, beets and dried apples often enough to have something good every meal. He has some tomatoes to issue, so report says, this morning. We buy condensed milk of the sutlers and have milk in our tea and coffee all the time and it don't get sour in hot weather, either. I have bought dried apples and just lived lately. The men in the regiments never had such fare as they have had since the close of the summer campaign.

And yesterday came the most glorious news of the war. The identical flag that the gallant Anderson and his seventy-three brought safely away from Fort Sumter, again floats proudly over its battered walls.* The fort is a ruin, but the Union is not. And better than all, fifteen great guns are throwing their shells over all the hostile works into Charleston itself. Their boasted "street by street and house by house," "last ditch" defense is played out. If they don't surrender or evacuate, the city will be battered down about their ears by men so far away they can't see them. Oh, but I feel jubilant! I hope they will fight till the "last ditch" is taken and nothing is left of Charleston but a grease spot.

**Note.*—Error: Probably a newspaper rumor. Sumter was not captured until 1865.

How are you, copperhead? How does that news suit you? Abolitionists are at work down there. They are "good looking" and they will "come in."

Captain Judson arrived some days ago with two hundred conscripts for the Eighty-third. He has gone back for more and soon the Eighty-third will be a full regiment again. The old army of the Potomac is filling up fast, but these new men desert awfully. I think they will quit that after a hundred or so have been shot. Three are to be shot in our division next Saturday. They were to be shot yesterday, but it was postponed. I think it will not be put off again. The whole division will be paraded at the execution. The men belong to the One hundred and nineteenth Pennsylvania (Philadelphia Corn Exchange), First Brigade.

Colonel Rice, who has commanded the brigade since Colonel Vincent fell, is appointed Brigadier General and assigned the command of First Division, First Corps. Our new commander is Colonel Chamberlain of the Twentieth Maine, a very fine man (formerly professor in college), but not much of a military man.

I still keep my position through the changes in the administration, and I have not much fear of losing it now.

E. writes quite often. Seems to like his place first rate. He has been home once on a visit.

I am most ready to send you my little diary, if you want it. I have sent to New York for a new one. Expect it Saturday or Sunday. When it comes I can send the old one. You won't find it a very nice book. It is worn and discolored by sweat and rain and it is very brief. Much of it is no more than a record of the weather and of my correspondence, written in haste with a pencil after a long day's march, but it will be a good reference if I ever get home, and I may write a more extended narrative from it. I am writing what I can in just such a book as this now and I am going to send it to E.

Now do write as soon as you can. That your life may be happy, with many returns of your birthday, is the fervent wish of your brother.

Beverly Ford, Va.,
Aug. 30, 1863.

Dear Sister L.:—

We may remain here a month yet, and we may not stay twenty-four hours. I see no present indications of a move, unless the fact that the boys begin to feel like wild colts is a sign.

The grub beats all I ever saw in the army, and last week to cap the climax they gave us beets and pickled cabbage. The latter was splendid, put up in mustard.

The late news from the south has put everybody in the best humor and camp life now is tolerable.

The last few nights have been almost cold enough for frost. The days, too, have been cool, but we shall get more hot weather soon, I suppose.

How is it that you did not notice Uncle Legrand's name in the list of drafts? It was in Alf's paper.

That diary I mean to send as soon as I get another. I expect it every night now. It won't be anything great as a literary curiosity, but the most I value it for is its account of the dates of our movements. You'll find out all about my correspondence now. Don't let it get destroyed.

I'm very much obliged for your offer to send me berries. If you do send any, dried ones would be the best. They would last better. The "perfumery" was all right, but happily I have no present use for it. E. sent me some, too, some time ago.

The great event of last week was the execution of five deserters from our division, which took place yesterday afternoon.* So much better descriptions will be given in the papers, that unless you want me to I won't try it, but will send you a paper, and if I can, an illustrated paper with a sketch in it. I saw Frank Leslie's and Harper's men both sketching it. If you see anything in the account about the "bugler," that's me. General Griffin sent for me to bugle.

Note.—They were George Kuhn, John Felane, Charles Walter, George Reinese and Emile Lai.

Beverly Ford, Va.,
Sept. 7, 1863.

Dear Friends at Home:—

I am enjoying good health now, "and I hope these few lines will find you the same."

The weather has been very cool for a week or so, and the nights so cold that we can hardly be comfortable under two blankets. It is growing hot again now, though I think the hottest weather is over.

I see no prospect of an immediate move. Every one seems to be settled as though he intended to make a stay of it, and yet for aught I know we may be up and off before night. We have been here a month to-morrow and the men are rested and supplied with clothing and just as ready to move to-day as they will be in another month, but the men I hoped to see here by this time filling up the skeletons of the old regiments have not come. Two hundred have been received in the Eighty-third. That is all in our brigade. They are all armed and equipped now and doing full duty and the Eighty-third looks something like a regiment again, but all the others need recruits as much as we.

This three-hundred dollar provision don't suit me exactly. Not that it is a hardship, but it seems to me mistaken kindness on the part of the government. The practical working of the system is that the government gets $2,700 and one man for every ten men drafted. Very few men are unable in some way to raise three hundred dollars, and as a rule they raise it. The government may get considerable money to bounty volunteers, but they will be too late. We want the men now to finish up the job this fall. The papers say they are coming at the rate of a thousand per day, but I "can't see it." Of course I don't know about the rest of the army, but they don't come to our corps at the rate of a thousand per month.

Deserters continue to come over from the rebels, and if one could believe the stories they tell, it would not take many troops to wipe out Lee's army, but I put but little confidence in them. Their statement of the feeling of the army is always colored with their own dissatisfaction. No doubt,

Lee's army is in a measure disheartened and the rank and file would be willing to accept any terms of peace, but their leaders have a way of dealing with that sort of enthusiasm so different from ours that we shall find a pretty large "obstacle" any time we start for Richmond, and for that very reason we want the men.

Every paper that I see lately is telling how nearly used up the rebels are and how soon the war will end. I think they are taking the wrong course, raising hopes and expectations that will be disappointed. Charleston is not taken yet and Richmond is not taken, and they won't be for some time. I am now entered on the last of my "three years" and am not building any very big castles on what I am going to do before that is served out. There are few who have stronger faith in the ultimate triumph of our arms, but this thing of "a few days," "starved out," "no men," "worthless currency," and all that is played out. It will take a long pull and a strong one well backed up to finish the job yet. So much for the prospect.

My letters from E. inform me that he has changed his base. Bidwell dismissed him one day without a word of warning. From what E. writes, the only motive he could have had seems to be the fact that he was paying him more than he earned, and his excuse was shabby enough. Of course you have heard the particulars before this. I always thought E. had made a big bargain to begin with, and I think if the man had told him so and reduced his pay some till he could earn more, E. would have consented. Well, he won't have that to contend against now, at all events. I don't know what you will think of the propriety of his going away so and making a new engagement without consulting his parents. Perhaps it was not right, but I must say I admire the energy and self-reliance he displayed in thus looking out for himself, and the determination to do something in spite of disappointments. One thing is certain, he won't have much temptation to dissipation on his "margin" of twenty-five cents per week, and his employer little temptation to discharge him for over-pay. I sent him one of my watches Saturday and the other one I can't sell or give away to advantage now. I send five dollars in this and think I won't send any more now, unless we are paid soon. I don't expect any more till about New Year's. It was the 26th of January last year before we were paid again.

I see that you, Mother, still talk about sending me something to eat. Now, I don't think it will pay at all. I am doing well enough. Sometimes I think I would like a little butter or fruit, just as you wish you had the thousand and one things you don't have and can't get. But it don't make any great difference to you in the long run, and it don't to me.

H., your receipt for cooking "growley" isn't worth a picayune. Soaking don't help 'em.

Headquarters Third Brigade, First Division,
Monday, Sept. 28, 1863.

Dear Sister L.:—

We are still near Culpeper. The big fight has not come off yet and does not seem so near at hand as it did a month ago. The camp is full of rumors that the Fifth Corps is going to Texas. The Eleventh and Twelfth have gone somewhere, probably to help Rosecrans, and the supposed plan is to leave four corps for the protection of Washington, abandon the attack on Richmond and transfer the seat of war to the southwest. What do you think of my going to Texas? It is quite a distance from home.

I am glad you got the diary. I told you there wouldn't be much in it. The most it is good for is for reference. I could make quite a story with this for a text. I am keeping one now a little more detailed. My book is a little larger. The one I sent to E. was more of a narrative. It seems strange to me that he does not write to you and to me, too. His address was "care of Ketcham & Barker, Toledo, Ohio." All the reason he gave for Bidwell's turning him off was that he thought he could not make a merchant of him. I think the reason was that E. could not earn the wages he was paying him. I thought so when E. wrote about his bargain and I could hardly understand about it.

I had got so far when the melodious voice of our adjutant general was heard pronouncing my name in tones considerably above a whisper. I reported and was ordered to saddle my horse quickly. The brigade was flying round, getting into line, drums beating and a big time generally. Colonel Chamberlain mounted and put for the brigade post-haste and I began to think the rebels might be coming. On ascending the hill I saw it was only a review by General Meade and a civilian whom I took to be Senator Wilson of Massachusetts. We had not had a review for some time and it was quite a novelty. It passed off very well. Casualties none, prisoners none and not much of anything else but dust.

Home of the Sanitary Commission,
Washington, D. C., Oct. 15, 1863.

Dear Sister L:—.

My mind has been in such a muddle since I came to Washington that I cannot remember whether I have written to you since I came here or not. I know I have answered your last letter, but I believe I did that in camp, and though I have not heard from you since, it seems time to write again, so here it is.

First, what I am doing here. If you have not heard, you are wondering if I have at last got into a hospital. Not very, at least I am not under medical treatment.

You know that, with my restless disposition, I could not be contented as brigade bugler while there was a possibility of doing better. As long ago as last May I began to work for a commission in a colored regiment. I wrote to Galusha A. Grow for advice. (I presume you noticed the record of that in my diary and wondered what that was about.) I heard nothing from him till this fall, when I received a letter recommending me to the notice of C. W. Foster, Major and Assistant Adjutant General, Chief of Colored Bureau, and requesting that I might be examined. It was dated September 21st. I immediately made an application to Major Foster, enclosing this letter, and in due time received an order from the War Department permitting me to appear for examination before the board of which Major General Casey is president. I reported to the board on the 1st of October and was informed that I could not be examined for a week or two yet, and was sent to this place to stay in the meantime.

Second, my prospects. When I first came here I had a very poor idea of the qualifications requisite to pass a successful examination. I knew I was as well qualified as half the officers of my regiment and I hoped to get through. Now I find that none are commissioned who are not qualified to hold the same rank in the regular army, and I begin to feel very small indeed. A man is required to show, first, a thorough knowledge of Casey's Tactics (and the examination is very severe in this), then a good knowledge of geography and history, arithmetic, algebra and geometry. Then the "Army Regulations," "Articles of War," muster and pay rolls, etc., etc., in fact be fully as well posted for second lieutenant as colonel of volunteers. Since I have been here two lieutenant colonels and many line officers have been rejected as unfit for second lieutenants.

After all this comes a searching physical examination, and no matter how well a person is posted, if the surgeon does not pronounce him sound in every respect, he is rejected. Knowing all this you may believe that my hopes of success are very small indeed. However, I shall try, and if I succeed shall be very agreeably disappointed, and I shall consider it no small honor, either. I am studying all I can, but I cannot fix my mind to study as I once could. Two years and a half in the army vetoes that.

I left the army at Culpeper. To-day they are reported at Bull Run, and the air is full of rumors of another great battle on that already famous field. For the first time, if so, the "Third Brigade" has been in a fight without me. I confess to no little anxiety for the result. Our army, I know, is weakened. The Eleventh and Twelfth corps have been sent to Rosecrans, and the First, Second, Third, Fifth and Sixth comprise the whole of our army. The papers say that "Meade is only falling back to seek a field," but I don't believe it. If he had the force, the fields at Culpeper are just as good as those at Bull Run, where the rebels have the memory of two victories. However, I will not croak, but hope for the best.

From Pennsylvania and Ohio we have glorious news. Curtin is re-elected by 30,000 majority and Brough has beat Vallandigham 100,000. That is a greater victory for Pennsylvania than the battle of Gettysburg. It is a victory for the country. Copperheads are nowhere and the elections speak in unmistakable terms of the determination of the people to support the administration. It cannot but have its influence on the South and on the war.

No. 374 North Capitol Street,
Washington, D. C., Oct. 15, 1863.

Dear Mother:—

My examination has not taken place yet and probably will not till next week. I have been here two weeks already, and I am not yet prepared. I am studying all I can. Today I have been up in the President's room in the Capitol with another candidate for strapic honors, reviewing and cross-examining on the tactics. Imagine my feelings, transferred from my shelter tent on the Rapidan to the royal magnificence of our republican President's private room in the Capitol. Pier mirrors twenty feet high on three sides of the room, marble top table, luxurious chairs, and, oh, such paintings!

It may be that I am very verdant, but a ramble through the Capitol puts me in mind of the fairy palaces of the Arabian Nights. The vaulted roofs, beautifully painted and frescoed, the marble columns (white and variegated) polished till they look as though they were covered with glass, the labyrinthine passages so puzzling it is almost impossible to enter and come out the same door, the glorious historical and portrait paintings, all make up a scene of wonder and grandeur to a plain republican like me, such as I never have seen and never expect to see again. In the Patent Office I saw Washington's sword, the one he carried in the Revolution, his dress suit, his writing case, tent, cane, bureau, mirror, etc.

I visited the Smithsonian. I won't try to tell what I saw there. It set my brain in a whirl that I have not got over yet. It is near supper time and I must close. I will say that nothing but my eyes will keep me from a commission. If I can convince the board that they are right, I shall be all right. If they throw me out on that, I have half a mind to demand a discharge on that ground. I cannot see why my eyes should disqualify me for an officer and not for a private.

374 North Capitol Street,
Washington, D. C., Oct. 28, 1863.

Dear Father:—

The great day for me was yesterday. After waiting almost a month the door swung on its hinges to admit Private O. W. N. to the presence of the arbiters of his fate who would transform him to a "straps" or send him back to his regiment to be the butt for the ridicule of his companions.

Well, it is all over with and I breathe freer. My examination occupied forty-five minutes, and in that time I missed only two questions, and those on points which I had stated to the board that I was not prepared to answer. My examination was unusually long. Many have been commissioned on a ten or fifteen minutes' examination and very few privates or non-commissioned officers stay in over half an hour.

I was the last one examined, and after I left the room to be examined by the surgeon, a sergeant heard the general remark that they had "not had to reject a man to-day." So I am satisfied that I am all right if the surgeon was satisfied with me. In testing my eyes he sent me to the corner of the room and the clerk covered one of my eyes at a time while the doctor held up something and asked me what it was. I had played sharp on him by taking an inventory of the articles on the table. I could see just enough with one eye to tell a pen from a paper knife, and a pair of scissors from a cork. He discovered that I was a little near-sighted. He asked me if I could march twenty-five miles and not be sick. That was a thrust at my "shanghais," but I told him with emphasis I could and had, and he seemed satisfied. He wouldn't look at my captain's letter, probably thought he didn't want any assistance in determining my physical ability.

I went down this morning to try to learn the result, but I could not.

Washington, D. C.,
Oct. 28, 1863.

Dear Sister L.:—

I have just time to tell you the result of my examination, which came off yesterday. Just as I expected, the result depended on the surgeon's verdict. Before the board I passed without trouble, unless study be trouble, and I hope I satisfied the doctor that I could see a commission. It tried my eyes to do it, though, I assure you of that.

I tried this morning to find out my fate. I could not satisfy myself, but those who pretend to know the ropes and who have heretofore been correct, say I am booked for straps, "First Lieutenant—First Class." If so I am content. It was what I worked for. Many of my comrades here express surprise that it was not a captaincy. I am not surprised, and should not have been if it had been second lieutenant. It is no boy's play to satisfy that board that you can make even a lieutenant.

However, it may be all moonshine and perhaps I am rejected after all, but if I am, the surgeon did it.

I return to the army to-morrow, and in the course of a week or two I shall be officially notified of the result, when I will lose no time in informing you. I hope to be able, if successful, to get leave of absence for a few days to come and see you. You would be glad to see me, wouldn't you? My letters from the army haven't been sent up. No doubt there is one or more there from you. If there is not I shall think you don't care much about me, anyway, and shall not care to come home.

Camp near Warrenton, Va.,
Monday, Nov. 2, 1863.

Dear Sister L.:—

I got back to camp last Thursday night. Next morning early we marched about six miles and brought up on the Branch railroad, about three miles from Warrenton. I do not as yet know any more of the result of my examination than I wrote you from Washington. My papers have not arrived yet.

Headquarters Third Brigade,
Kelly's Ford, Nov. 11, 1863.

Dear Sister L.:—

I have another name to put on my battle pin (when I get it), that of "Rappahannock Station, November 8th." Soldiers have a fashion of counting up their battles, with an honest pride when they reach a certain number, and I will count up mine and then tell you a little about the last. Hanover Court House, a battle then, a skirmish now, Mechanicsville, Gaines' Mill, which no one calls less than a battle even now, Savage Station, White Oak Swamp, Glendale, Malvern Hill, then the greatest battle of America, Second Bull Run, Antietam, Shepherdstown Ford, Fredericksburg, the slaughter pen, skirmish at Richards' Ford, Chancellorsville, Loudon Valley, Gettysburg, Jones' Cross Roads, and Rappahannock Station.

Quite a little list, and as I have always been there when the Third Brigade has, I do not feel ashamed of my record.

About four o'clock last Saturday morning the reveille sounded and in half an hour the camps of our division were all astir, brilliant with fires, bristling with preparation for the march at daylight. Daylight came and we began the march toward the river. The day was cold and windy and very dusty, but we marched rapidly and by noon we reached the rebel pickets, or our advance discovered them a mile from the river. We halted for an hour or two, while the generals made their dispositions, and then formed in line. Our division came next to the railroad, on the south of it.

On the other side was the Sixth Corps, Second Division of the Fifth Corps on our left and Third Division in reserve.

At 2:30 p. m. the line advanced. The skirmishers soon ran on to a cavalry picket and fired, and the way the rebs did "git" over the little hill was a warning to slow horses. We advanced steadily and soon came to a line of rebel skirmishers thrown out to meet us. They fired and fell back and soon the artillery opened on our line, but oh, such firing! Shells burst all around and over us, but hardly one in the right place. On our side of the river just above the railroad was a fort mounting six or seven guns and the opposite bank of the river was bristling with field batteries.

Griffin's battery (our favorite) got into position to send a message to the nearest fort and our skirmishers advanced. The rebs opened on them and the aforesaid pet opened on the rebs, and over the rampart went our boys and out went the rebs. Some of them jumped into the river up to their necks, but they had to come back. The result was sixty-five men and five officers prisoners, and seven guns (all in the fort).

The paper states that the Sixth Corps took the fort. It may be so, but men who were the first in say that only one sergeant and one officer from the Sixth were there, and I know that the Eighty-third and Forty-fourth took the prisoners, because I saw and counted them myself and heard Colonel Connor's report when he brought them to Colonel Chamberlain.

Well, that was about all of it. It was after sundown when the fort was taken and we could not cross the river till morning. Our casualties were very small, twenty killed and wounded in the brigade, three wounded and none killed in the Eighty-third.

We went back into the woods to bivouac. No fires were allowed, but a good many were made, nevertheless, and I made out to get a cup of coffee. I tied my horse to a fallen tree and lay down close by him, and the rascal kept me awake half the night. He pulled my haversack out from under my head, pulled my blankets off, and once I woke and found him with my bugle in his mouth chewing the tassel.

By daylight we were on the move down the river to Kelly's Ford, crossed on pontoons and back into the country three miles and bivouacked. Monday we lay all day in bivouac and at sundown got up and came back this side the river. Our First Division did. The rest of the corps remained.

We had big times that night for fires. We had no wood, camped on a plain where there had been an old camp, and not a stake for our horses or stick to burn could we find. The wind blew furiously and it began to snow.

The mounted orderlies and I after unsaddling put out and finally found a pole thirty feet long half a mile away. We took that, carried it up and laid it on the ground to tie to. The other boys had got some brush afire and we got coffee and lay down. That night it snowed an inch deep on our blankets. Next morning we moved back into the woods, where we are now and expect to stay a few days to watch guerrillas.

I have heard nothing from the War Department yet. Begin to think I am rejected. Write again soon.

Kelly's Ford, Va., Nov. 13, 1863.

Dear Sister L.:—

I received your and Charlie's letter. Your expressed wish to see me will not yet be gratified, I fear. I have heard nothing yet from Washington and I would take about ten cents for my chance of a commission. I do not entirely give it up yet, but my expectations are dwindling fast. One of the Forty-fourth New York, who was examined the day after I was, got First Lieutenant, First Class. That I am morally certain of, and he has not got his appointment yet. Until he gets his I shall not entirely give it up.

I copy a portion of the last "General Order" in relation to the fight at Rappahannock Station:

"The enemy was attacked in an entrenched position of great strength in enclosed works, defended by artillery and infantry, and compelled to surrender, after a sharp conflict, to an assaulting column actually inferior in numbers to the force defending the works.

Four pieces of artillery, four caissons filled with ammunition, the enemy's pontoon bridge, eight battle flags, two thousand stand of small arms, one thousand six hundred prisoners, including two brigade commanders and one hundred and thirty commissioned officers, are the fruits of the victory."

National Hotel, Washington,
Nov. 19, 1863.

Dear Sister L.:—

Perhaps you think my long silence bodes no good. If you do, dispossess yourself of that idea immediately.

I am half "luny" with delight. Do not think that because I would not allow myself to think or speak of coming home, or listen to you, that I cared nothing for my home or my friends. No, indeed! But now times are altered and I shall be with you next week, God willing. "How? Why?" Because I am "First Lieutenant, Eighth Regiment, United States Colored Troops, Philadelphia, Pennsylvania," and have leave of absence for fifteen days, signed by the Secretary of War, in my pocket.

I shall go to New York to-night to buy some clothes and see my friends. I shall stay till Monday night. Then I come to you. I will stop on my way to Michigan to call for E. and take him home with me.

This is good news to you, I know. It is to me. I hardly expected to get home, but last night I went down to see Major Foster, stated my case and asked ten days. "Why, you can't go to Michigan in ten days; it will take you all the time to go and come." I thought, you see, that if I asked too much, I wouldn't get anything. "Make your application in writing and I will see what I can do for you." I made the application this morning for fifteen days and got my papers through the whole red tape in an hour.

E. made the most sensible remark I have read since the talk of my promotion. Said he, "I shall think no more of you than I did when you carried a musket, but the world will." Straps are honored, and already I see the advantage of wearing them, though I have not got them on.

Camp Wm. Penn, Philadelphia,
Thursday, Dec. 10, 1863.

Dear Sister L.:—

I have just time to write you a line. I had just two days to spend at home. Trains not connecting and being behind time delayed me. I got here to the camp last Monday and was immediately assigned the command of a full company.

Next day I was put on as "officer of the guard" and my letter writing and everything of the kind are coming out slim.

My regiment is full. The field officers are Colonel Chas. W. Fribley, Lieutenant Colonel N. B. Bartram, formerly Lieutenant Colonel Seventeenth New York, and Major Loren Burritt. The second lieutenant of my company is Jas. S. Thompson.

The regiment is in barracks, just moved in on Tuesday. We are eight miles from Philadelphia, but the cars pass frequently and it is not too far for camps, twenty minutes trip.

I was officer of the guard the day we moved and not allowed to leave my guard, and when the officers' baggage was unloaded some one took my valise and I cannot find it. It was worth sixty dollars to me at least, and all my papers were in it. It may come to light and the end of the world may come in 1867. One is as probable as the other.

The weather is clear and very cold. I must close. Will tell you more next time. Write soon. Address "Lieutenant O. W. N., Company K, Eighth United States Colored Troops, Camp Wm. Penn, Philadelphia, Pennsylvania."

Camp Wm. Penn, Philadelphia,
Dec. 26, 1863.

Dear Sister L.:—

A Happy New Year to you if it isn't too late. Christmas in camp went "merry as a marriage bell," big dinner, sham battle, etc., etc.

At night I went to the theater in town. Saw Edwin Forrest in "Metamora." I send you a "phiz." Will send

LIEUTENANT OLIVER W. NORTON.
December, 1863.

you a full length when they come. I have just time to say I have been appointed Acting Quartermaster on the staff of Major Burritt, commanding three companies Eighth United States Colored Troops, to be sent to Delaware on recruiting service. I shall have a horse to ride, of course. Write soon and direct as before till I send my new address.

Philadelphia, Dec. 29, 1863.
Dear Sister L.:—

I am waiting yet for the final order to start for Delaware. The weather has been very stormy for the past three days, but this morning it has cleared off beautifully. Probably we start to-morrow morning. I send the promised photo, also two others. One is Captain Bailey of Company B, the other Lieutenant Schiffelin, same company. He is going as adjutant of the expedition to Delaware.

LETTERS OF 1864

Seaford, Del., Jan. 4, 1864.

Dear Sister L.:—

We came by boat from Philadelphia to Wilmington. New Year's day our whole detachment was feasted in the town hall at the same time with the First Delaware Volunteers, home on furlough. We had good times there.

On the 2d we came down on the cars to Seaford, one hundred and thirty-three miles south of Wilmington. I saw Governor Cannon in Wilmington and had quite a talk with him. He is enthusiastic on the subject of negro soldiers.

Arrived here at dark, found a man at the depot waiting, who offered us quarters in a negro church and a school house and all were comfortable.

Sunday morning I got my tents up from the cars and we pitched a camp in one of the most beautiful pine groves I ever saw. Our camp was thronged with visitors, and darkies who wanted to enlist. There are hundreds of them, mostly slaves, here now, anxiously waiting for the recruiting officer. The boys are singing—

> Rally round the flag, boys, rally once again,
> Shouting the battle cry of freedom.
> Down with the traitor, up with the star, etc.

They sing with the heart, and the earnestness they put into the words is startling. Cool as I am I found myself getting excited as I heard their songs this afternoon and saw the electrifying effect on the crowds of slaves.

The officers here are lions. I am afraid I'm guilty of putting on a little style. Not with the men of the regiment, though. I was shaved by a woman this morning.

Seaford, Del., Jan. 9, 1864.

Dear Sister L.:—

I have just time to-night to write you some important

news. Important so far as you and I are concerned. An orderly arrived in camp to-night with a dispatch from the Secretary of War ordering the detachment to return to Camp Wm. Penn, and the United States Colored Troops will proceed as soon as practicable to Hilton Head, South Carolina. We shall be off next week.

There is joy in camp to-night over the news. I hardly know whether to like it or not. On some accounts I shall. Almost any place is preferable to Virginia. I shall be far away from home and friends. Letters will be like angels' visits, few and far between. But bid me God speed, L. Far or near, my heart will be with thee. Don't write till I send my address.

St. Lawrence Hotel, Philadelphia,
Jan. 17, 1864.

Dear Sister L.:—

The regiment started for the sunny south last night, leaving me behind. I shall go to New York before I go and I would like to see you once more first, but it would require too liberal construction of my orders to find any business in Chautauqua. I am left to settle my business as quartermaster and to take command of a squad of men not yet reported to the regiment.

Jacksonville, Fla.,
Monday, Feb. 29, 1864.

Dear Sister L.:—

You will probably see accounts of the battle of Olustee, or Ocean Pond, in the papers. I have ordered a copy of the Brookville Republican, containing a letter from Dr. Heichold, descriptive of the battle, sent to you, but I will give you some of my own ideas about it, too; you always express a preference for them, you know.

Well, the morning of Saturday, the 20th, found us at Barber's Ford on the St. Mary's river ready to march and loaded down with ten days' rations. Our force consisted of the One hundred-fifteenth, Forty-seventh and Forty-eighth New York Regiments, Seventh New Hampshire and

Seventh Connecticut (repeating rifles), Fifty-fourth Massachusetts (colored) of Fort Wagner memory, the First North Carolina Colored and the Eighth, twenty pieces of artillery, one battalion cavalry and the Fortieth Massachusetts (mounted infantry).

We started marching in three columns, artillery in the road, flanked by the infantry on either side. After marching twelve miles we halted near a few desolate houses called Sanders and while resting heard a few musket shots in advance. We supposed our cavalry had met a few of the enemy's pickets. Their force was supposed to be at Lake City, twelve miles distant, so we moved on up the railroad. The skirmishing increased as we marched, but we paid little attention to it. Pretty soon the boom of a gun startled us a little, but not much, as we knew our flying artillery was ahead, but they boomed again and again and it began to look like a brush. An aide came dashing through the woods to us and the order was—"double quick, march!" We turned into the woods and ran in the direction of the firing for half a mile, when the head of the column reached our batteries. The presiding genius, General Seymour, said: "Put your regiment in, Colonel Fribley," and left.

Military men say it takes veteran troops to maneuver under fire, but our regiment with knapsacks on and unloaded pieces, after a run of half a mile, formed a line under the most destructive fire I ever knew. We were not more than two hundred yards from the enemy, concealed in pits and behind trees, and what did the regiment do? At first they were stunned, bewildered, and knew not what to do. They curled to the ground, and as men fell around them they seemed terribly scared, but gradually they recovered their senses and commenced firing. And here was the great trouble—they could not use their arms to advantage. We have had very little practice in firing, and, though they could stand and be killed, they could not kill a concealed enemy fast enough to satisfy my feelings.

After seeing his men murdered as long as flesh and blood could endure it, Colonel Fribley ordered the regiment to fall back slowly, firing as they went. As the men fell back they gathered in groups like frightened sheep, and it was almost impossible to keep them from doing so. Into these groups the rebels poured the deadliest fire, almost every bullet hitting some one. Color bearer after color bearer was shot down and the colors seized by another. Behind us was a battery that was wretchedly managed. They had but little ammunition, but after firing that, they made no effort to get away with their pieces, but busied themselves in trying to keep us in front of them. Lieutenant Lewis seized the colors and planted them by a gun and tried to rally his men round them, but forgetting them for the moment, they were left there, and the battery was captured and our colors with it.

Colonel Fribley was killed soon after his order to fall back, and Major Burritt had both legs broken. We were without a commander, and every officer was doing his best to do something, he knew not what exactly. There was no leader. Seymour might better have been in his grave than there. Many will blame Lieutenant Lewis that the colors were lost. I do not think he can be blamed. Brave to rashness, he cannot be accused of cowardice, but man cannot think of too many things.

Some things in this story look strange. Officers should know exactly what to do, you may say. Certainly, but it is a damper on that duty when there is a certainty on the mind that the commander does not know. When, with eight or ten regiments ready, you see only two or three fighting, and feel you are getting whipped from your general's incompetency, it is hard to be soldierly.

I saw from the commencement of our retreat that the day was lost, but I confess to you that I was in doubt whether I ought to stay and see my men shot down or take them to the rear. Soldierly feelings triumphed, but at what a cost!

Captain Dickey was shot early in the fight and the command of the company devolved on me. He was not seriously wounded, a ball through the face.

Captain Wagner was standing by me when he fell,

pierced by three balls. I seized him and dragged him back a few rods and two of his men then took him to the rear. I carried his sword through the fight. Several times I was on the point of throwing it away, thinking he must be dead, but I saved it and had the pleasure of giving it to him and hearing that he is likely to recover.

Of twenty-two officers that went into the fight, but two escaped without marks. Such accurate firing I never saw before. I was under the impression all the time that an inferior force was whipping us, but the deadly aim of their rifles told the story.

Well, you are wanting to know how I came off, no doubt. With my usual narrow escapes, but escapes. My hat has five bullet holes in it. Don't start very much at that—they were all made by one bullet. You know the dent in the top of it. Well, the ball went through the rim first and then through the top in this way. My hat was cocked up on one side so that it went through in that way and just drew the blood on my scalp. Of course a quarter of an inch lower would have broken my skull, but it was too high. Another ball cut away a corner of my haversack and one struck my scabbard. The only wonder is I was not killed, and the wonder grows with each succeeding fight, and this is the fifteenth or sixteenth, Yorktown, Hanover, Gaines' Mill, Charles City, Malvern, Bull Run, Antietam, Shepherdstown Ford, Fredericksburg, Richards Ford, Chancellorsville, Loudon Valley, Gettysburg, Manassas Gap, Rappahannock Station and Olustee, to say nothing of the shelling at Harrison's Landing or the skirmish at Ely's Ford. Had any one told me when I enlisted that I should have to pass through so many I am afraid it would have daunted me. How many more?

Company K went into the fight with fifty-five enlisted men and two officers. It came out with twenty-three men and one officer. Of these but two men were not marked. That speaks volumes for the bravery of negroes. Several of these twenty-three were quite badly cut, but they are present with the company. Ten were killed and four reported missing, though there is little doubt they are killed, too.*

A flag of truce from the enemy brought the news that prisoners, black and white, were treated alike. I hope it is so, for I have sworn never to take a prisoner if my men left there were murdered.

This is the first letter I have written since the fight, and it is to you, my best beloved sister. It is written in haste, in a press of business, but you will excuse mistakes and my inattention to the matter of your own letter. You may pray for me—I need that, and do write to me as often as you find time.

Jacksonville, Fla., Tuesday, March 1, 1864.

Dear Father:—

On the 20th we fought our first battle at Olustee, or Ocean Pond, as some call it. They might as well call any other place in these pine woods some high sounding name, for this country is all alike. Since leaving Jacksonville I have not seen five hundred acres of cleared land in a journey of forty-five miles to the west. The country is covered with scattered pines, most of them blazed for turpentine. The ground between the trees is covered with a dense growth of coarse grass and palmetto shrubs. At intervals there are swamps, not deep, but broad and wet. Once in about ten miles is a small collection of dilapidated looking houses on the Florida railroad, and the people—the most abject, stupid, miserable objects.

I have ordered a copy of the Brookville Republican containing an account of the battle by Dr. Heichold, to be sent to you, because I have not time to write it myself. I have not yet seen it, but I presume it will be correct, as the doctor had better opportunities for learning the facts than I had.

I shall give you more particularly my own ideas of the

Note.—The regiment went into the battle with five hundred and fifty-four officers and enlisted men. Of these, three hundred and nineteen were killed or disabled by serious wounds. Many others were slightly wounded, but remained on duty.

performance of our own men. I want to be true and I cannot endorse all that has been said of them. First, I think no battle was ever more wretchedly fought. I was going to say planned, but there was no plan. No new regiment ever went into their first fight in more unfavorable circumstances. Second, no braver men ever faced an enemy. To have made these men fight well, I would have halted them out of range of the firing, formed my line, unslung knapsacks, got my cartridge boxes ready, and loaded. Then I would have moved it up to the support of a regiment already engaged. I would have had them lie down and let the balls and shells whistle over them till they got a little used to it. Then I would have moved them to the front, told them to get as close to the ground as they could and go in.

Just the other thing was done. We were double-quicked for half a mile, came under fire by the flank, formed line with empty pieces under fire, and, before the men had loaded, many of them were shot down. They behaved as any one acquainted with them would have expected. They were stunned, bewildered, and, as the balls came hissing past or crashing through heads, arms and legs, they curled to the ground like frightened sheep in a hailstorm. The officers finally got them to firing, and they recovered their senses somewhat. But here was the great difficulty—they did not know how to shoot with effect.

Our regiment has been drilled too much for dress parade and too little for the field. They can march well, but they cannot shoot rapidly or with effect. Some of them can, but the greater part cannot. Colonel Fribley had applied time and again for permission to practice his regiment in target firing, and been always refused. When we were flanked, flesh and blood could stand it no longer, and Colonel Fribley, without orders, gave the command to fall back slowly, firing as we went. He fell, shot through the heart, very soon after that. Where was our general and where was his force? Coming up in the rear, and as they arrived, they were put in, one regiment at a time, and whipped by detail.

It is no use for me to express my feelings in regard to the matter. If there is a second lieutenant in our regiment who couldn't plan and execute a better battle, I would vote to dismiss him for incompetency.

The correspondent of the Tribune who was present said he dared not write a true history of the affair here, but he should do it in New York, and it would be published.

You may judge of the severity of the fight by this: Of fifty-five men in Company K who went into the fight but two came out untouched by balls. Of twenty-two officers engaged but two were untouched. I got a ball in my hat that made five holes and just drew blood on my head. Another took off the corner of my haversack.

Colonel Fribley was shot through the heart. Major Burritt, gallant fellow, had both legs broken. Captain Wagner fell pierced with three balls, but got off, and I hear is in a fair way to recovery.

March 2nd. I had to stop here and fall in the company for a review by General Gilmore, and just after that the alarm was sounded and we all removed inside the trenches.

Last night I was out all night in the rain in command of a detachment cutting and carrying trees for abattis work, and I feel owly to-day.

This afternoon we have inspection and I must close to prepare for it.

Jacksonville, Fla., March 9, 1864.

Dear Father:—

We are still at Jacksonville, and the whole force is hard at work nearly all the time, either on the fortifications or on picket. Last week we were moving every day. One day we would go outside the works and bivouac, and the next the pickets would fire a few guns and we would hustle inside again, to go back the next morning, and so on.

Saturday afternoon we moved into our present position and have remained here so far since.

Ever since the battle the men have slept with their shoes and equipments on, and they fall in every morning an hour before light and stand in line till sunrise. This looks to me very much like "locking the stable door," etc.

Vague rumors reach us of all sorts of stories in the papers in regard to the battle. The Herald (of unquestionable veracity, so they say) says that the Eighth retired in confusion after Colonel Fribley fell. There may be some truth in it, but not as most persons would take it, i. e., meaning a complete rout. From all I can learn it appears that the regiment was under fire for more than two hours, though it did not seem to me so long. I never know anything of the time in a battle, though.

The veracious "Lieutenant Colonel Hall, Provost-Marshal, Department of the South," is probably the author of this story. He was the first to inform Mrs. Fribley of the death of the colonel, and he chivalrously and consolingly added that his death was the result of his own rash exposure and that the officers of the regiment were "as badly scared as the men" and he "rallied the regiment himself." It is all an infamous lie, and there is more than one officer in the regiment ready to tell him so at the first opportunity. He was seen riding about the field with his pistol cocked and shouting to every wounded man to halt. The man who could coolly tell a poor widow alone in this country that her husband was killed by his own fault, is a brute to say the least. Colonel Fribley exposed himself no more than was necessary. He dismounted as soon as the line was formed and was in the rear of the regiment when he was shot.

I want to see justice done the regiment. I don't claim that they fought well, only as well as they could, and that the officers had all they could do to get them to fall back at all after the first halt. The "confusion" in which they "retired" was owing to this, that there was no line and the men would only leave the trees, behind which they were firing, on direct orders to do so. The regiment had no commander after the colonel and major fell, and every officer was doing the best he could with his squad independent of any one else.

I have been on a court-martial for the last week and

probably will be for some time to come. Two cases have been finished thus far—Corporal Smith of our regiment, for mutiny in shooting his sergeant while in discharge of his duties, and another case similar. I am considered rather fortunate in being detailed, as it relieves me from other duties which are very onerous just now.

We are having beautiful weather, very much like our own July. We have not had forty-eight hours of rainy weather since we came here.

Julius Tyler writes that Dennison, Newton Bushnell and several others from Ararat are down in Tennessee in an engineer corps constructing a railroad.

News from New York and Brooklyn is all about the Sanitary Fair. Brooklyn is wild over it and the Independent is full of it.

I wish you would send me that money, $10 at a time, in letters to Hilton Head. I am getting short. Kiss ye babie for ye boy who fights ye rebels.

Jacksonville, Fla.,
March 11, 1864.

Dear Sister L.:—

Somebody has said that is the sweetest word of endearment in the language, and I believe it. Beside it other terms seem to me in my present mood mawkish and sentimental. Since that April day when the red dawn of this cruel war was just breaking over our country, and with tear-wet face you bade me good-bye and God speed, no other woman has been so dear to me. Perhaps my letters and my language may not have shown it, but it is true. There may be a touch of Lara or Conrad the Corsair in my character. I know my heart is not often visible in my face, but when I came home and you were so glad to see me that you could not think even where your husband was, do not imagine that because I was not affected in the same way, or that there were no tears of joy in my eyes, I did not feel one of the greatest joys of my life that day.

H. has never seemed to me like you. Perhaps the greater difference in our ages may account for this, and she is so shy and strange, she is really getting to be almost a stranger. She has changed very much since I left home, and I have not kept pace with the changes, so infrequent have been her letters, and her letters, too, are not a part of or like herself. They are only the family gossip, but you, in all this time of absence have been my dear sister, and, when sitting round the camp fire a comrade has spoken of his sister, I have mentioned mine with reverent love and tenderness. And often I have thought but not spoken of how she has followed me in her thoughts and dreams, mayhap, over weary roads and through the smoke and din of battle, or in the tiresome hours of winter quarters followed me with the untold wealth of a sister's love.

Often I have thought and felt I was not worthy of all that wealth of sisterly pride and affection lavished on me, but, because I was not worthy, I have craved it all the more. Brothers are not like a sister. Perhaps I may be wanting in natural affection, but my younger brothers never seemed so very dear to me. At home I used to be impatient of their restless freaks, and though I would have resented very quickly a wrong done to them by an outsider, yet I never troubled myself much about them. E. is getting to be a man, and, as his strength and manhood develop, my admiration for him increases. In fact, to see our letters, you would think we constitute a mutual admiration society, but E. is not a woman and not my sister. And as a proof of my love for you, have I not written you often? And how anxiously I have watched the mails for your letters, you will never know.

Jacksonville, Fla.,
March 15, 1864.

Dear Sister L.:—

I send you a copy of an army paper containing some interesting matter about Olustee. I enclose a specimen of the gray moss that covers these trees. It grows in locks six, eight and even ten feet long and a foot thick hanging all over the branches, yet it has no root. It is an inextricable snarl. It seems to feed on the air, for it can get life no other way. It is the most singular vegetable I ever saw. I will try to send you some orange flowers when I write next.

Jacksonville, Fla.,
March 22, 1864.

Dear Sister L.:—

I send you another copy of the Free South, printed this time on wrapping paper. "Necessity is the mother of invention." There is no news. All quiet along the lines. The alarm I mentioned was caused by about forty rebel cavalry making a reconnoissance along our lines. Our men withdrew at first, then rallied and chased the rebels a mile beyond the original line without a shot being fired on either side. The court is still in session.

Jacksonville, Fla.,
Sunday, March 27, 1864.

Dear Sister L.:—

Again the mail has come and no letter from you. Nine days have I waited in the confident expectation that if that boat ever did come I should certainly get some letters. It comes and I get a short note from Father only. My papers come, so I know that it is not the fault of communication. What is the matter? Has some one reported me dead, and have you got on mourning for me already? Am I set down in your mind as an inmate of the Libby, and are you torturing your brain with thoughts of the fate of a "nigger officer"? If you are, cease now and henceforth. Do you never believe I'm dead or in prison, even if you see all the particulars in the papers. Wait till you get the news in writing from Captain Dickey or Lieutenant Thompson. Both have your address and will be sure to write immediately in case anything occurs to prevent my writing.

Rumor says to-night that we have a new commander, General Hatch. I hope it may prove true, for whatever may be General Seymour's talents, he certainly does not possess the confidence of the officers or men of this department, and without that it is difficult to succeed in anything.

Do you want to know how I spend my time here? Well, in the first place I am a member of a court-martial that meets every morning at 10 o'clock. If there is business enough we sit till 3 or 4 p. m., and then adjourn, but usually we get through much earlier. Then I come back to camp, and after dinner I read or write or play chess. I play a great deal lately and the more I learn the more I like it. It is a noble game and I am determined to be no mean player. I have already beaten the best player I can find in the regiment, and I mean to get so I can do it every time. Last winter I used to play "euchre" or "old sledge," but it never improved me much. Chess on the contrary is a never ending study. Dr. Franklin called it the "King of Games."

After I get through the chess, I wonder when the mail will come and whom my letters will be from. It is very easy to tell whom the last were from, or rather whom they were not from. By George, I shall be driven to the necessity of advertising in the Waverly for correspondents or initiating another cousinly affair.

Tell me if you get a paper every two or three days, a letter once a week, a package of Florida moss, an envelope of orange blossoms. All these I've been sending.

I wrote to you that I had found Almon Ploss and the Wait's Corners boys.

Jacksonville, Florida,
Sunday, April 10, 1864.

Dear Sister L.:—

It is a beautiful Sunday morning, gloriously fresh after yesterday's rain. The sun is not high enough yet to be uncomfortably warm. The weather is very much like northern June. Such a delicious freshness about the morning air, and as the sun mounts up, a glow that makes a cool shade appreciated.

The "Sunday Morning Inspection" is going on now. Being on "special duty" myself I am excused from that, and while the captain and Lieutenant Thompson are examining guns and knapsacks. I am sitting in the tent writing to you.

The band of sable performers is discoursing "Hail Columbia" and "America," and they play well, too, very well for the length of time they have been practicing.

Since I wrote to you we have moved our camp. We had the most beautiful spot in the vicinity. A high point of land overlooking the river and fringed with magnificent live oaks, and dotted here and there with orange trees and magnolias. It did not look very well when we first went there, but then we soon fixed it up.

When we got well fortified, Colonel Hawley concluded we were not strong enough to hold the place, and ordered us to change camps with the Seventh Connecticut, his own regiment. Our present camp is on a perfectly level plain of sand regularly laid out, and the streets are lined with pine trees which the men have set out, giving it a very pretty appearance. We have one wall tent for the officers of each company. We have the fly of ours stretched in front of the tent. It makes a very nice place to sit in the heat of the day. We are to have it paved with brick, which are plenty hereabouts, but we have not got it done yet. Behind the tent is our mess-room roofed with shelter tents, where at stated hours Dickson serves up the staff of life and ham and potatoes. Also the dwelling of Dickson himself and his brick cooking-range. Around the whole is a double row of pines. Can you see by that little description our surroundings? Inside we have our bed, our table and bookcase. On the table are books and writing materials, my flute and chess, the last Atlantic and the papers, read till they actually get thin.

The court still continues to meet every day from 10 till 4 o'clock and I do little but attend that.

I met Almon in the street the other day. He was looking well. Spoke of a projected raid across the river in which he was to take part. A raid after the enemy's fresh beef, to be converted of course to the benefit of the Yankee invaders.

Jacksonville, Fla.,
Thursday, April 14, 1864.

Dear Mother:—

Any news of special importance is simply out of the question. The rebels, after taking out of Florida all they cared for, have abandoned the state to the Yankee invaders. Only a few roving bands of cavalry remain.

This morning two regiments left us for the Army of the Potomac. Rumor said that all the white troops in this district were to be sent there, but I believe that is one of Madam's incredible stories. Certainly no others have orders yet.

The court-martial, which has been in session the last six weeks, was broken up by the departure of the judge advocate, who went with his regiment, but I hear it is the intention to appoint another to fill his place and continue the court.

Judging from appearances, it is not the intention to abandon this place soon. The general is having the streets re-planted with shade trees in places where the fire killed them. Fatigue parties have been at work draining the swamps in the immediate vicinity, and they have succeeded well. A high signal tower has been erected to communicate with vessels outside the bar at the mouth of the river.

Jacksonville was before the war as large or larger than Jamestown, and built mostly of brick. Sutlers are doing a heavy business in the stores which survived the general wreck. Everyone is occupied and there are two eating houses in operation. I notice one good thing—no liquor is sold in the town. Neither officer nor soldier can get a drop. As a consequence nobody gets drunk, a very satisfactory state of affairs.

Beyond this there is little to say. The regiment, so far as I can judge by observation (having had nothing to do with it for the last six weeks), is improving rapidly. I think another fight will give them a different story to tell.

We have received a list of our wounded in the enemy's hands and find that quite a number supposed and reported to be dead are alive, and some left alive have since died.

The furnishing this list was the act of Major General Patten Anderson, "Commanding Confederate States Forces in Florida," and was entirely of his own free will, and shows a disposition that I wish was more general.

Mr. Rockwood is the only useful chaplain I ever saw in the army. He is doing the regiment much good. Besides preaching he is furnishing the men books, teaching and encouraging them to read, and working all the time as hard as any other officer to improve the regiment. He is very much liked, or at least respected in the regiment.

Yellow Bluff, Fla.,
April 23, 1864.

Dear Sister L.:—

The change of place indicated in my date is an accomplished fact. We came down here last Sunday. Yellow Bluff is on the north bank of the St. Johns about seven miles from the mouth. We have a fort here, a stockade and some rifle pits.

Our regiment garrisons the post and there are no other troops here. Having no other commander we have things all our own way. Captain Dickey is provost marshal of the post and I am commanding the company. Companies K and B are at post headquarters and do post guard duty and river patrolling.

Our court-martial, after a six-weeks' session, was disbanded the day before I came down here, and on arriving I was sent on picket. Imagine a slashing of five hundred acres with an impassable swamp on each side, woods in front and the camp in the rear, and you have my field of operations. After posting my line, I selected a log in the center for my headquarters and awaited developments. They came. Development No. 1, a commotion among the darkies on the hill, the discharge of a musket, and beating the ground with clubs, ending in the reception at picket headquarters of a black snake seven and one-half feet long and thick as my wrist. No. 2, similar to No. 1, except the musket and the kind of snake; No. 2 being a brown cottonmouth five feet long. No. 3, 11:30 p. m., a bellow that beats all the bulls of Bashan, shakes the ground and huddles the darkies in heaps. Boys think it is a bear, but I conclude it is an alligator. No. 4, a buggy containing a woman, five children, a trunk and a box of tobacco, and drawn by a Florida pony arrives at the line. The woman wants to "Come over to you-all." She is admitted and sent in to headquarters. No. 5, Lieutenant Young relieves me and I return to camp.

Well, as I told you, Company K is provost guard and river patrol. About all the duty I have is to patrol the river one night in three. The steamers Maple Leaf and General Hunter have been blown up by torpedoes, and our business is to prevent the rebels from putting down any more of them between here and St. Johns Bluff, six miles below. We have four boats' crews beside the guard in the two companies. I come on to-night and I will give you an outline of the night's work. About dark I shall leave the wharf with a crew of seven men and run down the river among the islands and past the mouths of creeks and bayous to St. Johns Bluff, keeping a bright lookout for any strange boat. I shall get out on shore, build up a fire and wait an hour for my oarsmen to rest, then come back again, reaching camp about midnight. Then I shall take a new crew and do the same thing over again, getting back at sunrise.

To-morrow night Lieutenant Griffin will go with his company, next night Lieutenant Thompson, and next I go again. After breakfast I shall take a snooze, then get up and play a few games of chess with the adjutant or somebody else, or perhaps go fishing. Fish are abundant here, and strange fish some of them are, too. Catfish just like our bullheads, weigh thirty pounds. Sheephead, shaped like a pumpkin seed with teeth exactly like a sheep's, and lips too, for that matter. Garfish with a bill like a duck's only hard and full of sharp teeth, and eight or ten inches long. Sea trout—Thompson caught one the other day that weighed twenty-six pounds, delicious eating. When one of them bites, it is a fair question which is caught, the fish or the man. Sea crabs and oysters are plenty, too. Don't you think we can live?

The regiment is camped rather scattering. Two companies are in the fort, two at the stockade, and two here, two in reserve and two down at St. Johns Bluff. There are three or four houses here. One is used for headquarters, one as hospital, one commissary. Lieutenant Thompson and I have a tent with a fly in front and a floor under the whole. Captain Dickey has a tent for himself and one for his office. The men to-day are putting up "A" tents and discarding the shelter tents. Altogether we intend to be comfortable while we stay here.

The white troops are all gone or are going north and we are to stay and hold the river to prevent smuggling. Next time I will give you some description of the country and river scenery.

I am collecting some beautiful shells and curiosities to send you if I ever get in reach of an express.

I've got three little alligators a foot and a half long in a tub. I keep them for playthings.

Yellow Bluff, Fla.,
May 10, 1864.

Dear Sister L.:—

Everybody is talking now of the event of yesterday, the destruction of the little steamer Harriet Weed by a torpedo. It occurred about four miles above here. Captain Dickey, who was coming down from Jacksonville on the Boston, saw it. The Boston is quite a large boat and carried a large party of excursionists or "inspectionists" from Hilton Head. There were some fifty ladies on board. The captain for some whim ran a little nearer the shore than the regular channel. He had never done so before. The Weed, however, was just behind, and she kept the regular channel and was blown to atoms. She sank immediately. There were ten killed and wounded. The rest escaped unhurt. The gunboat Mahaska had been lying there for some time and her launches patrolled the river, but the day before she went up to Jacksonville. and the first night she was gone two torpedoes were planted. We received orders last night to patrol that part hereafter. It brings it pretty hard on us. I am very glad it did not occur on our part of the river. Much blame is or would be attached to us if a torpedo should be found in our part. Under the circumstances it would be unhealthy business for a strange boat to be caught on the river here. I would shoot first and court-martial afterwards. This is the third steamer blown up on this river already, and any amount of torpedoes have been found.

The paymaster came on Saturday with his $7 per month. Not half the men would sign the rolls or take their pay, and those who did, did so under protest. It is too bad. Seven dollars a month for the heroes of Olustee! I received two months' pay, deducting the tax, $213.49. Some difference between that and $26. My expenses besides clothing, etc., are about $6 a week and I hope to save some money now.

We are living very quietly, enjoying ourselves as well as we can.

The weather is extremely warm in the middle of the day, July and August weather, but the evenings—O, how I wish you could be here to enjoy a few! When the moon rises red as blood and throws across the river a long shining path; when the air is so balmy you seem to float in some other element. And then to go out on the river where your oars drip pearls or drops of fire, and the sparks fly from the prow of the boat as she plows her way along. I suppose it is electricity in the water. I know it is beauty.

A man just down from Yorktown says there is a bigger army on the Peninsula than was there before, and as many as the old army along the Rappahannock. The advance was at Bottom's Bridge, ten miles from Richmond, when he left. I have no doubt that is the route to Richmond, notwithstanding McClellan's failures, and Grant is the man to go in. Even now, for all I know, the North may be in jubilee over his victory. The rebels seem to have accepted our discarded "scatteration" policy, and Grant works on the concentration. Richmond must be taken. No doubt they will blow up the prison where our soldiers are, but God pity the prisoners we take after that.

Yellow Bluff, Fla.,
Monday, May 16, 1864.

Dear Sister L.:—

My letters from home bring the news that you have another brother in the army, but of course you will have heard that long before this reaches you. I am not sorry he has gone. One hundred days of a summer's campaign will be apt to knock some of the romance out of him. He thinks he has none, but the remark that he has paid $10 for a pair of boots "like yours, military, you know," shows how his mind runs. He has been running over for three years with the desire "to be a soldier like Oliver," and now I hope he will get his fill of it. No doubt he will make a good one and would fight like a tiger on occasion, but a little experience will change a good many of his ideas. He is not likely to see any harder fighting than a brush with guerillas. I am afraid he will consider himself in for the war after his hundred days are up, which is just what I don't want him to do, but I won't borrow trouble.

I hear from the Eighty-third that it is nearly full to the maximum. Captain Woodward is mustered as the Colonel and Captain McCoy as Lieutenant Colonel. All the old members of Company K, except five have re-enlisted, so Captain Hechtman writes. According to my figures "all but five" is just four, for when I left there were but nine of the old boys left.

This mail brings us the good news that colored soldiers are at last to get their dues in the matter of pay. The paymaster was here a week ago and offered the heroes of Olustee $7 a month. Most of them would not take it. Only those very much in need of money did so.

Yellow Bluff, Fla.,
Saturday, June 18, 1864.

Dear Sister L.:—

Last week I sent you something pretty. I made myself

happy imagining your expressions of wonder when you get the pen box, and of delight when you see the exquisite beauty of the little shells it contains. I captured them at the house of a rebel colonel, which we burnt down. He was the gentleman who fitted out the nest of torpedoes, one of which blew up the Harriet Weed. Did I tell you about my finding the box of powder (one hundred and fifty pounds of cannon powder) in his family graveyard? It was a little brick enclosure deep in the woods near Cedar Creek. In the corner was a box nailed up. On the box was a heavy set of dinner plates and a pitcher. Inside the box was another one covered with leather, and inside that in pound bags of red flannel was the powder. Of course, I destroyed it. Near the graveyard, hid in the bushes, I found two barrels of sugar and one of molasses, which I threw into the creek.

It was on this march that I took my first rebel prisoner. We had surrounded a house just before daylight, and while the others were searching the house, I concluded to peep into an out-building, and who should I see but Mr. Johnny just getting into his "don't-speak-of-'ems." He "allowed it was all up with him," and I allowed ditto. He was a pretty fine fellow, belonging to the Second Florida Cavalry.

I suppose Almon-d (what about that "d"?) is somewhere about Gaines' Mill now. They had another terrible fight there, and I see a long list of wounded in the One hundred and twelfth. I did not see his name. Colonel Drake was among the killed, and Hubbard, Cushing and Tillotson wounded. I think Grant is bound to win this time.

I received a letter from E. at the same time I got yours. He was on detail then in Toledo after deserters. His regiment was at Johnson's Island guarding rebel prisoners and he expected to return the next day. Chauncey Ayres is chief bugler of the Ninth New York Cavalry.

Oh, but I do wish you could see the flowers I have on my table this morning! Beside a grand magnolia I have a Spanish bayonet, a cone-shaped or egg-shaped flower two feet high and a foot in diameter. It is shaped like this:

(SKETCH OMITTED.)

One solid head like that emitting an exquisite perfume. If you could slice one down the middle, the transverse section would look like this:

(SKETCH OMITTED.)

From the main spike stems radiate in every direction with a bell-shaped flower at the end of each stem, and they are so close together as to present the appearance of a beautiful white cone, with proportions that in a flower are magnificent. By putting oleanders, jessamines and roses in among the stems you can have a beautiful bouquet of gigantic dimensions.

Yellow Bluff, Fla.,
Friday, June 24, 1864.

Dear Sister L.:—

The greatest excitement here is caused by the advent of our new regimental commander, Major Edelmiro Mayer. He is a South American, and has been ten years in the army in foreign countries. He speaks several languages, the English poorest of any, and with his inexhaustible fund of anecdotes and his quaint remarks, keeps everybody in the best possible humor. Ever since the battle of Olustee the regiment has been under command of Captain Bailey, who though a very nice man and good company commander, couldn't "keep a hotel" or command a regiment. He allowed himself to be led by the nose by the doctor, who virtually commanded the regiment, had his say in everything, and bullied and interfered in all possible ways. The new major "has broken the doctor's nose" and given him to understand that his duties are to attend to the sick and not to act as "General Adviser." Of course the *medi-cuss* is not "sweet on" the major, and of course everyone else is jubilant that "Othello's occupation's gone."

Hear the major specifying the duties of the day: "After the reveille he (the soldier) shall bathe himself in the river and from 7 o'clock till 9 he shall drill in the company for perfect himself in the mechanism of his little duties. From 9 o'clock till 3 is very hot and he shall eat his dinner and in his tent stay, with that little divertisement—what you call 'em scratch himself. From 3 o'clock till 5 is battalion drill and after—dress parade and supper."

He gets right down to the bottom of things and our regiment is going to improve under his direction.

Yellow Bluff, Fla.,
June 30, 1864.

Dear Sister L.:—

I know something how near to you the death of Almon comes. He was a comparative stranger to me. I had seen him but twice, once at home and once at Jacksonville, and of course I could not know him very intimately. His comrades spoke well of him and esteemed him highly, and he seemed to me like an excellent soldier and a good young man. I sympathize with you in your sorrow. Your grief is mine and your joy also.

My last letter from E. gives the intelligence that he too is among the host pressing on to Richmond, and I tremble lest in these days of terrible slaughter the next one may bring the news of a fearful wound, or some strange hand may tell me of his death in the field. I feel more anxious for him than I ever did for myself. You know how I have always felt about his going out and I have expressed my views freely to him, but now he is there, he shall hear no discouraging word from me. I have written to him to do his duty fearlessly and faithfully, and if he falls, to die with his face to the foe. He will do it. You will never blush for the cowardice of your brother, and my only fear is that he will be too rash. I glory in his spirit, while I tremble for his danger. Oh, I could hardly bear to give him up now, and yet I suppose his life and his proud young spirit are no more precious, no more dear to me or to you than thousands of others who have fallen and are to fall are to their friends. But I will not look forward to coming sorrow, but hope for the best.

This is the last night in June and very swiftly the month has passed away. The weather has been delightful, not near so warm as May. Almost every day we have had a refreshing shower.

We are in hopes to be ordered to Virginia, or we should not be disappointed if we were ordered there. The Seventh U. S. C. T. started day before yesterday and the Thirty-fifth went by to-day. It does seem hard that I should be lying here in idleness while my old comrades are marching on to victory or death. Perhaps it is for the best.

I have just been looking with pride at E.'s picture. Why cannot I look at yours? Isn't it worth while to take a little trouble to send it to me? There must be a photographer in Panama.

Jacksonville, Fla.,
July 23, 1864.

Dear Sister L.:—

The "District of Florida" is cursed by a commander called Brigadier General Birney.* It seems to be a sort of dunce block for the government—a place where they send men good for nothing in any other place. They began with Seymour—his performances you have heard of. Then they sent Hatch. He couldn't hatch up any disaster and they sent him somewhere else. Next came Foster. He was a pretty sensible man, so he did not stay a week. Then at last came Birney, the *summum malum,* a man afflicted with the St. Vitus' dance, in a military point of view. He is utterly unable to be quiet or let anybody else be. He came early in June about the time most of the troops were sent away, and immediately began to stir up things. He thought there was not much force near Charleston and he would make a reconnoissance. He took the splendid steamer Boston, put a regiment of infantry and two pieces of artillery on her and started up one of the small rivers near Charleston. He ran aground, the rebels fired into the boat, he set fire to her, and the regiment jumped overboard and took to the woods. The steamer was lost with the two guns, all the arms of the regiment, and stores, in all $100,000

Note—Not the General Birney of the Third Corps.

of property. By and by he started again, went up to James Island and—came back again. Didn't lose much that time but a great deal of patience among his officers and men. On the Fourth of July there was some difficulty between the Third and Thirty-fifth Colored Troops in town here. He would punish the Third. He didn't like the Eighth very well. He would punish the Eighth. The Third was in the forts here and had been drilling all summer in heavy artillery and understood it pretty well. He ordered the Third to Yellow Bluff and the Eighth to the forts at Jacksonville. Next day he ordered a raid. There was a steam sawmill belonging to a rebel on the Nassau River about twenty-five miles from here, and he started nearly all the force in the district to capture that sawmill. Three steamers loaded with troops left here a week ago to-day, landed the troops at Trout Creek above Yellow Bluff, and they marched across the country while the Alice Price, one of the most valuable steamers in the department, went round to go up the Nassau. He marched one day's march into the wilderness and concluded he didn't need so large a force, so he sent them all back but one hundred men. The Price struck a snag in the Nassau and went to pieces, a total loss of $40,000, and he hasn't got the sawmill yet. He came back and ordered the Eighth out of the forts and the Third back again. He ordered us to camp on a place that was an equine cemetery, and didn't see the joke till he had been told half a dozen times, and then he ordered us to change again over by Fort Hatch where we were last spring. We had not got tents pitched before the order came to "Prepare to march immediately. Six days' rations, etc." The regiment stood in a pelting rain for two hours on the wharf and then were ordered back to camp. This morning they started again, and after waiting two hours again in the rain, at last got on board and started. They are off on a cow-hunting expedition to Indian River, a hundred miles down the coast. You will ask why I am not with them. I was not able to march and am left in charge of the camps. I gave out on the sawmill expedition. We marched eight miles through the pine woods (which keep off the wind but give no shade) without a halt, with the mercury above 100 in the shade. At the end of that time I fell in the road, sunstruck, and I haven't been worth much since. It was terrible. Twenty-five men and three officers had given out, and we all came back together towards night. So my boast of never being excused from duty is done. I was not well when I started and went further than I should have done, but for my pride in never "falling out." There is a limit to human endurance and I found mine there. I can stand any reasonable hardship and I believe little things do not daunt me, but that was altogether too much. I never heard of such a thing before as marching men in such weather. Why, they do not allow a sentry to stand without a shelter, but men can march and carry six days' rations on wild goose hunts well enough. There is no pretense of an enemy. There are not seven hundred rebels in the state of Florida.

General Birney seems to consider the Eighth as a sick child that requires nursing, and block and tackle by which to hoist his favorites into place and power.

Major Burritt was badly wounded at Olustee and has not been able to be with the regiment since (Colonel Fribley is dead and Lieutenant Colonel Bartram promoted to another regiment); he is the true commander of the regiment. Captain Bailey commanded in his absence for a long time, but the general had one friend (only) in the district, a South American major, ambitious and unprincipled, and he wants to make him colonel, so he sends him to command the regiment, on the ground that Captain Bailey is not competent. Then he proposes to have Major Burritt (who has appointment as Lieutenant Colonel, but cannot be mustered till he takes command) mustered out of the service, Major Mayer promoted to Colonel, and a Captain Hart to Lieutenant Colonel of the Eighth. Major Mayer has already made recommendations of officers to be promoted who are entirely out of the line of promotion, and, to cap the climax, the general yesterday sent Captain Hart to command the regiment, which stirred up such a breeze that he had to send him back. You do not understand why, I presume. Suppose the captain of my company to resign, or be promoted, or die, or get out of the way in any other way. Of course, I would expect to be promoted to fill his place, the second lieutenant to take my place. That is, if I were senior first lieutenant (having appointment of earliest date). Now, if an officer from another regiment is made the captain, that throws me and every officer out of promotion. Of course, that does not work smoothly, being opposed to the regulations, and such performances are demoralizing the Eighth very fast.

I have wished many times this summer that I was back in the Army of the Potomac. We would probably knock about more there than here, but it would be to some apparent purpose and we would have the satisfaction of trying to do some good.

I expect before Birney gets back there will be another steamer blown up by torpedoes and we will be hurried down to Yellow Bluff again to guard the river.

Jacksonville, Fla.,
August 1, 1864.

Dear Sister L. :—

My last was written on the 23d, and in that I told you that the regiment had gone on another expedition and that I, being unwell, had been left behind in command of camp. I am much better now, so you may dispense with any extra anxiety you may have felt on my account.

The expedition did not go to Indian River as we expected, but went up the St. Johns thirty miles, landed and struck across the country to Darby, on this railroad and seven miles west of Baldwin. It then turned and came back this way. The rebs had quite a little force behind three miles of intrenchments at Baldwin, and if Birney had moved right on he might have captured the whole of them, but he waited while they got ready to move, and only captured a dozen or so, and three officers. The regiment came back on the 28th, Thursday, and next day we were ordered to embark on the Cosmopolitan at 11 o'clock.

We have the only band in this district, and under the leadership of the colored Professor Anderson, it has got to be a good band. The officers pay the professor $100 a month to lead and instruct the band, and they take some pride in it. We found that we were going to Hilton Head to stay, and just as the regiment embarked he ordered the band ashore. Being enlisted men they were subject to his orders, but their instruments were the property of the regiment and the officers piled them up on deck. General Birney said they might be our instruments, but they could not go on a government boat. We told Professor Anderson to come with us, as he was not a soldier. General Birney ordered him off the boat as he was a citizen, and so it went, but the general finally beat us and we left the band.

He was determined that the regiment should not stay at Hilton Head, so he did all he could to make us appear to disadvantage, and immediately on landing he attacked General Foster and kept at him till he succeeded in getting us sent back, and here we are again. While he was gone, Colonel Noble in command here did something. He captured a locomotive and a train of cars on the Cedar Keys railroad which crosses this railroad at Baldwin. We expect to start on another expedition to-morrow. Our trip to the Head was a nice little excursion, take it all round, especially for those who did not get seasick. There are but few more troops there than here, but it is headquarters of the department and a busy place. I was much amused while I was there at seeing the contrabands. It was market day (and is every day) and they were coming to sell the melons and other vegetables. They all came in boats, and the beach is so very flat that their boats cannot come near the shore. The men come in every day costume, but the women put on their brightest bandanas and calicoes. Arrived at the end of their voyage, they run their boats up as far as they can, and then the men get out in the water and shoulder the women and carry them ashore and return for their cargoes. The process of transportation affords excellent opportunities for taking photographs of "black-legs," etc., for the Rogues' Gallery. I saw one of "de pretty yaller gals" dressed in the extreme of fashion, silk dress, white skirt, gaiters, etc., standing on a board on the beach surrounded by a group of lesser lights (or shades) who paid their homage by respectful "how dye's." She had evidently donned some of her "missis'" garments and I but do her justice in saying she looked well in them.

My! But I did lay in the ice creams, soda waters and melons up at the Head, like a fellow who hadn't had any in some time.

E. says his time is half out (more too, now) and if anybody gets him out in the infantry again, he'll be a smart man. Oh, ho, ho, I told you so, but don't tell him I told you so. His patriotism is not much less, but the poetry of war sounds better at a distance.

Its "Hottentotissimus" down here now. Thermometer past 100 degrees—a heap. I stand it much better than I expected and so does everyone else. I wear woolen clothes —woolen shirt and drawers all the time, too.

*Jacksonville, Fla.,
August 4, 1864.*

Dear Sister L.:—

I wrote you a few days ago, but important items occurring and having occurred, I embrace the opportunity to drop you a line.

I think I wrote on the first that we were ordered on an expedition into the interior. That night I cut my foot badly with a broken tumbler, which little interruption will no doubt lay me on the shelf for some time. The regiment started next morning but I remained behind.

Now the camp is full of rumors. General Birney is reported to be relieved by General Hatch and ordered to the Army of the Potomac and that two regiments are to go with him. She points her shaky finger at the Seventh and Eighth as the two regiments. The Eighth is still at Palatka, though expected down to-day. Some say the Seventh and Ninth, the regiments Birney organized, are the ones to go, but the Ninth is at Beaufort out of his district, and unless he can take us there and exchange us for the Ninth, they are not apt to go. Of course, I like the prospect of going— Grant, Glory and Richmond—I've fought and stumbled around there too long not to wish to be in at the death when the death is in prospect. I may meet E. too. Hurrah, for the Army of the Potomac! Still, I'm whistling before issuing from the sylvan shades. We are not certain to go after all.

Bermuda Hundred, Va.,
August 13, 1864.

Dear Father :—

I've just time to drop you a line in great haste.

We left Florida on the 5th, arrived at Hilton Read on the 7th. Left there on the 8th, arrived at Fortress Monroe, after a lovely passage, on the 11th. Anchored off the mouth of the James that night. While there the One hundred and thirtieth Ohio National Guard passed on their way home. E. or somebody else called my name as they faded away in the distance.

Yesterday, the 12th, we landed at Bermuda Hundred and marched to the front on the right of Butler's line. This morning the rebels opened a heavy fire on us and after a time we were withdrawn. Our sergeant major and some others were wounded—none killed in the Eighth, some in the Seventh. To-day our baggage came up and we sent ten wagon loads up to be stored at Norfolk or "else whair." I sent my valise to New York by express.

We are under orders now to be ready to march at a moment's notice and are ready. My foot is sore yet, but I march if there is any fighting to be done. I've cut my finger, which rather injures my penmanship, in my haste, but I guess you can read it. Grant has "several" reinforcements, and orders look like work. Good news from Mobile. The rebels got the worst of the shelling this morning.

Chesapeake Hospital, Fortress Monroe, Va.,
Monday, August 22, 1864.

Dear Sister L. :—

You will no doubt be somewhat surprised to receive a letter from me dated at a hospital. It is a novelty for me, but the proverb says, "every dog has his day," and mine has come now.

I wrote you a line from Bermuda Hundred saying that we had arrived in the old Army of the Potomac and that I was ready for what might come. I thought I was. I have been trying this long time to deceive myself into the idea that I was well enough, but I had to give it up. I have a fancy that my night duty along the marshes of the St. Johns affected me more than I knew at the time. It first showed itself in that attack of sunstroke, and ever since that time any exertion of consequence has found me wanting. I am weak and enervated, unable to endure fatigue as I used to in the old campaigns. I was taken sick on a night march, Saturday night a week ago, and though I kept up a while I was forced at last to lie down under a tree. Sunday morning I went on from the bridge over the James, where I had slept, to the front where they were having a brisk little skirmish, but learning that our regiment was in reserve, I came back and found them near the river. On Tuesday they marched again, and I was left in camp too weak to go. Wednesday I stayed there, and on Thursday the adjutant came back and put me on his horse and took me to the Tenth Corps hospital. On Friday I was put on a boat and sent down here, landing on Saturday. The Chesapeake is a large hospital exclusively for officers. The building was formerly a large seaside hotel overlooking Hampton Roads and is admirably adapted to hospital purposes. There is plenty of pure sea breeze and good food. Officers are charged $1 a day for board and attendance. In the card at the head of my bed my diagnosis (or symptoms) is set down as "General Debility," so I suppose that's what's the matter with me.

We had a lovely passage up from the Head. The Collins is not a passenger boat, but the weather was fair and the officers slept on deck in comfort. Her little table would seat just ten, so we had first, second and third tables, but plenty of good food, for which Mr. Steward charged us fifty cents a meal, or $1.50 a day. We were four days coming, and to while away the tedious hours we had whist parties and story clubs, and in the evening our band discoursed sweet music. We would have been selfish to have wished a better time.

Well, I'm too weak to write much and must close. We are much nearer together now than when I was in Florida, and I hope to hear from you often. I want to hear how you get along on the farm, and the thousand and one things you know will interest me. Give my love to C., and write as soon as you can after receiving this. Direct to Lieutenant O. W. N., Chesapeake Hospital, Ward 1, Fortress Monroe, Va., exactly. Don't put on my regiment.

Chesapeake Hospital,
August 26, 1864.

Dear Father:—

This letter of yours has been to Hilton Head I suppose, and then to the Army of the Potomac, and next day, by the kindness of Captain Dickey, to me here. He is a captain, that same Dickey. His good qualities wear like steel.

Twenty days old this letter is. In that time you must have received several from me, not all addressed to you, but to the family, some of them, papers for the boys, and one I sent to Mother with a little note about the picture. I don't believe they can all have miscarried. Well, one thing is certain, it won't take a month for letters to pass now, and I comfort myself by thinking that you will be reading this about Monday or Tuesday next, and by and by all this *arriere* will be straightened up.

After hearing what you have had to occupy you lately, I recall my impatient remarks about your want of interest, etc. Indeed, they were not leveled at you. Though you give every other reason I know that you do not like to write letters. You sit down to it as to a job that must be done and I do not expect you to write often.

I had an idea that I had a sister out there who (if she follows the track of young persons of her sex) must be quite a young lady by this time. Young ladies are supposed to wield a ready pen, to be familiar with the state of the family and to love to gossip about it. They generally have time enough, but despite all my ideas, hypotheses, etc., I find a married sister with a husband to take care of, a house to sweep, the stockings to darn, and the slight care of a dairy—I find her writing to me every week, while this young lady finds time about once in six months. E. is a "brick." He writes as often as he can, and, though I haven't received any from him of very late date, I lay it to the bags. I hope soon to hear from him that he is back in the hardware in Toledo. "What would you think," he says in his last, "if I should get as large a salary as Father's?" He got a stomach-full of the army in one hundred days. If he goes again, it will be with a strong impression that he can't help it. I wrote to him, directing to Brooklyn, thinking of course he would be at home a few days, or at least you would know where he is. He said Mr. P. was very anxious he should come back to his store, but he himself did not seem very anxious to accept so advantageous a situation.

I am very sorry to hear of your trouble about the house; however I suppose it is all over now. I hope so at least. I should think with such a scarcity of dwellings some Yankee would be putting up houses to rent. I had very much such a time as yours approached, just before coming here. Getting sick in camp, I was left behind unable to march. "In camp" in the Army of the Potomac now is a pleasant fiction, meaning any place a regiment bivouacs on over night. So they moved away and left me, our efficient medical staff making no provision for sick. Two days I stayed there, living on the kindness of some sick men from Maine. Then our adjutant came and mounted me on his own horse, like a good Samaritan, and took me to the corps hospital. The medical director wanted to see my papers. I must be committed like a pauper to the poorhouse. I was "liable to be arrested" for absence from my regiment without authority. You may understand it was trying to my temper to be called a skulk the first time I came near a hospital in more than three years. I turned away from him in disgust and lay down under a tree on the bank of the river. The adjutant left me there and said he would not rest till he had got the order sending me to the hospital. So there I lay and my thoughts were not pleasant. By and by I heard a rattle of musketry and knew my regiment was "in." Then it blew and began to rain. I curled myself up in my gum blanket and felt miserable enough, sick, weak, and no place to shelter my head.

The next afternoon a doctor came and asked me who I was and how I came there. I told him my story and he had the kindness to be shocked—"didn't see into it—anyone could see I was sick—didn't need any papers" and he immediately wrote the papers I enclose and sent me on the boat. I feel very weak, have only been out doors once. If it were any use I would apply for leave of absence as soon as I am able to travel, but it is not. I would be ordered to Annapolis and put on court-martial or some other light duty. It is next to impossible to get leave of absence.

The Eighth has redeemed any reputation it lost at Olustee. It was the Eighth before which "eighty-two dead rebels were counted after the battle," according to Birney's dispatch.

Chesapeake Hospital,
Sunday, August 28, 1864.

My Dear Sister L.:—

I have passed the week mostly on my bed—been out of the house but once. That was yesterday, when I went down to the fort (in the cars) and that little exertion was almost too much for me. I am very comfortably sick—have no pain except an occasional headache, but spend most of my time quietly, feeling a great aversion to the least exertion.

My bed is a little iron cot with a mattress on it, my table a light stand. I draw it up beside the bed and write my letters and then lie back and read or sleep. Three times a day my tormentor comes with quinine and whisky disguised as "tonic solution," and soon after come preparations for a meal from the "low diet kitchen." This is managed in a way called in military parlance "by detail," e. g., first installment for dinner (after the "tonic solution") 10 a. m., nurse with cup and saucer. Then at intervals of half an hour the following articles—10:30, knife, fork and spoon; 11, milk, cup and mug, with one spoonful of sugar; 11:30, teapot and plate of corn starch (good); 12 m., plate with leathery toast, dab of butter, boiled beef and a slice of beet or dried sweet potato. Regularity and system are indispensable in hospitals, so this routine is never departed from, and it is just two hours every time from the arrival of the cup and saucer to "Ready, Sir," the signal to fall to. I assure you there is no waste of food among the low diet patients. I always take all the sugar to make out. I do not seem to gain strength at all. In fact, I lose strength every day, but I hope to improve soon.

We have a new surgeon—came this morning. The one that left yesterday was a very nice man, and this one seems a good man too, as well as I could judge by ten minutes' talk.

I used to say that if I ever got in a hospital I should want to get home. So I do now, and I expect—to want. No use in trying that here. But as soon as I am able to travel, I mean to apply to be sent to Annapolis on light duty and from there I think I can get home. I have lost twenty pounds of flesh and I do not intend to go to the field again till I regain that and my full strength. It would be useless and might result in a more serious fit of sickness.

E. had not got home when Father wrote, and I have not heard a word from him since he passed me on his way north. I am not uneasy about him though.

I had a letter from D. F. a day or two since. He said nothing about Etta, but Lizzie and the baby had gone to Maine, so I have strong doubts about your seeing anything of Etta this summer. I wrote to D. to send you "Very Hard Cash" as my birthday present. If you have read it, it will be rather *mal apropos*, won't it? I do not think you have, as it has not been out long and novelties don't find their way out there very fast. You will, if I am not mistaken, find it one of the most absorbing stories you ever read. It is made up almost wholly of impossibles. For instance, his heroine, Julia, is one never seen except in a novel, but she is only an exaggeration of many sweet and lovely women. His best character, I think, is David Dodd, the nearest approach to a possible. Dr. Sampson is well drawn and an original person. I could not succeed in appreciating the saintliness with which he finished Jane Hardie. Her brother's comments on her diary seemed to me too just, and his motto for the diary might as well apply to her life; *"Ego et Deus meus,"* or I and my God.

But the lesson of the story is a good one, and the consummate skill with which it is wrought out makes one jealous of the author for being an Englishman. Why have we no one on this side the water to write an American story like that? In one thing he fails. In impossibles he is better than Dickens, but when he caricatures Yankees and negroes, he shows an ignorance of the originals. Vespasian is his poorest impossible, and Fullalove is not much better. But enough of this. When you have read it, tell me how you like it and how you like my comments.

From the front the news is always encouraging. Lee has been making desperate efforts to regain the Weldon railroad and so far without success, and every day lessens his prospects of success. He is reported to have said he must have it if it took every rebel soldier. He is welcome to it at that price. Sherman is waiting for Farragut to take Mobile or draw off a part of Hood's force to defend it, and things seem to be almost at a deadlock all round.

Chesapeake Hospital,
September 1, 1864.

Dear Mother:—

I was very much surprised to hear that E. had not got home, but was to stay here till the 7th of September, and I don't begin to understand it yet. The One hundred and forty-second Ohio National Guards, which must have been formed after his regiment, has gone home, and I was sure the regiment that passed us that night answered "One hundred and thirtieth Ohio—hundred days' men." "The Norton" which was heard might have been imaginary. I may see him yet before he goes.

I am glad to report that I am getting better. I was out yesterday, went down to the fort in the horse car, weighed myself and found my "mortal remains" to be just 109 pounds avoirdupois.

We had a change of surgeons a few days ago, and the new one said my liver was out of order and gave me calomel, salts, quinine, whisky, fever pills, sulphuric acid, etc., enough to kill a man with a less vigorous constitution, but I really believe it did me good. He has stopped all but the quinine and whisky now, and I feel a great deal better. I have gone to the "full diet" table now, with an appetite like a horse.

I am very glad to hear that you have succeeded in getting a roof between yourselves and "the starry decked heavens above you." Father was quite anxious about that when he wrote, and I cannot see how you do manage to live on his slender salary. I can't support myself in my present position on that. My full pay is about $100 a month; $11 of that is allowance for a servant, which I get if I have the servant. If I get a boy he will eat more than he earns and in the first battle throw away my overcoat and blankets. If I get a man over sixteen, Butler or some other man will take him away for a teamster or soldier. If I employ a soldier, I must pay $25.50 per month, or just what it costs the United States, $13 wages, $9 subsistence and $3.50 clothing.

Since January 1, Captain Dickey has employed one of the company as servant and the amount was stopped from his pay. Lieutenant Thompson and I had the benefit of his services and shared the expense till June. Since then, Thompson has been detached and the captain and I have stood the whole.

We have not settled for July and August yet, but we cannot employ a soldier any more. It is the general custom in the army for officers to employ soldiers and then certify on their payrolls that they have not done so and draw their full pay. It is done in every regiment and has been ever since I've been in the service. In that way some officers send home an immense amount of wages.

It costs me $1 a day for board, saying nothing of clothes or servant. If I want a coat, it costs from $25 to $30, pants $15, boots $12 or $15, hat $10, shirts $10 a pair.

Chesapeake Hospital,
September 11, 1864.

Dear Sister L.:—

I received a letter to-day from Captain Dickey dated "In the trenches before Petersburg, September 7th." He says the regiment is forty-eight hours in the outer line and forty-eight off alternately. It is certain death to show a head above the works. Some one is killed almost every day. Captain Walker, a particular friend of mine in the Seventh, was killed by the sharpshooters a few days since. We have lost one killed and four wounded in our company. It is a pleasant thing to have the respect and good will of your comrades. I will give you an extract from the captain's letter. After speaking of Lieutenant Thompson's being detached as Ordnance Officer, he says: "So you see, I am all alone, and a sweet time I've had of it, making muster rolls (they were finished an hour since), monthly returns, etc., with my books and papers all locked up in Norfolk. Hasn't it been a delightful job? But with you matters seem less promising. I am sorry to hear you improve so slowly. Seems to me a milder treatment would be better, but a man in the doctor's hands must follow prescriptions. But keep a cheerful tone of mind. There is no necessity for you to fret or worry the least about your duties here. You have the sympathy of all the officers. No one intimates that Norton is 'playing off.' No one intimates but that you did your duty and your whole duty. On the contrary, many are of the opinion, and among them your humble servant, that it would have been better for you if you had left your post sooner. You ought to have done it, and yet I know very well how you felt. I know one is loth to leave his command during active operations, and is perhaps as unwilling to trust his judgment then as under any imaginable circumstances. I have no doubt you felt unfit for duty long before you left it. Norton reasoning with Norton, thought himself sick, but declared he wouldn't be sick. Felt that he ought to be excused, but resolved not to be excused."

The captain is nearly or quite right in that last remark. Still, where so many "play off," a man's character is worth a good deal, and I am not very sorry I did not give up immediately, though it might have been better for my health. I think I am on the gain slowly.

I was writing to H. on the morning of the 7th, when I had an interruption. It came in the shape of one of Uncle Samuel's rebellion smashers, called for short "E." He was on his way home, and while the boat stopped at the fort for coal he came up here to see me. I was "tolable" glad to see him. He looked quite like a "vet."—a little thin and very dirty, perfectly soldierly. He says Phillips will give him $600 a year to come back in his store, and it's my opinion he will accept that as quickly as the good Lord and his parents will let him get to Toledo. If P. backs out he won't lack employment. Barker, of Ketchum & Barker, spoke to him of coming into his store again, but I think Mr. P. will be glad to get him.

Chesapeake Hospital,
September 28, 1864.

Dear Sister L.:—

I am getting some better, not much, but some, and I am going to the front soon now. I have stopped taking medicine and attribute my gain to that. The last prescription was soap pills. (?) Think of that! "Throw physic to the devil." "Overhaul your catechism for that." my dear, "and when found, make a note on." I did, and my "promise to pay" relates to my hospital bill and my respects to our new colonel. I took only one of the "soap pills." It started me.

Another motive to hasten my return is the prospect of a horse to ride. There have been several promotions lately among the "straps" "of ours," including the quartermaster and adjutant to captains. Both the desks are vacant and my chance for one of them is good, better if I'm there to take it.

You will be glad to hear that I have a horse, when I do. So will I. I prefer the adjutant's, but will not decline the quartermaster's. The pay is $10 better, promotion from the line to the staff. Both are First Lieutenants.

I have just come back from a trip to Norfolk. I left at 9 o'clock yesterday on the Baltimore boat. Arrived at 10:30. I rambled round the town some till I got tired. The main street reminded me of Canal street, New York. Do you remember how that looks, crossing the others obliquely? It used to be quite a town. Intensely *secesh*, it shows the fruits of rebellion.

In the evening I attended the theater to see "Faust and Marguerite," a German drama. Do you know the story? How the old philosopher, Faust, sold himself to the devil for a new lease of youth? Mephistopheles gave him youth, beauty and riches, and assisted him to win and ruin Marguerite, an orphan, and finally claimed him as his own. It was tolerably played. The devil was on hand in person pretty much of the time and played some queer tricks. At the finale, he seized Faust with a horrible leer and descended into the pit amidst lurid flames and smoke, while Marguerite was borne aloft on angels' wings. I send you the picture— a black impression. The scenery was beautiful, but the angels traveled by jerks. The machinery was a little out of order, and instead of sailing grandly through the heavens, they went up like a barrel of flour into a storehouse.

Coming back I saw the captured rebel ram, Atlanta. She looks like a vast turtle on the water.

Jones' Landing, Va.,
Sunday, October 9, 1864.

My Dear Sister L.:—

You will be glad to know that I am out of the hospital. My adventures in getting away ought to form a chapter in the secret history of the war, that the people may know how rascality flourishes in high places. They were making about fifty cents a day out of me, and of course did not want me to leave, and I was a full week in settling up. First, my bill must be paid, but when I applied for the papers to enable me to get my pay, they put me off with trivial excuses time after time, till at last I got my "back up" and told the surgeon that if my papers were not forthcoming by the next morning (Wednesday) I would desert to my regiment, report to General Butler, and learn why an officer must be detained after he wished to join his command. I went back to my room and in five minutes after, an orderly appeared with my papers all ready and signed.

Wednesday I started for the front, reached the regiment at noon of Thursday. Found them occupying a line of works about five miles from Richmond on the left of the Tenth Corps. They seemed very glad to see me. The regiment is very short of officers. Three were wounded in the battle of the 29th, Captains Cooper and Richardson (late Adjutant) and Lieutenant Cone. He, poor fellow, lost his leg. I found Lieutenant Evans in the adjutant's place. Had I been two days earlier, I would have had it, but now I have something full as good while it lasts, of which more anon.

The accession of several new regiments of colored troops to our division made the formation of a new brigade necessary, and it was made of the Eighth and Forty-fifth United States and Twenty-ninth Connecticut Colored Troops. Colonel Ulysses Doubleday of the Forty-fifth commands. Burrows, our regimental quartermaster, was appointed quartermaster of the brigade, and yours truly was selected to fill the vacancy made by the promotion of Burrows, and now I am Acting R. Q. M. of the Eighth United States Colored Troops. These capitals I suppose are unintelligible to you and I will tell you about them. R. Q. M. is Regimental Quartermaster. His duties are to supply the regiment with rations, forage and clothing, take charge of the officers' baggage and attend to the transportation for the regiment. Of course he is mounted, a fine thing for me, and a fine thing for my friends is that a quartermaster is not a fighting man. His duties faithfully done are as necessary to success as those of any branch of the service, but they are not dangerous and he does not receive the credit for it that a fighting man does. I have had a good share of duty in the line and can afford to let some one else win the glory now while I take it easy.

It will be a relief to you to think you can read the lists of casualties after a battle without the dread of seeing my name among the killed or wounded. I mean to master every detail of the business if I remain in it any time. You will notice that I am only "Acting" quartermaster, Burrows still holds his appointment of R. Q. M., but is acting in his new capacity. I cannot get the appointment of R. Q. M. till he vacates it by promotion or otherwise, but while acting I have all the privileges and immunities of a full quartermaster. One of the former is being nine miles in rear of danger, seated in my tent by a good fire—a big thing on such a day as this.

Jones' Landing, Va.,
October 17, 1864.

Dear Sister L.:—

I am just as busy as I can be all the time now; not much time to write letters. The trains are some nine miles in rear and I have to go to the front almost every day. I have no clerk and have all the office business to do myself, which is no light job.

I am happy to say my health is first rate now. Riding and exercise seem to agree with me.

Since I wrote you last we have had another battle and more loss in the regiment. Forty-seven men and four officers are the casualties, and the saddest part of all to me is that Captain Dickey is among the killed. I spent an hour during the fight on the very spot where he was struck. I had no business there, but I did not consider it dangerous, and I wanted to see how the fight was going. Soon after I left, while the regiment was being relieved, a shot passed right through the captain's head. He continued to breathe for thirty-six hours, but was unconscious all the time. I took his body to the embalmer's and to-day have been down to send it to his mother. His death is the saddest loss I have known in the army. He was almost a brother to me, and was beloved and respected by all who knew him. His loss to the regiment is irreparable. Another of our best captains was wounded, mortally, I fear. Another lost his left arm and will probably never come back. We have less than one officer to a company now, and when we came out we had three.

Deep Bottom, Va.,
October 22, 1864.

My Dear Sister L.:—

You are the most faithful correspondent I have, but your letters are as unfortunate in their travels as any that start me-ward. Your detained letter of the 2d, with P. S. of the 14th, arrived last night. It found me making myself comfortable. Do you remember the extract from the "C. S. Catechism," in which it was laid down as the first duty of a quartermaster to make himself comfortable, and the second was like unto it only more so? I have my wall tent nicely floored and a jolly fireplace in it, my bed and mattress with sheets and blankets, my arm chairs and my desk. Burrows, the brigade quartermaster, with whom I mess, goes a step ahead of me. He has his floor nicely carpeted and a rug before the fireplace.

You have often wished to send me something good, and I have concluded to give you the opportunity. If you have a pair of sheets that are rather old and not too much so, they would just suit me to a T. These I am using now belong to our surgeon, who is home on furlough, but he will want them when he returns. I am in a position where I can carry a few such things now, and I think it will pay to have them, but do not go to sending me a pair of new sheets now. Then, if you are running over with dried berries, etc., if you could stow in a few of them in a little box beside the sheets, it would help me to make a nice supper several times. I hope you won't do as some people do who send boxes to the army—put in a lot of sweet cake that will spoil before the box is delivered—and don't send me any peaches. I am cloyed on peaches, and as soon as I get over it there are plenty here that I can get. I have so little doubt that you will send it that I will tell you how to direct it—Lieutenant O. W. Norton, Eighth United States Colored Troops, Third Division, Tenth Army Corps, Bermuda Hundred, Va. The charges will have to be prepaid and I will send you the money when you let me know the amount.

Your letter was the first intimation I had had of Conway's death. I received one from Alf at the same time and one from Lucretia. She spoke of it as though she supposed I knew it. What a shame it is that Charlie B. could allow himself to get drunk under such circumstances!

You may have noticed often in my letters that I have spoken of my captain as a good man. He was killed in the engagement on the Darby Road, on the 13th, shot through the head. I had spent more than an hour with him on the very spot where he was killed, and had but just left him when a ball came along and struck him down. He was the best friend I had in the army and was almost a brother to me. I had only known him since last fall, but there was time to learn to love him. I am not accustomed to weep at the sight of death, but I shed some tears over his body. He was a widow's only son, and it will be a terrible blow to her. I had the body embalmed and sent to her, the officers paying the expense. We had four officers lost then, or lost to us for the present. One captain lost an arm, another wounded in the abdomen, a lieutenant in the hand, and Captain Dickey killed.

There is a captaincy waiting for me in the regiment, but the idea of stepping into a dead man's shoes is not pleasant to me. If my health would permit of my roughing it as I used to do, I would accept it, though, but as it is I shall hesitate some before doing so. I have some hopes of getting Alf Ayres into the regiment as second lieutenant. I think he has served in the ranks long enough to deserve promotion.

Chapin's Farm, Va.,
November 9, 1864.

Dear Sister L.:—

My position in the quartermaster's department does not afford the leisure I used to have when my business was to blow "Dan! Dan! Butterfield," or even when I was in the company with the captain there. There is forage to haul and rations to issue. The colonel wants me to go to Bermuda Hundred for axes; the colonel wants logs hauled to build him a house, and he wants this and that, and the status of the poor quartermaster may be graphically described as "on the bob" from morning till night, and his letter writing must be put in edge-wise to all this work.

My experience is that there is a difference between navigating a ship on the ocean and guiding a mule team through Virginia woods and over Virginia roads, and the difference is in favor of the ship. There is a significance in the "Ya-a-a-e mool" and "Now git" of the American teamsters of African descent, that to a novice is unintelligible, but the animals with the ears seem to understand the animals with the gum and ivory, and from the mutual understanding results much good to the animals with the muskets.

I have a very limited idea of what is going on over at the Weldon railroad, but in this part of the army everybody is going into winter quarters. To be sure they are under the old orders to be ready to move at a moment's notice, and line of battle is formed every morning an hour before light, but log houses continue to grow like mushrooms on a damp night. Generals and "two rows of buttons" generally are demolishing the residences of the "F. F. Vs." and working them in with logs into cozy quarters. There is no certainty of their being occupied any length of time, but there is a possibility of it, and so they are built. Lieutenant Burrows and myself have been putting up a log stable for the brigade teams one hundred and eighty feet long, with two wings of forty feet each. It would not be considered in Broadway an imposing edifice, but it will impose an amount of comfort on the poor mules that they never dreamed of in connection with their fate in the army as "means of transportation."

My health is not what it used to be. I am not sick abed any of the time, but I feel weak and lack energy. Any unusual exertion tires me out. My stay in the hospital did not seem to do me much good.

To-day I suppose there is almost as much excitement as yesterday. The returns from elections will be known, and at telegraph stations they will have the news—of Abraham's election. We believe it here, but it will be vastly consolatory to have our belief confirmed.

I may have mentioned to you that I was trying to get Alf Ayres into the Eighth as second lieutenant. If he is as competent as I think he is, I could get him appointed on sight, if he could only come over and see our colonel. The colonel's recommendation would secure his promotion, and I would like to see him in the regiment.

Chapin's Farm, Va.,
November 11, 1864.

Dear Sister L.:—

This afternoon I rode down to see Lieutenant Ellinwood, Nineteenth Wisconsin, a cousin of Captain Dickey's. He was out in charge of the picket line, so I galloped out there, and as I pulled up at a squad by the roadside a man just a little way ahead sung out, "Take that horse back." The lieutenant got up from beside a stump and I asked him if that was an outpost of his. "That is a Johnny," said he, "here is my line." I sent that horse back. The reb did not shoot, but I did not want to give him too big a temptation. He was so near I could hit him with a stone, but he seemed very peaceably disposed.

I am not yet able to say that Alf Ayres is second lieutenant of the Eighth, but I hope to be able to do so in my next. I think all that is necessary is for him to come over and see our colonel in order to be recommended, which amounts to success.

I am running the quartermaster's department of the

Eighth very much to my satisfaction and so far as I know to that of the others.

My health continues so-so, able to be around all the time.

Chapin's Farm, Va.,
Sunday Eve., Nov. 27, 1864.

My Dear Sister L.:—

I have been pretty busy the past week in getting my new house done in addition to my other duties, and to-day I have just moved in. I could not get my "details" to-day, being Sunday, so I had to turn to myself and put the floor in this morning. Perhaps you think it bending the Sabbath to build while I should be at church, but I cannot see it in just that light. The colonel burned up his tent the other day and to-morrow we have a new major coming and I have to give up my tent to him, so I made the excuse of necessity, rolled up my sleeves and finished my house so that I could occupy it, and moved in, and I am so comfortable to-night! I have a little the most gorgeous residence I have had since I came to the army. It is about the size of your parlor, perhaps a little larger, with a canvas roof which also serves for window, and then the beauty of it is the fireplace, a regular old-fashioned kitchen fireplace that I can have a group sitting around and enjoying themselves.

To-night while I am writing Lieutenant Colonel Cooper, One hundred and seventh Ohio (Captain Cooper of the Eighth), is with me making out his returns preparatory to leaving for his new command, which, by the way, is down in Jacksonville, where we left them. They are supposed to be having a soft thing down there.

I was just sitting down to dinner when a gentleman of color approached bearing in his arms a box which he desired me to accept and give him a "ceipt" for it, which I proceeded to do, and opening it I found the sheets and the fruits and the pickles, etc., in the tip-toppest order. You sent just what I wanted, and you may congratulate yourself on having accomplished a feat that very few who send boxes to the army do. Almost every one sends something that will mold or sour and spoil the rest. I had not the least idea when I asked you to send me sheets that it was going to cause you much inconvenience. Shows how much I know of such things. You must thank Mrs. Ploss for me and remember that I did not think of sending to her for sheets.

Did I write you that Williston Tyler was dead? He died in Louisville, Ky., where he had gone to work for the Government. Denny took the body home. I received a letter from him yesterday containing his photo. He looks just as he used to. Frank says she has heard from you after a long silence.

I suppose you have heard about the Thanksgiving dinner sent to the army. Our part of the army did not get theirs till Friday, but it was good when it came—most of it. The "Field and Staff" of the Eighth got two turkeys, one of which came into my mess, and a cake with a pretty name and Jersey City address and "'Tell me how you like my cake" on the bottom of it. I shall proceed to praise the cake (and it would bear praising) after finishing this.

I have got your picture framed and hung up in my new house, and Ed's and Etta's and several others.

Chapin's Farm, Va.,
December 7, 1864.

Dear Sister L.:—

The move I spoke of has taken place. Our regiment moved only about forty rods, but enough to oblige them to leave all their nice log houses they had been so long building. We moved into the camp of the Fortieth Massachusetts, which was a much smaller regiment than ours, and there were not quarters enough for us. I do not move, as I am about as near the new camp as the old one, and could gain nothing by moving.

Last night just as I got into a comfortable doze between those sheets the brigade quartermaster came into my house and said: "Are you aware, young man, that we have orders to be ready to move at a moment's notice, teams harnessed and ready to hitch up?" Well, I had not been aware of it, but it did not take me long to become so. Then at midnight I had to get up and issue two days' rations to the regiment, and was up and down all night, so to-day I feel rather blue. It is 10 o'clock and we have not moved yet and perhaps we may not, as it began to rain at daylight this morning and there is a prospect of its continuance. We have had most delightful weather lately, dreamy Indian summer weather, but treacherous as the Indian. You cannot tell on one warm, bright, dry day that the next will not be cold, wet and awful for outdoor work.

The "Corps d'Afrique" is organized and there are a thousand rumors. The Sixth and Nineteenth corps landed at City Point a day or two ago and some say they will relieve us and we be sent to Wilmington or Savannah or Florida, and others that the Dutch Gap canal is all done but blowing out the end, and that is to be done at once and a grand rush made for Richmond with "Cuffee in advance," so the rebs say, so altogether we are in a state of great uncertainty.

My coming home is very doubtful. In fact I do not care to leave till I get my appointment as regimental quartermaster. I am only acting now, but our regimental quartermaster expects promotion soon, and if some one else is acting when he gets it and I am off on leave, my chances for stepping into his shoes will not be so good as though I was here on hand. That is one reason. Another is that when he gets his promotion he will be absent for some time settling up his accounts as regimental quartermaster and I shall probably take his place as brigade quartermaster, and in the time I am acting I shall be showing if I am competent to be Captain and Assistant Quartermaster, which may come in due time. Perhaps you don't understand all this, but you know I am a little ambitious and you can understand that "Captain and Assistant Quartermaster" is *parlance militaire* for quartermaster of a brigade or division.

Chapin's Farm, Va., December 18, 1864.
Dear Father:—

A sentence in S's letter has troubled me considerably

lately. He says, "Father is growing old fast. His hair is white as snow, and his old complaint, the diarrhea, is troubling him very much." Mother had written me that a very good physician there had entirely cured you of that and I was somewhat surprised to hear such news from him. Is this true? I wish you would write me freely about your health and condition, and prospects among your people. I had formed the opinion from the family letters, particularly Mother's, that you were getting along better there than ever before. I heard of some trouble about a house and of some political difficulties in the church, but I did not suppose these things were serious enough to wear upon your health as some old troubles have done.

Do you make out to live upon your salary these hard times? The family is some smaller with L., E. and me away, and I should judge from reports that S. and C. earned nearly enough to feed and clothe themselves, but with everything you have to buy. at double the old rates, I cannot see how you manage.

Yesterday was my birthday, and I am twenty-five years old. It is time I was a man if ever I am to be one, but there is much of the boy about me yet. Still I dread growing old, and the years fly by all too swiftly. I begin to have that feeling already that I am too old for what I have accomplished and I am looking forward anxiously to know what I shall do when we have peace once more. Till that time my duty is plain, and I do not remember to have had at any time any other purpose than to remain in the army till peace is won, if my life is spared so long. Then comes the thought, what then? The war may last another year and I shall be twenty-six and be ready to start in life for myself, with no capital but a small stock of brains. Sometimes, when I think of these things, I wonder if I can have missed it in giving these four starting years to my country. There is Chapman, who was my class and roommate during my last term at school. We were then as nearly on a par in almost all respects as could be. Both sons of poor ministers with ourselves to depend on. He pursued the course I had marked out for myself, went down to Ohio teaching, and then to college, and he has worked his way into his senior year. He has spent three months in the army and we have maintained a correspondence all the time. Next year he will graduate and marry and settle down to law. He says he envies me my record of the past four years, but I rather think it is his friendly style of flattery, for he had as fair a chance to make that record as I. Now is he better off than I? My spirit would hardly brook the thought in coming years that while other young men were giving their time to their country I was giving mine to myself, and no doubt the man who has fought this war through will receive from the community all due honor, but honor is not going to support him, and what is, is a serious question. Another serious question is at what age can I marry? Very few young men set out with the intention to remain single and I am not among the few, but I have always thought I would not marry till I had something to support a wife on, either money, or money and educated brains. I have a horror of being the head of a poverty-stricken family. Now I have given up my hopes of a college education. It is too late, and my education must be such as I am getting now, and I am not sure but it is better so. Some hold the opinion that a young man can do better on the same means with a wife than without—that the right sort of wife is not an expense but a help to him. I want your opinion about that in my own case.

Chapin's Farm, Va.,
December 26, 1864.

My Dear Sister L.:—

This will not reach you in time to present my respects in a "Merry Christmas," so I will wish you a "Happy New Year" and many returns of the season, and tell you how I spent my Christmas. There are so few Sundays in the army that the occurrence of the holiday on that day was no drawback. The military part of the festivity was a Division Dress Parade and the social, or our social part was a dinner at "Ye Quartermaster's." Lieutenant Burrows is a capital hand at carrying out anything of that kind and he determined to do the thing up right.

We had two guests, Colonel Samuel C. Armstrong,* of the Eighth, and Lieutenant Colonel Mayer of the Forty-fifth, two men who would be considered acquisitions in almost any social circle. Colonel A. was born in the Sandwich Islands and Colonel M. in Buenos Ayres, South America, and both are full of stories of adventure, travel and society. Mayer is the hero of half a dozen duels, which is not much of a recommendation. I know, but the custom of his country makes it a very different thing from dueling here.

I will not undertake to describe our dinner in detail, but we had oyster soup, fish boiled, roast fowl (chicken) and mutton, potatoes, peas and tomatoes, oysters, fried and raw, and for dessert mince pie, fruit cake, apples, peaches, grapes, figs, raisins, nuts, etc., and coffee, and for wassail a rousing bowl of punch. The band of the regiment played in front of the house during dinner, and the leader says he played three hours. The long and short of it is we had as elegant and *recherche* an affair as often comes off in the army, enjoyed ourselves thoroughly and nobody went home drunk.

Do you know that since my last letter to you I have passed my twenty-fifth birthday? And now I am beginning my twenty-sixth year. My years would indicate that I ought to be a man, but I must confess to much of the boy in my nature yet. To be sure I have grown some in strength of character since I was twenty-one, but I seem to be a long way off from the condition of a man in society. Do you think I will be married before I am thirty? I don't see much prospect of it. I am twenty-five and not in love yet, and sometimes I think it is the best thing that could have happened to me that I have been beyond the reach of temptation in that line, until I had strength of character enough to look at this matter as a man should. God willing, I mean to have a wife and a home, but when, is beyond my knowledge.

Note.—Founder of Hampton Normal and Agricultural Institute. He was for more than thirty years at the head of this institution, which has done so much for the colored race. Booker T. Washington was one of his pupils.

I send you an excellent picture of my late captain. I send it to board only, for money would not induce me to part with it if I lost my others. I think you have a picture of Lieutenant Thos. Young, who is now captain of "K" Company.

I have again been obliged to decline a captaincy, for the present at least. It is gratifying to me to have had it offered to me, but, in the present state of my health, I told the colonel I did not think I ought to accept it. I would rather be a quartermaster on duty than a sick captain.

LETTERS OF 1865

Chapin's Farm, Va.,
January 8, 1865.

My Dear Father:—

On New Year's my friend Richardson, late captain in the Eighth (resigned), arrived and put up with me. He is from Roscoe, Ill., and has just come from home, where he had been to recover from wounds. He has resigned and come down to settle up his business, and we had many things to talk of while he was here, so that I had little time to write. When he left Lieutenant Burrows went with him "on leave" and I was appointed brigade quartermaster.

The clothing for the brigade had just arrived and I had it all to issue. I suppose there was forty thousand dollars worth of it and it behooved me to be careful in my issue, for a small proportion of it unaccounted for would absorb the little four months' pay due me now. After attending to that I had the clothing to issue to my regiment, for as I do not expect to be brigade quartermaster permanently, I preferred doing the duties of both positions to turning over my property. I got through it all in good shape; did not lose anything. I have now over a hundred horses and mules to feed and a large train to care for, and that includes a deal of care, for in these roads shoes will get off the mules, and wagon tongues and axles will break and something needs attention constantly. I rather like the extra labor and responsibility. It gives me an opportunity to exercise all my powers, and it has always seemed to me before that I had not that. You will see, however, that I have not much time for writing, and excuse short letters on that account.

I am very glad to know that S's statement of your health was too strong. I did feel quite anxious on that account.

And you really are doing better than I could expect. You support your family on a deal less money than I support myself. I'm afraid I should find it hard to get so prudent a wife, or a wife who could make my money go as far as yours does. I am not spending much money now, I notice, for the excellent reason that I cannot get it to spend.

I shall look for the remainder of what you have to say on the subject of my last letter in your next. I suppose you would laugh to hear us young fellows discuss this matter. Richardson, Burrows and I are about of an age, and very similarly situated, and we have been discussing the matter in all seriousness.

Chapin's Farm, Va.,
Sunday, Jan. 15, 1865. midnight.

Dear Sister L. :—

My diary has ceased to be. It is now the middle of January, 1865, and I have made no entries in it since I left the hospital, and as I am about to send it to you lest it share the fate of my other diaries in the early part of the war, and in the hope that some of it may interest you, I can think of nothing better than to fill up a few more pages with some recollections, and records of the regiment, and of myself.

As you know from my letters, I reached the regiment on the 6th of October, having left the hospital before I was strong enough for duty in the line, with the expectation of being regimental adjutant. I found Lieutenant Evans already in the office, and while Major Wagner was deliberating whether it was best to return him to his company and make me adjutant, Lieutenant Burrows was made brigade quartermaster and the major at once detailed me to act as regimental quartermaster in his place, and "A. R. Q. M." I have been ever since.

The regiment was then lying in the works to the right of the rebel Fort Harrison, which was taken by our forces on the 29th of September, and the name since changed to Fort Burnham, in honor of Brigadier General Burnham, who was killed in the charge which captured the fort.

On the 13th of October the reconnoissance on the Darby Road was made. As a military success or a movement of importance in any respect, it is not worth mention, but it is a memorable day to me on account of the death of my dearest and best army friend, Captain A. G. Dickey.

The "Eighth" was deployed as skirmishers early in the morning and covered the front of the division. Three companies were held in reserve and Captain Dickey had command of those companies. I left my place at the train on learning that fighting was in progress and came up to the front to learn what was being done. I found the division in a belt of woods facing a line of the enemy's works and the skirmish line pushed well up to those works. The reserve was a few rods in rear of the line and they had remained in that position some three hours. The skirmishers were pretty well concealed and kept up a desultory fire wherever they could see any of the enemy, and the rebels did the same. An occasional bullet cut through the bushes near the reserves, but I did not think it a place of particular danger, or having no particular business I should not have been there. As it was I sat down on the ground by the captain and stayed two or three hours, and then thinking that not much more would be done that day and that I should have little enough time to get back to the train before night, I started to return. The captain said to me as I left, in that bantering style so common among soldiers, "Take care of yourself, Norton, this is no place for quartermasters," and I retorted in similar style. It was the last word he ever spoke to me.

That night as I sat in my tent, a lieutenant told me that one of our captains was killed, and on my mentioning their names he said it was Dickey. I could not believe it, but the next morning the news was confirmed.

It was too true. Not ten minutes after I left, one of those occasional bullets had crashed through his brain. He lived, or breathed rather, for forty-eight hours after, but I could not go to see him.

By and by they brought him to me—all that was left of my friend lay before me on a stretcher in an ambulance.

Just after the battle of Olustee he had given me the address of his mother (he had no father) and his sister, and I had given him your address and my father's, and we promised each other that if anything occurred, (we expressed it in that way with the natural dread of speaking of death) that if anything occurred to one, and the other was spared he should write to our friends the sad news. The sad fulfilment of the promise was mine, and I took his body to the embalmer's and had it prepared and sent to his friends, as I knew he would have done for me under like circumstances. It was all I could do, and now I sit and gaze on his picture and think of all his noble, manly, generous qualities and I know how his mother and his sister must mourn for him, but our grief can never return him to us.

> "They, who the tasks of life took up so gladly
> And bore them onward with exultant palm,
> Now graveyard grasses wave above them sadly,
> Their still hands folded to a changeless calm.
>
> Gone! Gone! The gay leaves twinkle in the summer shining,
> The light winds whisper o'er the grassy lea,
> And song and fragrance gentle links are twining,
> But oh! beloved and lost ones, where are ye?"

Well, dear sister, I send you my diary, such as it is. There will be much of it that you cannot understand and much that would not interest you if you could. There are many references to persons who are strange to you, and but very little of any part will pay you for the reading. To me, I have a fancy that it will be very interesting in after years. It will recall to me scenes and incidents that without it I should have forgotten. I have kept it in a careless, desultory manner, and with no expectation that it would interest any but myself. Indeed a diary would be more appropriately named an "I-ary," for there is little else but "I" in it. Still, if you find any amusement or enjoyment in it, it will be an additional source of pleasure to me. I ask you to keep it for me, and perhaps at some future time we may look it over together and pass a pleasant hour in so doing.

Chapin's Farm, Va.,
January 19, 1865.

My Dear Sister L.:—

I have not much news to write. It seems to me my letters must have changed in their character, as I have in my habits of thought since the early part of the war. I remember how I used to write elaborate descriptions of reviews and parades, marches and incidents of camp life. I seldom do this now. These things have come to be a part of my everyday life and have lost the charm of novelty. Not entirely so, either. I found myself the other day at a division drill dashing here and there in the capacity of staff officer with orders from the brigade commander, and I remember well, when I was in the ranks with a musket, how great a thing it seemed to be on the staff. Ah, well, such is life.

Chapin's Farm, Va.,
February 12, 1865.

Dear Sister L.:—

You seem to be having a very severe winter. All the soldiers who have been home say, with a shrug of the shoulders, "It is terribly cold up there." It is cold enough here. To-day the wind almost takes the roof off my house. It is, however, the most windy day we have had.

Military operations just here are pretty quiet, though they have been moving on the extreme left of the Army of the Potomac. The Eighty-third was engaged, I see, and Alf's regiment.

Lee tried a most brilliant dodge a week or two ago. We were such fools that we did not see our danger till the papers told us of it. I make a little "plan" of it. (*Sketch omitted.*) Lee sent a force estimated at 20,000 down to the right of our line, and when they were all ready sent the gun boats to run by Fort Brady and go down and break our pontoon bridges and thus cut us off, and when this was done the 20,000 was to break through our line on the right and gobble us all up. It was an excellent plan. The gun boats succeeded in getting by the fort and then got stuck in the mud. One of them was blown up and the others were glad enough to get back safely. They supposed that our boats had all gone to Wilmington, and they were pretty near right, but we upon the line did not know that, and the whole thing was a mystery to us, and it proved a failure. My little rough plan will give you some idea of our position here. Our division is on the right of the corps and just after the C. in "25th C." I have marked an X. That is the camp of the Eighth, and just across the creek southwest from the 2, in "24th C." is another X. That is the location of my domicile.

Chapin's Farm, Va.,
February 17, 1865.

Dear Father:—

The war seems to be moving on with irresistible grandeur. Its progress is like the motions of the planets—almost imperceptible, but steady and sure. We see it more by its results than anything else. Who can tell when this nation determined to uproot the cause of our troubles? We know they had not so determined two years ago, and now we know they have passed the point of that determination. The power that opposes us is just as steadily crumbling away. One by one, its cities, its arsenals, its railroads, its armies are slipping from its grasp. Its approach to the "last ditch" is steady, and by and by it will be tumbled in, and when the bells of peace ring out over the land their wild, glad notes, we shall have thrown the last spadeful of earth on the bloody carcasses of slavery, aristocracy of color, state rights, and all the demons of that ilk that have troubled us so long.

This is a glorious age. There is something grand in the way Honest Old Abe is steering the ship of state through the breakers of the revolution. He may be a very common man now, but school boys to come will revere him as at least the step-father of his country.

Chapin's Farm, Va.,
February 25, 1865.

My Dear Sister L. :—

Yesterday I issued clothing and I have had no time till to-night to post up my books. Just as I finished, the order came to break camp and prepare to march in heavy marching order, which little phrase means—prepare to leave your snug quarters, take up your bed (and any other little matters you ever expect to see again) and walk—seek a new home in the field. Well, of course, I went to work and in two hours I had my wagons loaded, and soon after the regiment marched out. The wagons parked behind the stables to wait orders, and at midnight the teams were unhitched and I turned in on the floor of my house. The troops marched a mile and bivouacked in the field, and all night it rained. This morning the doubts about the destination were solved by an order to occupy the camp vacated by Russell's brigade, about two miles to the left of our old camp. I did not move my quarters and shall not for the present. So much for so much.

But, oh! Glory, Hallelujah! What news! Victory! Victory!! and without the long lists of killed and wounded. Sherman captures the capital of South Carolina. Charleston is ours, and the identical old flag floats again over Sumter. Fisher, Anderson and Wilmington are ours, and now to-night Petersburg is evacuated and Grant holds the South Side railroad. That seems too good to be true, but it is sent as "official" by General Weitzel.* Do you know that means Richmond will be evacuated? Perhaps I shall be in Richmond before I write again. Lee would not have abandoned that line till he was driven from it unless he meant to leave Richmond. He may be intending to gobble the Army of the James, but I think he has gone to meet Sherman. Well, perhaps he may meet him more and sooner than he wishes.

**Note.*—Error. General Weitzel's bulletin was inaccurate. Charleston was evacuated with Sherman's army many miles distant. Petersburg was not abandoned nor the old flag raised over Sumter until some time later.

Baltimore, Md.,
April 15, 1865.

Dear Brother and Sister:—

I am only so far on my way as yet, and take the opportunity afforded by my detention till this afternoon to drop you a line. I bought my ticket to Philadelphia, via Elmira, and arriving at Elmira found I could not get through that way. I return the ticket to you, Charlie. It was nothing less than a swindle to sell it to me. Take it back to the office there and demand the fare from Elmira to Philadelphia. They are obliged to take it up, as they knew that no trains had run over that road for two weeks.

I went to New York, stopped over night, got my pictures and went on to Philadelphia. Stopped there to get my pay for March and went up to Camp William Penn. Came on here yesterday and leave for Richmond this afternoon.

The news of Lee's surrender is true. Better than all my hopes was the prospect of the end of the war. It was ended on the 9th and every one admitted it. New York, Philadelphia and Baltimore were jubilant. Joy on every face and tongue. I could not see or hear of a secession sympathizer. At the theater last night a band from Lee's army was present and played "Hail Columbia" and the "Red, White and Blue," and here in Baltimore those tunes were vociferously cheered. I went to bed happy, thinking of the glorious change, and came down this morning to be astounded by the news that President Lincoln was assassinated last night at Ford's Theater in Washington and Secretary Seward and his son were stabbed at almost the same hour. The Secretary will perhaps recover, but his son cannot live. The President was shot through the head by a man who entered his private box from behind, shot him and then leaped upon the stage brandishing a dagger and disappeared behind the scenes, escaping at the back of the theater before the audience knew what had occurred. The President died at 7:22 this morning.

It is too terrible to think of, and I cannot imagine the consequences. We could have spared him better at almost any other time. What can we do with such a President as Andy Johnson? What effect will it have on the question of peace?

Well, we can do nothing but wait. The nation's joy is changed to mourning and to mutterings of vengeance on the cowardly assassins and the infamous plotters who arranged the murders. J. W. Booth, the actor, is said to be the assassin of the President, and it is hoped he will be arrested to-day.

Spotswood Hotel, Richmond, Va.,
April 19, 1865.

Dear Sister L.:—

Long ago I promised to write you from Virginia's capital, Richmond, and here is the fulfillment of my promise, though it can be but a few words. My regiment is at Petersburg and I go there this afternoon.

I have been all through Libby and its filthy horrors, through the Capitol building, been to see Jeff Davis' house, but General Ord and family are occupying it and I could not get in. I have seen Belle Isle and all the other places of public interest.

Relics are scarce. I can only send you a picture of Stonewall Jackson, which I bought of the artist who took it. Good-bye. Write me soon to my army address.

Spotswood Hotel, Richmond, Va.,
April 19, 1865.

My Dear Father:—

To-day completes the fourth year of my efforts to reach Richmond, and I am here. You will have heard that I started for home the 23d of March, but I could not enjoy my visit while such glorious events were in progress, and as soon as I knew that Richmond was ours I came back, hoping to come home to stay in a short time. I arrived here yesterday and go to Petersburg to join my regiment this afternoon, when I will write you more at length.

I found the Libby prison in charge of an old friend of

mine, who gave me every facility for exploring its horrors. I visited Jeff Davis' house (outside). General Ord and family occupy it. I went through the Capitol and have visited the principal places of interest. Relics are scarce. I send a picture of Jeff Davis, which I bought of the artist.

Lighthouse Point, James River, Va.,
Sunday, May 7, 1865.

Dear Sister L.:—

The regiment moved a short distance the morning after my arrival, but far enough to break up everything, and with the expectation of remaining there some time we began preparing camp for permanent quarters, and I drew and issued a larger amount of clothing than I had ever issued at one time before. This and my share in fixing camp occupied my time and I had just got through and began to think of writing some letters when marching orders came. We moved early on Wednesday morning, passing through Petersburg, and were detained in town (the trains were) a long time by the passing of the Fifth Corps on its way home. I sat on my horse and watched them pass and it was one of the happiest days I've seen in the army.

I saw Colonel Rogers of the Eighty-third first in the morning. He told me they were coming and after a while I met in the street Milo, my old chum, who is still carrying the mail, and by and by the regiment came along. I should never have known it for the same regiment. Not a dozen of the old men who were in the ranks when I left remained, but there were a few and that few greeted me joyfully. The old "Charlie" I used to ride was at headquarters yet, and not killed, as I heard.

They would not believe they had started for home, but knew they were going to Richmond, and now they know they are going home, marching overland to Washington, over the roads they have marched before so many weary days.

My faith was too weak when I left you to believe the rebellion could so utterly collapse in one short month. Sherman's army has started for home. They are to march to Washington via Petersburg and Richmond. Two corps were left in North Carolina and two of the Army of the James are left here, the Twenty-fourth at Richmond and the Twenty-fifth Corps here. There are rumors already looking to the final disposition of the colored troops that I expected to be made. They will not be discharged till Congress has made some provision to incorporate a portion of them into the regular army. The men are to be re-enlisted, those who choose to do so, and the officers are to pass a far more rigid examination and receive commissions in the regular army. There are to be no more "U. S. C. T." but "U. S. A." Twenty-four regiments of two thousand men each are to be organized—so says General Casey.

Well, we may say the war is over—"this cruel war is over." The joy of the nation is tempered by its grief at the base assassination of the President, but we can console ourselves by the thought that he had accomplished his work. His murderer is also dead, and Jeff Davis, the instigator of the fearful deed, is fleeing from the wrath to come—proclaimed an outlaw and $100,000 offered for his head.

From home I have bad news. Mother has been sick some time and Father is afloat again. It is too sad to think of, but its frequent recurrence has made it seem almost a thing of course. The saddest part of all is that his trouble in the church was caused by copperheads who hated his war preaching. My indignation at that has no bounds. I cannot say I am astonished. A copperhead is fit for any meanness this side of hell. If there is a hell they are on the road to it, and the sooner they arrive at their journey's end the better it will suit me. They had better leave or turn strong war men before that old Army of the Potomac gets north, for, my word for it, those old veterans I saw marching through Petersburg the other day will not listen quietly to any of their balderdash. I can listen with a quiet smile to the sad story of a rebel soldier who has fought bravely through the war for a bad cause and acknowledges himself beaten. That is punishment enough for him, but for the villain at home too cowardly to fight for the cause he helped with his tongue and influence, I have only infinite scorn and loathing. I curse him from the bottom of my heart. Earth is too good for him and hell is full of just such men.

Well, my sheet is full and I must close. Write to me soon—same address.

Camp Lincoln, Va.,
May 16, 1865.

Dear Sister L.:—

"Camp Lincoln" is the camp of the corps at Lighthouse or Jordan's Point and vicinity, and it is becoming the "A No. 1" of camps. Matters are arranged *a la* regulars and we are becoming regulars as fast as possible. Cannot tell whether we will be discharged this summer or not—most likely "or not." Every man has a scheme of his own for disposing of us, and they will all hold good till Congress meets and takes the matter into consideration.

Jeff Davis is captured. The country doesn't seem to get much excited about that, but I have my own jubilee. I never expected it, but I am most happily disappointed, and if the villain doesn't stretch hemp, I shall be disappointed less happily.

I send you to board a photo of my quartermaster-sergeant James Duty. The cap rather spoils the face, but it is not a bad picture. How's that for a "naygur"?

I had strawberries and cream for dinner with a late *secesh* maiden—how's that, too?

I have been busy and am not done yet in fixing our headquarters. I send you a plan. How do you like it?

It is my plan and my execution. The colonel's tent faces up the avenue, and the others in toward the center. The court inside is all to be covered with a shade or booth of pine boughs. The "O O" at the rear corners are servant's quarters. Well, it is midnight and I must wind up. Write to me soon. Camp is all right but won't write. Tell his mother.

Steamer Warrior, James River, Va.,
Monday, May 29, 1865.

Dear Sister L.:—

I take the opportunity before we get beyond the reach of mails to drop you a note to say "good-bye, I'm off."

The last of the second division sailed on Friday to rendezvous in Hampton Roads, and I was left behind in charge of the transportation and private horses of my brigade. It was the hardest job by far of the whole embarkation, but they are all on board and I am on my way to Texas or elsewhere.

The Warrior is one of the largest ships of the fleet—carries three hundred horses and mules and one hundred army wagons, and being the senior officer on board I shall command the ship during the voyage—that is, the military part of it. Of course the captain sails his own vessel.

U. S. Steamer Illinois, off Fort Morgan, Mobile Bay,
Thursday, June 8, 1865.

Dear Sister L.:—

I've just time to write a line to say we are so far on our voyage in safety. I was transferred from the Warrior the day we started. Had a lovely trip—couldn't be better. Shall disembark here to clean the ship—and coal and water again—and then—ho! for Texas or elsewhere.

U. S. Steamer Illinois, off Ft. Morgan, Mobile Bay,
Thursday, June 8, 1865.

Dear Sister L.:—

I wrote you a line this afternoon just in time to get it off by the New Orleans boat. I could not write much in the few minutes of time I had before the boat left, and so to-night I will write a little more extended account of our voyage.

I wrote you from the Warrior expecting to go down in her, but on arriving at Fortress Monroe, the general concluded he couldn't dispense with my company, and ordered me to the Illinois. I was not sorry to make the change, as my regiment was there with the general and staff, and the Illinois is a floating palace.

I spent a day in Norfolk and then removed my traps to the Illinois, and on the 31st we weighed anchor and steamed out past Cape Henry lighthouse and off to sea. The next morning we were out of sight of land, and steaming southeast to cross the Gulf Stream; our ship drew nineteen feet of water, and we could not go next the coast, so as it would not pay to go against the current all the way, we were forced to go outside. The time passed merrily away. A few were sick enough to make amusement for the others, but none enough to be thoroughly wretched. We had plenty of books, and in the evening we gathered in the spacious saloon and had whist parties and quartettes of euchre or old sledge, and such like abominations.

On Sunday morning we came to the Bahama Banks, where the waters changed from their indigo blue color to azure, light green, purple and almost all the colors of the rainbow. The water was so clear we could see the bottom at thirty feet, and the finny monsters were disporting themselves regardless of the curious eyes that looked at them for the first time. At noon Memory Rock rose in bold relief against the horizon, lone, stern and grim, a sentinel of the sea. In the afternoon we passed the Bahamas, a line of long, low, sandy islands, uninhabited except by a few wreckers, and not very inviting situations for a cottage by the sea. But at dark we saw the cottage by the sea, indeed. It was a little hut on a lonely rock, where dwells the keeper of the Isaac Island Light, an English lighthouse. He has a spice of solitude, he has. State's prison is nothing to it. I mused on the pleasures of solitude, as I watched his lonely light flash and fade in the darkness, and I concluded that it must be very sweet to have someone to whom you can say—"how sweet is solitude!"

On Tuesday we sighted, away off in the dim distance, the heights of Cuba, and that afternoon passed the Florida Keys and the Dry Tortugas. The last is the penitentiary of the army, where mutinous and other desperate criminals have been sent. It rises like a great castle in the sea, and is a lonely place enough.

This afternoon we sighted the land off Mobile Bay, and at three o'clock we dropped anchor off Fort Morgan, and now I am writing on deck, with my portfolio on my knee, and the scene of the greatest naval battle of the world spread out before me. Within a stone's throw, I can see the ripple in the current which marks the spot where the ill-fated Tecumseh went down, right under the guns of Fort Morgan, and a little to the left the ribs of the rebel ram are rising above the water. Here the "gallant, grim old Admiral," ran the gauntlet of the terrible batteries. My words are too tame—I will not attempt to describe it. Read "Our Battle Laureate" in the April or May Atlantic, and you will get some idea of the inspiring scene.

Well, the sun has disappeared in a blaze of glory behind Fort Gaines, and I must bring my letter to a close for want of light and room for more.

To-morrow we disembark, and I hope before we re-embark to see how Mobile looks, but I may not make it out. The rumor to-night is that we are to go to Brazos Santiago, at the mouth of the Rio Grande.

U. S. Steamer Illinois, off Brazos de Santiago, Texas,
Thursday, June 15, 1865.

Dear Father:—

I have a few minutes in which to write a continuation of my note from Mobile Bay. The Illinois returns to New York to-morrow, or sails for there via New Orleans, and I must send by her.

We disembarked near Fort Morgan on Friday the 9th. Found on shore a family from Boston, with a piano and girls fond of music and dancing, and enjoyed ourselves immensely. Re-embarked the next morning and sailed at noon. Our trip across the Gulf had nothing of interest till on Tuesday morning we sighted land, the Isla del Padre, and at 9 o'clock anchored off Brazos. There are only nine feet of water on the bar, and as our ship draws nineteen, we could not get over and it has been too rough to transfer the men to a lighter till to-day, when we got them off on a schooner, though it was a perilous job. I expected to see at least one or two drowned, but they all got off in safety. I remain to unload the rations and stores, and seize the time the schooner is off to write my note.

Our brigade is to remain with division headquarters at Brazos. One of the other brigades is at Corpus Christi and one at Indianola. Brazos is an island at the mouth of the Rio Grande. Seven miles down the coast on the other side is Bagdad in Mexico, where several thousand French and Imperialist Mexicans are camped. One of our regiments will guard the ford, and as soon as I can get time I am going across to see how they look.

Brazos has not much to recommend it as a pleasant place to garrison, but we shall build barracks and live within ourselves and enjoy ourselves, I make no doubt. The worst feature is that we must use condensed water. I shall be busy for a time in fitting up, and in making up my papers, but I hope to have time to write some letters, and I hope some of you will write to me at least once a week. Change the address from Washington to New Orleans, but make no other changes.

U. S. Steamer Illinois, off Brazos de Santiago, Texas.
Thursday, June 15, 1865.

Dear Sister L.:—

I wrote you last from Mobile Bay, just as we were about sailing. Our trip across the Gulf of Mexico had nothing of special interest till on Tuesday morning we sighted land, the island "Del Padre" or Father's Island, as we would say, and at 9 o'clock we dropped anchor at Brazos.

My letter from Fort Morgan left us expecting to disembark the next morning, and the entry in my diary for Friday, the 9th, is "Disembarked at Mary Cove, Mississippi Steamer Swaim. Sand-flies. Swimming in the surf. Roast pork at the Hotel de Lawrence. *Soiree dansante*—minstrels—model artists—midnight orgies on the beach—school house."

To you, that collection of disjointed phrases is suggestive of bedlam, I presume. To me it is suggestive of a day long to be remembered for its unique pleasures. "Mississippi Steamer Swaim" recalls the image of the craft that took us off the Illinois to the wharf at Mary Cove—a lumbering awkward looking steamer, that could turn one wheel forward and the other back at the same time—that made a smoke suggestive of inferno—and that coughed like a consumptive Titan. "Sand-flies" is a compound word, and sand-flies themselves are a compound of all the disagreeable qualities of mosquitoes, fleas, lice, gnats and bedbugs. They are so small they are almost invisible till they bite, and it is no pleasure to kill them for they stand still to be killed with perfect equanimity, and for every one you kill ten more take his place. The only things to keep them away are mud and tobacco. We had a few of them at Mary Cove.

"Swimming in the surf" recalls a pleasant two hours of sea bathing, when big waves combed over us, or tossed us high on the beach, and when the sharks kept at their proper distance, which we were afraid they wouldn't.

"Roast pork at the Hotel de Lawrence" recalls our dinner. We had gone on shore expecting to starve, or live on salt air till the next day, but the adjutant and I with our usual inquisitive spirit, started on a prospecting tour, and catching a glimpse of some "delaine" that did not look exactly like the "cracker" style, we ran alongside, took a reef in our topsails, saluted, and invited ourselves to dinner in an insinuating way. Of course, ourselves included the colonel and major. We soon found that Mrs. Lawrence was a southern lady, the wife of an officer in our navy, who hailed from Boston, and that the lady and her two daughters and niece had just come from Boston, where they had been living since the war began. That Mrs. L. had kept a hotel in Pensacola, appeared from her conversation. That she had kept a good one was evident from the dinner she got up for us.

Soirée dansante recalls the evening. Imagine our surprise in finding in that low cottage by the sea, half buried in the sand, a piano, and a girl who could play with taste and skill, one who had played on the great Boston organ. We found it; we sent for our band after tea; we sent for the violins and guitar from the string band, and our "choir" came too. We had music, songs and dancing. At the first squeak of the viol, the girls said it sounded familiar, which was a hint that could not be resisted by a soldier. The floor was cleared and a cotillion formed in a reasonable time. Once the spell was broken there was no stopping it till the "wee sma' hours." The tall form of the colonel, with his riding boots, went round and round the *mater-familias* in stately Lancers or lively quadrille. Schottische and waltz pleased the daughters better, and we had a good time all round.

"Midnight orgies on the beach" recalls the bath before the bed in the school house. We enjoyed that surf some after being cooped up on a ship for more than a week, and then we slept in a school house. The very idea was novel, but we were not in Virginia, and they do have some school houses in Alabama, I believe.

Well, I have enlarged pretty well on that little page, but I have not written half those few disjointed words suggest to me.

The Gulf is full of sharks and the fierce monsters have been following us ever since we left Mobile. Yesterday we caught one about thirteen feet long, and raised him out of the water, but he straightened the hook and got away.

Last night at sunset we had a burial at sea. One of the men of Company F died and as it was impossible to land, and we could not keep the body, it was buried in the deep. The body was sewed up in a blanket and placed on a board on the guards of the ship, with heavy weights at the feet. The band played a dirge, the chaplain read the Episcopal service for burial at sea, and when he came to the words, "We commit his body to the deep," the plank was lifted and the body descended with a sullen plunge to the bottom of the ocean.

Brazos de Santiago, Texas,
June 27, 1865.

Dear Sister L.:—

By this time you will think I should be able to give you something of a description of this strange country. If you look at a map of Texas you may see down at the mouth of the Rio Grande, the name of Brazos de Santiago. There is a little strip of sand about ten miles long, dignified by the name island, and on the northern end of the island is the village. The village is a row of small wooden houses put up by the government for store rooms and offices, with a few occupied by sutlers.

There is a wharf and shipping. These form a very small part of the scenery—the rest is sand. There is not a spear of vegetation growing within sight of my tent. There is not a tree within fifteen miles. Just across the narrow strait is the Isla del Padre, another sand strip, seventy-five miles long. At the mouth of the strait is the bar and a dangerous one too. There is only about seven feet of water and the breakers roar and tumble over it so that at most times a small boat could not live ten minutes. The ships anchor outside and are unloaded by little sloops called lighters, which, with the Spanish names, Bonita, Dos Amigos, etc., and their Mejicanos crews are funny crafts. They rendezvoused here when cotton ran the blockade, and loaded and unloaded the ships, and now that their occupation is gone they come to Uncle Sam for employment.

I told you, I think, that our regiment was ship-wrecked when they came ashore. It was only such a peril as one likes to tell of when it is past, for no one was lost. The schooner though, lies high and dry on the beach. We have had terrible times for water. There is none on the island fit to drink—all salt. Two condensers are in operation, but they would not begin to water all the troops. Our men have gone nine miles up to the Rio Grande after water and got back the same night, rolling barrels of water all the way. Just think of that for getting your water. It don't rain here; or we might get rainwater. Now that all the troops except our brigade have gone up the river we hope to get water enough.

The sun is terribly hot. At noon it is directly overhead and if it were not for the constant sea breeze we could not live. The wind commences to blow from the southeast every morning about nine o'clock and blows till nearly daylight next morning, so that in the shade of a tent it is quite comfortable. The hottest time of day is from sunrise till nine o'clock when there is no breeze. About four p. m. it is comfortable walking and we go to bathe, keeping an eye out for sharks.

You must be well on in the summer now, and it is almost the Fourth. What glorious celebrations there will be this year!

Many officers are sending in their resignations, but none of them in this corps are accepted. I think I shall stay through the summer pretty well contented and see what turns up then.

July 1, 1865.

Dear Sister L.:—

I send you another "boarder." The time for distinction of color *per se* is past. The face you see is the counterfeit presentment of the "American citizen of African descent," Jefferson Chisum Brown, called for short (or surnamed) Jeff. Mr. Brown belongs to a numerous and highly respected family. The fact that his name is not descriptive of his condition is not uncommon, or at all remarkable. Though he is Brown, he is also "black as the ace of spades." That is a camp simile, which you will not understand, but it means very black. Mr. Brown's former residence was Charleston, and he belonged to the aristocracy there. He came over from there with Robert Small on the Planter, and though his trip will be an event commemorated in history, Mr. Brown himself can claim little credit for it, because as he acknowledges—"he didn't know whar dey was a fotchin' him to." Mr. Brown is at present employed as a polisher of metal (cleans the sword) and an artist (handles the boot brush) under the auspices of my friend Burrows.

Brazos de Santiago, Texas,
July 8, 1865.

Dear Sister L.:—

I have written of our voyages, its pleasures, and the shipwreck at the end. I have told you the features of the country here, its lack of vegetation and its abundance of salt and sand. There is not much more to tell, except that we are just about ready for a march away up the Rio Grande, into the wilderness of the Comanche country. I expect danger and hardship, heat, thirst and all the troubles and pleasures incident to a trip in the wilderness of this romantic country.

The rebellion is dead—we have no more rebels to fight, and the work laid out for us seems to be to garrison the forts and posts along the frontier, from the mouth of the Rio Grande away up into New Mexico. I saw an officer yesterday, who had just come down from up there, who said he had not seen a white man beside his own company for two years. Greasers (Mexicans) and Comanche Indians are the inhabitants up there. With us, it will be some different. We have a whole army corps to be scattered along the frontier, and there will be frequent communication.

You do well to talk about heat and rain. What would you think of a country where the average heat is from 96 to 100 and you lived in a cotton house where it did not rain for three months, and then the whole three months' rain came down in one day, where you would have to get your water by condensing the steam from sea brine? It wouldn't suit me for a home, but a sojourn here does very well for an episode in one's life. There is no use in your disliking my coming here. I was well on my way when you wrote the words, and here before I read them.

If you find the time when you can go on a visit to Michigan, you better go, without making any calculations of my going with you. Our "best laid schemes o' mice and men gang aft agley," and there is no telling what may happen to any of us. I have a plan in my mind now, which I intend to work out. The war is over, the object of my enlistment is accomplished, and I propose to resign about the middle or latter part of September, so as to start for home about the first of October. I shall go via the Mississippi River, make a visit to our parents in Michigan (I cannot say go home, because I have no home yet), then come for another visit to you, and about the first of January go for a term of instruction in the forwarding and commission business, to Eastman's Business College at Poughkeepsie. After that go to New Orleans or St. Louis and get a position as agent for some firm in the business, till such time as I get ready to go into business on my own account. An officer in the regiment, whom I have known intimately for nearly two years, will join me at the school, and we shall go together for better or worse. It is a business that can be carried on with less capital and produce surer and larger profits than any other I know of, and one which will suit my tastes better than a quiet country life. Now what do you think of my plan?

Ringgold Barracks, Texas,
July 28, 1865.

Dear Sister L.:—

I have just time to drop you a line before the mail goes, to say that I arrived safely at the end of my long tedious march, through the strangest country and oddest people you or I ever saw. By and by, when I have leisure, I have lots of material for letters.

I was appointed Post Quartermaster immediately on my arrival, and I have been so busy that I have not had time to eat my meals half the time since.

We have a large post and plenty of business, but it is rather a hard country to live in, I should say. Nothing in the way of vegetables to eat can be had, and we have to drink the Rio Grande mud, and are glad to get that.

A line is all I can write. You must take the will for the deed and make up by writing often to me.

Ringgold Barracks, Rio Grande City, Texas,
Sunday, July 30, 1865.

My Dear Sister L.:—

Having some leisure to-day, I will give you a description

of our march from Brazos, and my impression of the country as jotted down in my diary. We had been expecting the order to march for some time, but it did not come till on Monday, the 10th of July, and about 5 o'clock that afternoon we started.

Our road at first lay along the beach on Brazos Island, south, but just at dark we forded the channel to the main land, and began to cross the plain—moonlight on the plain. It was my first experience of the kind, and my first impression was of a beautiful scene, a boundless prairie, dotted here and there with prickly pears and Spanish bayonet. The prickly pear is a sort of cactus that grows all over this country. It looks like a set of green dinner plates, the edge of one grown fast to the next, and so on, and the whole so covered with sharp thorns that you cannot touch it with your hand. The pears grow round the edge of the plates, about the shape and size of pears, covered with thorns and of a beautiful purple color when ripe, and full of seeds like a fig. Most of the men devoured them greedily, but I did not fancy their insipid taste. Everything that grows in this country has thorns or horns. Even the frogs are horned, and the cattle have horns longer than their tails. Most of the grass I have seen is harsh, prickly stuff.

We bivouacked that night at 10 o'clock, at White's Ranch, having marched about ten miles. The next day was to be spent in camp near the river. A party of the officers strolled down the bank to swim. Few of us had yet been in Mexico, and as it was not far off I proposed to swim over. The current was very swift, six miles an hour, and my proposition was accepted by but one of them. We two started and did swim over. So my first exploration of a foreign country was *in puris naturalibus* and the result nothing worth mentioning, for the country was just like that we had left.

The next day at 3:30 a. m., we continued our march, and a terrible march it was. Part of the way the road lay through mesquit chaparral, impenetrable thickets of scrubby, thorny trees, too small for shade and too dense to admit a breath of air. Dry as parched corn was everything, no grass, no water. I have passed miles and miles of such road since, but nothing that seemed so desolate as that first experience of the chaparral. By and by we came out of it and entered a broad prairie of wild, coarse grass. A mile or two off we saw a drove of wild asses. A mounted man started to reconnoiter and it would have made you laugh to see those wild fellows scorn him with their heels. They waited till he got reasonably near, and they went away from him so fast that he stopped to look in sheer amazement at their speed. It is needless to say he did not catch any of them.

We halted about 4 o'clock, having marched sixteen miles. There was much straggling, and I could not blame the men, for it was impossible to march under such a sun. I had all I could do to ride my horse under it. Next day we marched eight miles to Brownsville, halted till four o'clock and then went three miles farther and camped. We spent a day or two there, and as it is the only town of importance in this part of the state I must give you some description of it. The population is mostly Mexican, ten to one Yankee. It is about the size of Jamestown, N. Y., and has one street, something similar to the main street there, but the balance is Mexican, all. I used to think that Ross Brown's delineation of Mexican life, in Harper's Monthly, was somewhat exaggerated, but I am satisfied now that his portraits are true to life. I went down to the river to swim, and was a little surprised to observe that it is the custom for whole families to enjoy that luxury together without the incumbrance of bathing dresses. All ages and sexes were indiscriminately mixed in the river, and as when you are with the Romans, you must do as the Romans do, I mixed in too.

The houses in town are adobe (mud brick) or "jacal," mud and sticks, with mud floors and roofs of thatched grass and cane. The prime requisite seems to be to keep cool, and I must admit that with their style of dress the result is attained. The little pot-bellied children go entirely naked till they are ten years old, when they attain to shirts, which seems to be the only garment worn till they are grown up, when the women add a petticoat or skirt, and the men a pair of leather breeches. I must do them the justice to admit that they are clean. Their beds, where they have any, are as clean as any I ever saw, but most of them sleep on raw ox-hides laid on the floor. Passing along the streets, one sees through all the open doors, the families reclining on these rawhides, in all stages of dress below semi-nakedness. These people are the genuine Aztec Mexicans—a race by themselves, neither negro nor Indian, but something like both. There are some among them who approach civilization. My first lesson in the language I learned from a pretty senorita—bright, intelligent, vivacious and pretty. She called at a jacal where I stopped a while, and addressed me with a "Buenos dias, Senor" (Bwa-nose-de-as-Sayn-yore) good day, sir. She took a bunch of "cigarros" (cigarettes) from her pocket, passed them around and lit one herself. The women all smoke. Of course I could not refuse to light my cigar at her lips, when so temptingly offered. She told me that horse in "Mejicano" (Meh-i-can-o) is "caballo" (ca-wal-yow); saddle is "silla" (see-yah); eggs are "blanquitos;" milk, "leche;" hens, "gallinas" (gah-ye-nas); rooster, "gallo;" chicken, "pollita chiquita."

In one day I had mastered Spanish enough to ask: "Tiene usted pollitas chiquitas?" (Have you any chickens?) "Si, Senor" (Yes, sir.) "Quanto es por dos?" (How much a pair?) "Un peso por dos." (A dollar a pair), and I could buy.

They are an exceedingly polite people, never omit the "Senor" in their conversation. My senorita, when I left, kissed her hand to me with "Adios, Senor," in the prettiest way.

I attended a "fandango," or Mexican ball, at the Brownsville market house. Many senoritas were over from Matamoras, just across the river, most of them well dressed and good looking. An American officer's introduction was to step up to one and with a bow say, "Dance Senorita?" "Si, Senor," is the invariable reply, and after a Spanish waltz or schottische, he is expected to give her something to drink and smoke a "cigarro" with her. They all dance well and the music of cornets and flageolets is far from disagreeable.

I have always been fond of the water, and swimming is a favorite amusement. There is another officer in the regiment, brought up "on old Long Island's sea-girt shore," who is equally fond of it, and we are often companions in swimming frolics. "Miller & Norton" are supposed to do just as much in the way of feats in water as can be done in the Eighth, so we always stump the company when we go in. At our camps above Brownsville we agreed to swim half a mile further in the river than anyone else, so we went two miles above the camp and took a boy along to carry our clothes, and then swam down half a mile below the camp. It was no great feat in a six mile current to swim two and a half miles in half an hour, but it sounded big, and left us champions.

The water in the river is very muddy, looks just like the road gutters after a heavy shower, but it is all the water we have to drink. In all our journey I saw but one well and one spring. The water in the wells if dug, is bitter. Every few miles on the road we came to "lagunas" or lakes of fresh water, that had no apparent outlet or inlet. They come from the overflow of the river, and the water collects in such large bodies that the wind gives it motion enough to prevent its stagnating and it is quite palatable, though I doubt its being wholesome. We camped usually near some laguna. As we came farther up the country we found more ranches. These are jacal houses, with enclosures for the cattle, sheep and goats. There are large flocks of sheep and goats together that feed over the country, with men or boys to guard them, and are driven up at night. There is one peculiarity about the Texas cows, that would be awkward in a dairy country—they will not milk till the calf has sucked and if the calf dies or is killed they immediately dry up.

I have heard before of snake countries, but till I came here I never saw many snakes. There are some here. I have counted on a day's march of fifteen miles, more than a dozen snakes. Not the little striped worms than run in

New York meadows, but black snakes and rattle snakes from six to eight feet long, killed by the troops and left lying in the road. The adjutant has a string of eighteen rattles that he cut off one snake. It was nearly eight feet long and four inches thick. I have killed several big black snakes myself, but those rattle snakes I'm going to let alone.

Another of the varmints in this country is the tarantula, an enormous spider, whose bite is more venomous than that of the rattle snake. The back of the beast is covered with a fuzz, like the inside of a chestnut bur in color and texture, and its legs as long as a man's finger and very thick and muscular. There are two fangs in its mouth, sharp and black, much like a cat's claw. I killed one when on the march, the only one I've seen. They are not very plenty, I believe. There are scorpions here, too.

In passing through some parts of the country, the chaparral cleared up and the mesquit trees with the wild grass under them, looked exactly like an old orchard of half-dead apple trees in a field of half-ripe oats, and the road winding through the grass, like some farm road in harvest time passing through a grain field.

There is abundance of game in the country—wolves, foxes, deer and immense rabbits, but there are no edible vegetables or fruits to be had, and I tell you it is tough living, and take it all in all, I would not live in this country if I could own a whole county. To all intents and purposes, this country is Mexico still.

Monday, 31st: I had not time to finish my letter yesterday and will add a few lines to-day and seal it up, to wait the arrival of the next boat. There is no telling when that will come.

Last night I was disturbed in my sleep by a strange noise, and rising up in bed to listen I made out that a pack of prairie wolves had made a visit, and were paying their compliments by making a most infernal noise about ten rods away in the chaparral, whining, howling and yelp-like a parcel of half-fed curs. They are cowardly rascals.

Well, I've written you a long rambling letter. Things

are jumbled up in it very much as they have been in my experience here, and it seems half like some ugly dream, but you can rely on it as being all true. About two months more of such life and I hope to see civilization again. In the meantime I hope to hear from you as often as a mail comes, which is seldom.

Office A. A. Q. M., Second Division, Twenty-fifth
Corps, Ringgold Barracks, Texas,
August 27, 1865.

My Dear Sister L.:—

I received your letter dated July 23d, by the last boat (23d) just a month from date. I cannot tell you how glad I was to hear from you again, but I can tell you that you must not expect many long letters from me, till I come home. There is not much to write, anyway. I have already written a tolerably full description of the country, and now I have no time to write anything but business letters. I am division quartermaster and post quartermaster at the same time, and you may judge I have something to do. Since the other quartermasters left I have worked night and day. To-day is Sunday and I and my clerk have written thirty-one business letters, besides inspecting my train. I am supplying forage to six hundred horses and mules, and have thirty-five six-mule teams of my own to take care of. I have estimated the value of the property for which I am responsible at $350,000 and I cannot take care of that without some work.

The only recreation I have taken lately has been to attend a ball over in Camargo, Mexico. General Cortinas and General Espinosa, of the liberal army, were in town, and the merchants got up a ball to bring together the United States and Mexican officers. The "baile" was "dedica a los Gefes y Officiales de los Estados Unidos del norte"— of course, you know what that means.

The senoritas were numerous and of rather a different style from these peon Mexicans. Their papas had thousands of silver "pesos" and they were as well dressed and well behaved as our girls at home, to say the least.

I am getting quite well acquainted in Camargo, where I am known as "Don Olivero el Quartelmaestro." Every one is known by his first name only. Charlie there would be "Don Carlos." Oh, how these girls can waltz, and how I can't! I didn't enjoy the dancing much, except looking on. I could only schottische a little.

It would amuse you to see what a man of consequence I am in Camargo. A brigadier general is nowhere beside "El Quartelmaestro." "Why?"—Because he don't make contracts for lumber, coal, grain and hay—the quartermaster does.

There are a thousand things I would like to tell you about, but I haven't time. I send with this the July Atlantic. I have had the August number two weeks and have not cut the leaves yet.

Ringgold Barracks, Texas,
September 10, 1865.

My Dear Sister L.:—

I have no letter to answer since my last, but I have a little time to spare to-day, being Sunday, and will devote it to you by writing.

I try to imagine what you are doing just now, and what is the change in the looks of the place since I was there. I presume that just about this time of day you are sitting in one of the slips in that "Podunk" or "Chachunk" (what do you call it?) "meetin' house," listening intently to the logical instructions of some "Elder Boanerges" and wishing between times that you had your big brother up there again to show him to those who were not sufficiently impressed by your first exhibition. Ah, well! You can't get him there to-day. Let me see. It is nearly the middle of September. We have been making garden. Our cucumbers are up and doing nicely—so are several other plants. You, I suppose, are just getting through harvesting. Charlie's barns are full to overflowing. The cows come up at night so full they lie down with a grunt, and all the country round shows the fullness and beauty of the early autumn. I have not learned to tell the season here. July and August have passed never so quickly, so coolly, so pleasantly before. Most of my time is spent in my office and, instead of the excessive heat being troublesome in the southern climate, I have never suffered so little from heat in New York. There is all the time a breeze, and the thick walls of my adobe house shut out all the heat of the sun.

I say the time has passed pleasantly. One reason is that I have had little time to think of unpleasant things, and another, I suppose, is that I am somewhat pleased with the power and influence of my new position. Except the commanding general, there is no one here so much looked up to by the citizens as "El Quartelmaestro," and then my business suits me. General Steele, Inspector General, has been inspecting my train, shops, storehouses, etc., to-day, and he compliments me highly on their appearance. From down the river I hear the same thing. "I like to consign a boat to a live quartermaster," says the quartermaster at Brownsville, "but how do you manage to unload your boats so quickly?" I do it by keeping things moving. I set seventy-five men with an officer in charge at work as soon as a boat is tied up, and when the load is off her papers are ready and she starts back. There is a pleasure in hard work when you see the results. That makes all the difference in the world. The way I punish an unruly teamster is to make him dig a big hole and then fill it up, dig it out and fill it up the second time, and that is enough for any man. It fixes them.

I should not write such a letter to everyone. It sounds a little like self-praise, but between us there need be no reserve. I tell you all because I know you like to know just what I am doing.

By the way, have I told you that I have at last dropped the "A" and my "pay handle" is "R. Q. M." of the Eighth? Burrows got his appointment in August and I stepped into his shoes at once. Rank from August 5th.

The prospect for getting out of the service very soon is not very good. As things are shaping I do not much think I shall try till after Congress meets. Wilson Camp has sent in his resignation and he will go out sure. The medical board that examines all officers pronounced him disqualified to perform his duties, by reason of physical disability contracted in the line of his duty. It is a big joke, for he is physically the ablest man in the regiment. Can stand more hardship than the whole medical board together, but he said "the doctors ought to know," and sent in his resignation on those grounds. I suppose I might do the same thing, but I do not care to do it.

The paymaster has paid us a visit and some greenbacks. I received $577.63 for four months.

Well, I will bid you good-bye, hoping to hear from you soon and as often as you can find time to write. Love to Charlie and all the good folks. Shall I bring home a doll from Mexico for your baby?

I enclose a missive I received the other day. Perhaps you can read it. It refers to a mule.

Adios, hermana mia,
DON OLIVERO.

RECOLLECTIONS

SEPT. 1 TO DEC. 31, 1863.

O. W. NORTON.

TO THAT DEAR SISTER, WHO FROM CHILDHOOD'S EARLIEST REMEMBRANCE HAS LOVED ME WITH A LOVE PASSING THAT OF EVERY OTHER WOMAN, THESE RECOLLECTIONS ARE INSCRIBED.—O.

I am writing, dear sister, in the summer of 1864, in the sunny "Land of Flowers," of times and friends in 1863, in war-cursed Virginia. The chivalry in their pride have called it the "sacred soil," and now indeed it is the "sacred soil"—consecrated by the blood of tens of thousands of the champions of right and liberty against slavery and wrong.

The first of September found the brigade to which I was attached, camped at Beverly Ford, on the Rappahannock. General Rice had just received his "star," and left us to command a division in the First Corps. He was one of the happiest men in the Army of the Potomac the day his commission arrived. He had been a faithful officer since the opening of the struggle, brave to rashness, generous to a fault, kind and even fatherly to his men, but till now senior officers had stood in the way of his promotion. The death of the gallant Vincent had sadly opened the way, and though sorrowing at the event, in common with all who knew the talented soldier, he was not the less ready to embrace the opportunity offered. Now, he too is gone. Vincent, glowing with patriotism, had exclaimed the night before Gettysburg, while the girls by the wayside sang "The Star Spangled Banner" to cheer our midnight march, glancing at our flag waving in the moonlight, "What death more glorious could any man desire than to die on the soil of old Pennsylvania fighting for that flag?" Words worthy to be set in letters of gold and pictures of silver for coming generations to study while they learn that it was not empty rhetoric, but the feeling of his soul, for he died with the triumph in his eye, and the smile of a glorious death on his lips. Rice, with the true soldier spirit animating him in the last hour, lying there in the Wilderness with his life-blood moistening the "sacred soil," said to the faithful drummer boys who attended him, "Turn me over, boys—let me die with my face to the enemy." And there he died. Thousands more were dead and dying there with the same spirit and in the same cause. Who shall say the "sacred soil" is mis-named?

But to return. The camp of our brigade was stretched along the river just opposite and above the dam. Colonel Rice, upon receiving his promotion, was assigned to another command, and was succeeded by Colonel Chamberlain of the Twentieth Maine. Our new commander was a tall, good looking man, who had seen but one year of military life. He was, before entering the army, a professor in a college in Maine, and a minister of the Gospel, but he doffed the ministerial black and donned the military blue with a good grace, and with credit to himself and his state. At Gettysburg, in command of his regiment, he evinced military talents of a high order, and did good service to his country.

The headquarters of our brigade were on a hill overlooking the camps and the river. In front was Colonel Chamberlain's tent, in rear and to the right of the colonel's was Captain Clark's, the A. A. A. G., and on the same line to the left was Lieutenant Rogers', aide-de-camp. In rear of these was the adjutant general's office tent, the four tents forming a cross, and a booth covered with pine boughs was constructed over the whole of them.

In rear of this and a little to the right was a humble dwelling constructed of poles and shelter tents, and occupied by your brother and his tent-mate. There were few at headquarters who understood and liked Theodore Roosen as I did. He was an orphan, born in Denmark. At the age of eight years he ran away from a cruel guardian and went to sea. He followed the sea in various capacities for ten years, visiting in that time half the seaport cities of the world, and at last was wrecked on the rock-bound coast of Maine. His experience on the sea seems to have satisfied him, and he settled down to the quiet of a farmer's life in Maine. It may be that the charms of a downeast maiden had some weight in influencing his choice, for I remember writing some letters for him to a certain Susan who shall be nameless. He had not been here long enough to write English much, though he wrote his own language well. What I most admired in him was his manliness and self-reliance, his determination to make his way in the world without dependence on others. He was strong in his likes and dislikes. One of his "likes" was me, and one of his "dislikes" was a "nigger." No amount of argument could convince him that a "nigger" was a man. He was a warm friend and faithful.

The first two weeks of September passed rapidly away. I was attending to my duties as bugler, writing letters to my friends, reading, and waiting for the orders to march. Lee's army was reported to be lying along the south bank of the Rapidan and his cavalry stretching from Culpeper to Orange Court House. On the 15th came the orders, and on the 16th at an early hour we broke camp and moved toward the enemy. After crossing the Rappahannock below the ford on a pontoon bridge, we struck across the country to Brandy Station, on the Orange and Alexandria railroad. Brandy Station has since become quite famous as the headquarters of Meade's army, but that is all that ever caused the name to be printed on anything but time-tables and schedules of a one-horse railroad. My recollection of the place is this: A low wooden shed with a whitewashed board with "BRANDY" on it, two dilapidated houses surrounded by a ruined fence, three or four ragged, towheaded children, and a cross-eyed woman. We followed the railroad from Brandy toward Culpeper. Half way between the two places, and half a mile from the road, was the residence of John Minor Botts, a neutrality man. He was opposed to the secession of Virginia, and would do nothing to help the rebellion, neither would he assist in making war on his native state. The rebels kept him in Castle Thunder a while and then released him.

Culpeper Court House is a rambling old town, about the size of Jamestown, New York. It was the home of the rebel General Hill, and a host of lesser lights among the chivalry. It used to be a place of fashionable resort of the F. F. V.'s, but alas! its glory has departed. The wives and daughters of the patrician families of the state were reduced to the dire extremity of keeping boarding houses for the Union officers, and bending their lady backs over washtubs containing their dirty clothes, to keep from starvation. Now that there are no officers to board and wash for, I cannot imagine what the first families do.

We went into camp three miles southwest of Culpeper. Headquarters were fixed in a point of woods on a hill overlooking the camps. The day before, there had been a cavalry skirmish on this ground, and just in front of the colonel's tent, under a spreading oak, was the grave of a Union cavalryman. Somewhere among the mountains of Pennsylvania a home was in mourning, but the mourned was taking a soldier's rest under the shadow of that oak. I spent two days in cutting out a head board and surrounding his grave with a fence.

Friday, the 18th, was a day long to be remembered in many homes. Desertions had become so common that energetic action alone could stop them, and on that day eighteen deserters in the Army of the Potomac were "shot to death with musketry" in the presence of their divisions. At half past two in the afternoon our division assembled to witness the execution of George Van, of the Twelfth New York

Volunteers. The day was dull and cloudy, and the ceremony took place in a lonely, wild valley west of the camp. The troops were formed in line on the hillside facing the valley, and soon after the line was formed the wild strains of the death march floated over the hill, and the condemned man came following his coffin down into the valley of death. Slowly they marched along the line—the muffled roll of the drum and the mournful shriek of the fife alone breaking the silence of that assembled multitude.

The coffin was set down in front of the grave, opposite the center of the line, the chaplain knelt and prayed for the soul of the doomed man, the provost marshal read the order for his execution, the prisoner seated himself on his coffin, thirteen glittering death tubes were aimed at his breast, there was a flash, a report, a smoke, and the prisoner rose to his feet, tossed his arms wildly above his head, and fell back on his coffin a corpse.

From that time till the 23d the weather was cold and overcoats began to come in play. We were undecided as to whether there would be a fall campaign or not. Our cavalry at the front were making reconnoissances and skirmishing every day, and the impression prevailed that Lee had been sending troops to Bragg, and that now was our time to attack him. We heard of an indecisive battle between Bragg's and Rosecrans' armies.

On the 23d I was electrified by the receipt of a letter from Honorable Galusha A. Grow recommending me to Major Foster in Washington and asking that I be allowed to appear before General Casey's board for examination.

I had written to Mr. Grow in the month of May previous asking advice about the mode of proceeding to obtain a commission in the colored regiments then beginning to be raised. I had heard nothing from him all summer and had given up the idea entirely, but this unexpected letter of recommendation revived my hopes and I immediately wrote to Major Foster making application for permission to appear before the board, and enclosing Mr. Grow's letter.

I said nothing to any one of what I had done. The sentiment of that part of the army in regard to colored soldiers was more favorable than it had been the winter before, when poor Joe Hatch had to hurry his departure to avoid the ridicule and jeers everywhere heaped on the "nigger officer." My most intimate companions, McKnight and Dickson, in the adjutant general's office, were moderately fond of sport at the expense of the nigger. On the 29th Captain Clark called me into his office and with a serio-comic expression desired to know if I had made application to appear before the board in Washington, and if so why I did not make it through the proper channel of communication. Of course I had, and the channel was the mail-bag. He then gave me an order from the War Department to report for examination to the board, of which Major General Silas Casey is president, sitting at 469 Fourteenth street, Washington.

Next morning I started about 9 o'clock for the capital. At Culpeper I took the cars for Alexandria, having first procured my transportation ticket from General Patrick, provost marshal. I was nearly all day traveling forty miles on that paragon of railroads, the Orange & Alexandria.

I arrived in the "City of Magnificent Distances" at 6 o'clock p. m. an entire stranger, with about $40 in my pocket. Coming in as I did, ragged and dirty from the field, I found it necessary to make some purchases of clothing before I could appear in a presentable condition before the board. I found a lodging place on Pennsylvania avenue, partook of my first civilized meal in more than two years, left my baggage and sallied out to visit the clothing stores. Two-thirds of the inhabitants of Washington being engaged in supplying the wants of our soldiers (for a consideration), and clothing being an important item in the necessaries, I was not long in finding the object of my search, and by half past seven I was promenading the avenue quite a respectably dressed private soldier.

The next matter for my consideration was how to spend the evening. The rough, hard life of a soldier in the field, followed up for two years and more, had predisposed me to a little relaxation and a little participation in the fashionable amusements of a city. I was nearly twenty-four years of age and had never seen the inside of a theater. The papers were full of the praise of Davenport and Wallack, the greatest "stars" who had ever played in Washington. Should I go to see them? Yes, so I decided, and went. The play was "The Stranger," one which usually draws well, and the "Washington Theater" was well filled. Of course I was pleased. Who was not on his first night? Knowing, or expecting, rather, that I should require all the energy I was possessed of on the next day, I did not stay to hear the after-piece, but retired to my lodging.

The next morning, after making my most careful toilet, knowing that much depends on first impressions, I reported to the secretary of the board, who, after examining my papers, informed me that my examination could not be had for a week or more, and in the meantime if I chose to do so I could receive board at government expense at the Soldiers' Home of the Sanitary Commission. I availed myself of the privilege, and as my examination was from time to time postponed, I spent nearly a month of pleasant days at that place.

By the wish of Captain Hechtman I called upon his wife at the earliest opportunity. I found her an exceedingly pleasant and sociable little woman, very glad to see me just from the front and bringing messages from her husband. I had seen her in Erie, as Corporal Hechtman's wife, and now I met her again as the wife of our respected captain. She expressed her warmest wishes for my success before the board, offered any assistance she could render, and urged me to call often during my stay in the city and drop in to take tea with her. So I had already found a friend, for her invitations were not conventional politeness.

The month at the Soldiers' Home passed rapidly away. There were from fifty to sixty applicants for examination constantly there, some leaving each day and new ones taking their places. Those waiting their turns made a practice of "plowing with the general's heifer" all they could. The examinations were all conducted on nearly the same plan and a certain routine of questions followed in every case. Applicants who had been examined were closely questioned on all points likely to benefit any future candidate, and they submitted with good humored grace, giving full details on all points likely to assist any one else. Had I known the ordeal through which successful candidates had to pass, I doubt if I had ever left the army to try it, expecting as I did to be examined immediately. The mornings were generally spent in hard study of the tactics and critical examinations of each other by parties who paired off for that purpose. After dinner we walked about town, visiting the lions till two or three o'clock, returning in time to catechize the candidates who had been examined during the day. In the evening we had a general class for examination in tactics, history, geography and mathematics, some one who had passed the board conducting the examination *a la* Casey. In this way much was learned that was of service in the ordeal to come, for ordeal it was.

Washington is very correctly called the "City of Magnificent Distances." It may be that the condition of the streets has something to do with that. Scarcely a score of streets in the city are paved. Pennsylvania Avenue is the Broadway of the capital. It is a broad street running the whole length of the city. At the head is the Capitol on an eminence overlooking the city. Two miles below the Capitol in an unfinished square are the unfinished Treasury buildings and other government houses; still farther below is the "White House." I visited the principal places of public interest during the month I was waiting my examination. Our boarding place was under the shadow of the Capitol and I spent much of my time there. My knowledge of architecture and my powers of description are both so limited that I will not attempt to describe it to you, but merely give you some of the impressions it produced in my mind. The first was its magnificent dimensions. It was by far the largest building I had ever seen, but like everything else in Washington it is yet unfinished. The whole neighborhood is strewn with blocks of marble and iron, and low sheds for the workmen, which do not add to the beauty of the prospect.

Inside, my preconceived ideas received another shock by the comparative smallness of the halls of the two houses of Congress. I had expected to find them occupying the greater part of the buildings, and I did find them only a small proportion of the whole. I have not the least doubt but that they are abundantly large, but I was disappointed much by my first view of them. The rotunda, of which so much has been said, is the base of the dome. In the center was a vast scaffold supporting the unfinished roof of that structure, and around the walls were various paintings, copies of which you see on the backs of notes of the national banks. I am no connoisseur in paintings and will vouchsafe no opinion of their merits, but the painting which most attracted my attention was that over one of the grand stairways, entitled "Westward the Star of Empire Takes Its Way." I studied that picture hours, and all the time discovering new beauties. I cannot describe to you the corridors and halls, the beautiful columns and fresco work. I can only say that since I have seen that all other buildings look tame and poor in comparison. In company with my friend, Powell, I spent much time in the President's room. It was a quiet place and we went there to study. To give you an idea of the magnificence of the place I will try to describe one column supporting a mirror. It was variegated marble, very much the color of castile soap, sixteen feet high and about four wide. The face was hollowed out into a niche and so beautifully polished that as I stood before it I really thought it was covered with a glass plate, and could not undeceive myself till I put out my hand and touched it.

Among the most interesting places to strangers in Washington is the Smithsonian Institute, founded by one Smithson, in the interests of natural science. It contains specimens of immense numbers of beasts, birds and fishes, and all manner of curiosities. I spent some time in looking over that. One curiosity was a young alligator, which at this present writing is not so much of a curiosity to me.

The Patent Office was another place I visited with much interest. Besides models of every known machine and a great many unknown ones, there were many historical relics of priceless value. The sword of Washington and his camp furniture, the original copy of the Declaration of Independence, the cane which supported the steps of Benjamin Franklin, the suit of clothes worn by General Jackson at the Battle of New Orleans, etc.

You must imagine an interruption of six months, a change of scene and season. I resume the "thread of my story" during the last days of 1864 once more in war-cursed Virginia. I do not know why I broke off, but this has lain quietly in my valise, waiting for me to complete it, so long that I have almost forgotten what I have already written, and if I repeat some things you will excuse me. I am writing now in my comfortable log house on the line of the Army of the James, about four miles from Richmond. The many changes that have taken place in our regiment have almost made another organization of it, and at this particular time I find myself occupying the position of regimental quartermaster. So much then for explanation, and I resume my story.

The 27th of October was the day which was to decide whether I was to return to my old position as a private soldier or assume the duties and responsibilities of an officer of colored troops, and you may well believe I awaited my examination with anxiety. My time came at last and I was admitted to the august presence of the board. An hour passed and my fate was decided, but not revealed to me. I returned to the Sanitary Commission rooms, and spent the evening in the hall, but tactics had lost their charm for me. I had been straining my powers of memory and steady thought too long, and the reaction had come. My study for the present at least was over, and I would only wait to try and learn the decision of the board before returning to the army. The next morning found me early at the examining rooms, and in receipt of the happy intelligence that it was "something," and the next morning I started for the army. The old Third Brigade was lying then a few miles south of Warrenton, and the depot was Gainesville, on the Manassas Gap railroad, where I arrived about 3 p. m., and after a rapid walk of seven miles I arrived at home just at dusk. I found McKnight and the adjutant's office in a log house, and headquarters in another, and all hands making themselves comfortable. They gave me a hearty welcome and Milo brought me a bundle of letters sufficient to occupy me till bed time, which was at an early hour, for I was tired, and marching orders for the next morning had been issued. In the morning I resumed my place as bugler, but several other things that I left when I started for Washington I did not resume. The bugler who had filled my place during my absence possessed the faculty of losing things to a rare degree. In the month of my absence he had lost my horse, my saddle, bridle, one spur, blanket, and worst of all, the mouthpiece of my bugle, a most excellent one, and impossible to be replaced. The horse had been restored to him and he had gathered apologies for most of the other things, but my bugle without the old mouthpiece was never the same bugle again.

We moved next morning at 8 o'clock, passing during the morning Auburn. Do not picture to yourself the poets' "Sweet Auburn." The village consisted of one house and some outbuildings in various stages of, I was going to say preservation, but decay is the better word. Some ladies with auburn hair were standing in the door as we passed, and the expression on their faces was suggestive of anything but joy.

The first week of November we were quietly resting in camp. I watched the regular channels of official communication pretty closely, but nothing came to me. I played chess with McKnight and Captain Hechtman, wrote a good many letters and waited for news from Washington. The army was stretched along the line of the railroad from Manassas Junction to Warrenton. The track had been relaid and trains were running to Warrenton, but rations and forage were coming up slowly and were somewhat scarce. The boys at our wagon train adopted a novel plan to increase their store of grain. There was quite a sharp upgrade in the track just opposite our train, and the cars often almost stopped in passing. One of the boys got a grappling hook and attached it to a rope fastened to a telegraph pole beside the track, and after well greasing the rails near the summit of the grade, waited for the train of grain. It came, a train of platform cars piled up with sacks of grain. It slowed on the up-grade and as the locomotive reached the greased portion the wheels slipped round and for a moment we had a stationary engine in motion. Just then the grappling hook was thrown into a sack of the bottom tier, and as an extra head of steam sent the train over the doctored track a dozen sacks of oats and corn tumbled off the rear car and disappeared among the wagons.

On the morning of the 7th of November our army was again in motion. Lee was holding the line of the Rappahannock. Most of his army was on the south side, but he had a few thousand on the north side near the railroad crossing. As day broke we struck the line of the railroad and marched towards the river, the Second and Third corps to Kelly's Ford and the Fifth and Sixth to Rappahannock Station. About 3 p. m. we met their pickets a mile or so from the river, and line of battle was formed immediately, the Sixth Corps on the right of the railroad and we on the left. On each side of the river just above the bridge the rebels had forts, and field guns on the south bank of the river commanded the approaches to the bridge. Our lines as soon as formed advanced and skirmishing began. The rebel cavalry who were in advance skedaddled for the river gloriously, without firing a gun, and we advanced as fast as the troops could march, the skirmish line driving the enemy, till we came within sight of the river. The forts and the batteries opened on us furiously, but their shells whistled harmlessly over our heads. The Eighty-third and Forty-fourth were next to the railroad, joining the left of the Sixth Corps, and when the order to charge was given, forward they went with a rush that carried everything before them. Into the fort they dashed and out of the fort went the rebs, some of them, and most of them surrendered quickly. Some jumped into the river and after getting thoroughly wet waded back towards the muzzle of a Yankee musket persuasively pointed at them. It was dark by the time this affair was over and operations ceased for the night. The Sixth Corps had the credit of capturing that fort, but I counted sixty-five prisoners taken in and about it by the Eighty-third, and our corps had about eleven hundred, and it would seem as though some troops beside the Sixth Corps had something to do with it. This was the last fight I witnessed in the Army of the Potomac, and though not very severe or bloody, it was a glorious victory. We bivouacked that night in line of battle where the fight ended, or rather in the woods just in rear of it. No fires were allowed, and the prospect bid fair for a cold supper and an uncomfortable night. It was very seldom, however, that I went to sleep without my cup of coffee, and I determined to have it that night. The rebel batteries were just across the river and the prohibition against fires was to prevent unpleasant attentions from them, so keeping the spirit of the order, but breaking the letter, I proceeded to make my coffee. I dug a hole in the ground behind a large tree, just large enough to admit my little pail, built a fire of twigs, put on my cup and then held my hat over it while it boiled. A cup of it offered to the colonel, his only chance of getting any, convinced him that no harm had been done, and I prepared for bed. My bed that night was on the most primitive principles,—a blanket spread beside a log. I tied my horse on the other side of the log, put my saddle down for a pillow, with a little bag of oats under it, and my bugle and haversack near it, and disposed myself for sleep. My horse seemed to think he had had a scanty supper, for he would not lie down, but devoted himself to finding something to eat, and at least three times he woke me and obliged me to remove from his mouth, first the oat bag, then my haversack, and lastly my bugle, the tassel of which he was mumbling in his mouth in the most innocent manner imaginable.

The morning broke at last and we looked for our neighbors over the river, but "nary reb" was to be seen. They had decamped during the night, and in excellent spirits we prepared to follow them. Instead of crossing the river there, however, we marched down to Kelly's Ford, where the Third Corps had already crossed on a pontoon bridge, crossed there and struck across the country in the direction of Culpeper. We marched about three miles from the river and halted on a magnificent farm that had been unvisited by soldiers till that time. There were miles of Virginia rail fence, and it melted away before that army of cold soldiers like snow in an April sun. We remained here only one day and then were ordered back across the river. I have very distinct recollections of this, my last march with the Army of the Potomac. We started a little before sunset and had three miles to march before reaching the river, and it began to snow just as we started. For some reason one regiment of the brigade was cut off by another brigade, and on crossing the bridge we were obliged to wait a long time for it to come up before we could bivouac. In the meantime the troops already across had gone into bivouac, and before we were ready to unsaddle every loose stick on that wide plain was burning under coffee cups or making soldiers comfortable in some other manner. We finally got settled, and two of the orderlies carried a long pole some half a mile to get something to fasten the horses to, while another and I gathered some brush to make a fire of. The fire made, and our supper cooked and eaten, we prepared for bed. Blankets were scarce and consequently in great demand, but we made quite comfortable beds on the frozen ground on that bleak plain. The wind whistled round our beds and for a time we were very cold, but it grew warmer, and in the morning we saw that nature had taken pity on us and sent us a white coverlid of an inch of snow. Very soon after the reveille we learned that we were to go into camp in the vicinity, and by noon a suitable place had been selected and the troops were in position.

Here for the first time since the commencement of the movement official documents began to come forward and I looked anxiously for something for me. It came on the evening of the 13th, an order from the Secretary of War, signed by the Assistant Adjutant General,

"Honorably discharging Private O. W. Norton, Eighty-third Pennsylvania Volunteers, from the service of the United States, to enable him to accept promotion." I was therefore a free and independent citizen after two and a half years of experience as a private soldier. The feeling was novel and exhilarating, mingled with a touch of sadness that it included a parting with the comrades with whom I had shared so many pleasant and unpleasant hours. Every one congratulated me. The feeling on the subject of colored soldiers had changed much since the winter before, when poor Joe Hatch left so abruptly to assume the duties of an officer in a colored regiment. On Saturday, the 14th, I attended my last review in the Army of the Potomac, a review of our division only, by General Bartlett, who had assumed command. I did not choose to avail myself of my discharge at once, but went on duty, feeling something like a volunteer aid, and loth to give up my old position. The review was nothing very grand or extraordinary. The principal feature that I remember was the appearance of the brigade commissary, drunk as usual, and his ridiculous efforts to maintain his position in the saddle.

On Sunday my appointment as First Lieutenant Eighth United States Colored Troops arrived and my order to report to Lieutenant Colonel Louis Wagner, at Camp William Penn, Philadelphia.

On Monday morning early I bade farewell to my comrades, turned over my dear old horse to my successor, and in company with Lieutenants Stewart and Storms, late of the Forty-fourth New York and Fourth Michigan, I started for Washington. We had a tedious time on that Orange & Alexandria, which I have mentioned before, and only reached Alexandria that night. Next morning we arrived in Washington. Being an officer, I was supposed to be able to provide for myself, and the Sanitary Commission was not an eligible locality, so I went to the National, the hotel where Buchanan and several others came near being the victims of poison, which might have been a better thing for the country than their recovery was.

Being short of funds, my first business was to settle my accounts with the United States. The balance in my favor was $138.40, which Major Taylor very promptly paid over. I then wrote my letter accepting the appointment, found a notary public and took the oath of office, and rested from my labors on a pretty good day's work. In the evening I attended Grover's Theater to see Lucille Western as Mary Tudor, the Bloody Queen. The next morning I went to see Major Foster to get permission to make a flying visit home before reporting for duty. He kindly got for me the permission from the Secretary of War. I had two weeks to visit and travel in before reporting for duty. Thinking I could make some purchases for my outfit at better advantage in New York than elsewhere, I determined to go there. I arrived before light and a cab set me down at the Astor House. After renovating the outer man a little by somniferous and sartorial appliances, I set out in search of my relatives with rather better prospects of success in the search than had Japhet in search of his father or Stephen in search of his mother, but with less certainty of my welcome in case of success, though I had very little doubt of it. I found Uncle Anthony in his office, and after promising to meet him at the close of business hours and go home with him, I returned to the hotel. To say that I enjoyed my visit there would be but a feeble expression of the fact. I had corresponded with Cousin L. as regularly as with any other person during my term of service, and felt already well acquainted, and she received me almost like a brother lost and found. Though I was anxious to meet the loved ones at home, the hours fled all too swiftly and I left them with regret. My journey to Chautauqua was "too tedious to mention," and I presume my visit with you is as fresh in your memory as in mine. You have not forgotten, I presume, the entire bewilderment of your faculties by the sight of me, and your ignorance of the whereabouts of your husband, who was innocently husking corn in the barn.

I left you in company with Uncle Rio to go west, after writing to E. to meet me at the Toledo depot and go home with me. The snow storm at that time had delayed trains so as to prevent them from making connections, and Rio and I arrived at Cleveland too late to go on, and in a painful state of impecuniosity. Uncertain as to the cost of the remainder of our journey, we dared not reduce our joint stock too much, and contented ourselves with supper and a bed, and in the morning lay in bed till it was necessary to depart without our breakfast in order to reach the cars in time.

To take leave in proper style we took occasion to rebuke the clerk for not waking us in time for breakfast before leaving, though a gong had sounded its mellifluous warning for full ten minutes in front of our chamber door.

At Toledo we stopped till the next train for E. He met us at the depot and I was at once struck by the change in his appearance. You seemed just the same, as though I had left you but yesterday, but he was much changed, and for the better. I left him a stout but uncouth boy, and found him grown and much improved in his manners and address.

We went on by the next train and had much to talk of by the way. Rio left us at some junction to go on to Milwaukee, and E. and I alighted from the cars to find Father waiting for us with his buggy. E., the sly rogue, had requested Father to meet him at the depot to take him home, and said in such a suspicious way that he would bring a friend with him that they all knew I was coming. Father was as much beside himself as a boy with a new pocket knife. Nothing would do but I must blow that bugle at every house like a fish peddler on a spree, to let the neighbors know that his son had come. And the old bugle rang out its war peals for almost the last time on that night. The whole house was up and anxiously waiting my coming, and such a greeting was worth all the service I had seen.

My stay at home was brief, only two days, but Father had determined that his son should be seen, and he had invited all the young people of his parish to meet him. They came, a house full, and some pretty girls among them, girls I would be glad to know, but I could only see them once, and I confess it was something of a bore, but I suppose it pleased the father and I ought to be satisfied. In looking back at my visit now, the most prominent unpleasant feature was my being made a lion of everywhere because I was a soldier. It may be part of the sacrifice for my country, and if so I accept it. Some instances were very amusing to me. At Jamestown, where I was compelled to stop part of the day, a little boy watched me passing up the walk and seeing me enter a hotel, he ran round the corner shouting, "Jake, O Jakey, come quick, here's a soldier," and presently a troop of boys came filing into the room and ranged themselves round the wall for a good look, and stood with their hands in their pockets and open mouths, getting what was evidently as good as a circus, and all without the customary twenty-five cents. One more bold than the rest, after walking all round me several times, seemed determined to know if I talked like a common man, and cautiously approaching me stammered out, "How d'ye do?" My reply, "I'm well, what's the state of your physical organization?" seemed to stun him, for after looking at me in silent wonder a few moments longer the whole party decamped.

But I am wandering from my story. I arrived in Philadelphia on my way to my new regiment and new duties on the night of the 6th of December, having come via Pittsburgh and Harrisburg. I stopped at the St. Lawrence Hotel, and I afterwards became quite attached to it as my home in town, but I left early in the morning, having ascertained that "Camp William Penn" was a few miles out of the city on the North Pennsylvania railroad. On the way up I fell in with some officers of the regiment, strangers then, but now dear friends and comrades, and with them I readily found my place of destination, and reported myself, per order, to Lieutenant Colonel Louis Wagner, who at once ordered me to report for duty to Colonel Fribley of the Eighth. As I came near the headquarters of the Eighth I saw a group of officers drilling, and among them a familiar face, Lieutenant Colonel Bartram, whom I had known as the commander of the Seventeenth New York, in the old Third Brigade, and who, I was much pleased to learn, was now to be my lieutenant colonel. He introduced me to the officers and I was at home as much as any of them. I can scarcely realize my feelings at my first sight of colored soldiers. It was all new to me. Everywhere dusky faces were flitting about and they looked so black. The little shelter tents were alive with negroes in army blue. They could not be called soldiers, but they were the raw material, and the great question of the hour was, can this material be worked up to the condition of efficient soldiery. We who had it to work were enthusiastic in our faith as to its success, but yet it was all theory. A year of trial has proved the soundness of our belief, and to-day after a year's experience I prefer, infinitely almost, black soldiers to white. I had some doubts at first, but they were soon swept away, and to-day the practicability of employing the negro race as soldiers is no longer an experiment but a fact, and a fact recognized by the very men who most vehemently opposed the experiment.

I was assigned at once to the command of a company. I had not expected this and the situation was embarrassing. I who had never had command of so much as a corporal's guard stepped at once to all the care and responsibility of commanding eighty men. I shrank from it, but there was nothing for me but to meet the responsibility. My own voice sounded to me in giving commands like a stranger's, and everything was new and strange. My men looked as much alike as a flock of sheep and I could only distinguish them by their size. This wore off by degrees, and in two weeks I had things in pretty good running order, and then the captain arrived. I liked him from the moment I first saw him, and I thought, there is just the man to put over two such boys as Thompson and myself. All my after intercourse with him but strengthened my first impressions. Always true, kindly, courteous and dignified, he was one of nature's noblemen, and though I was not long in learning to love and respect him, it was not till I lost him that I learned or realized how much I had lost. He died for his country.

Christmas is the negro's holiday, and Christmas at Camp

William Penn was a great day. The ladies of Philadelphia and the vicinity were very much interested in our camp, and determined to give the men a Christmas dinner, and they did it in excellent style. There was an abundance of the good things and every one was filled, and in return for their kindness the colonel determined to give them a sight of something as near war as peace could be, and after dinner we had a sham battle. There were skirmishers and lines of battle, volleys of musketry and furious charges. One line with their clothes wrong side out answered very well for rebels, and of course they were badly beaten and all taken prisoners. The ladies shrieked at the volleys of musketry and professed themselves much interested in the performance, though one of them remarked to me afterwards it was almost too dreadful to be very pleasant. I had been to the city quite often during the two weeks. It was only twenty minutes' ride and I began to feel less of a stranger then, and in the evening I went down with a party of the officers, spent a pleasant evening at the theater, and next day on coming back to camp I learned that I was to be detailed as quartermaster of a recruiting party that was to be sent to make a tour through the state of Delaware. We did not get off till the last day of the year. Went down to the city on the cars and thence by steamer to Wilmington. I have written pretty full accounts of our experience there in my diary for 1864 and with the close of 1863 I will end my story. It is not a very interesting one, or would not be to others, but you, dear sister, have always been interested in any thing connected with me, and I have written this for you. It is not the record of great deeds, but the simple story of a common soldier, one who has looked as much as possible on the sunny side of life, and who, remembering your constant interest and love for him, will always be

Your affectionate brother,

OLIVER.

APPENDIX

THE ESCUTCHEON illustrated on the opposite page bears the following inscription:

ENTERED SERVICE AS PRIVATE 83RD PENNA., VOL. INFY "ERIE REGIMENT" FOR 3 MONTHS' SERVICE, APRIL 21, 1861 REGT. ORGANIZED AT CAMP WAYNE, ERIE, PA., AND MUSTERED INTO U. S. SERVICE APRIL 28, 1861. MOVED TO CAMP WILKINS, NEAR PITTSBURGH, PA., AND DUTY THERE TILL JUNE. MOVED TO CAMP WRIGHT AND DUTY THERE TILL JULY MUSTERED OUT AT ERIE, PA., JULY 25, 1861. RE-ENTERED SERVICE AS PRIVATE 83RD PENNA., VOL. INFY., FOR 3 YEARS' SERVICE AUG. 28, 1861 REGT MUSTERED IN SEPT. 8, 1861, ORDERED TO WASHINGTON, D. C., SEPT. 10. CAMP AT MERIDIAN HILL TILL OCTOBER 1. ATTACHED TO BUTTERFIELD'S BRIG., FITZ JOHN PORTER'S DIV., ARMY OF THE POTOMAC, OCT. 1861, TO MARCH, 1862; TO 3D BRIG., 1ST DIV., 3D CORPS, ARMY OF THE POTOMAC, TILL MAY, 1862; TO 2D BRIG., 1ST DIV., 5TH CORPS, TILL JUNE; TO 3D BRIG., 1ST DIV., 5TH CORPS, TILL NOV., 1863

SERVICE.

DUTY IN THE DEFENSES OF WASHINGTON, D. C., SEPT., 1861-MARCH 1862. ADVANCE ON MANASSAS, VA., MARCH 10-15, 1862. MOVED TO HAMPTON, VA., MARCH 22. PENINSULA CAMPAIGN MARCH TO AUG RECONN TO BIG BETHEL MARCH 30. ACTION AT HOWARD'S MILLS APRIL 4. SIEGE OF YORKTOWN, APRIL 5-MAY 4. RECONN UP THE PAMUNKEY MAY 10. BATTLE OF HANOVER C. H., MAY 27 SEVEN DAYS BEFORE RICHMOND, JUNE 26-JULY 1 MECHANICSVILLE, JUNE 26. GAINES' MILLS, JUNE 27 SLIGHTLY WOUNDED. PEACH ORCHARD AND SAVAGE STATION, JUNE 29. TURKEY BEND AND GLENDALE, JUNE 30. MALVERN HILL, JULY 1 DUTY AT HARRISON'S LANDING TILL AUG. 16. ACTION AT GOGGINS POINT, AUG. 1 MOVEMENT FROM HARRISON'S LANDING TO FORTRESS MONROE AND CENTERVILLE, AUG. 16-28. BATTLE OF GROVETON, AUG. 29. BULL RUN, AUG. 30. ANTIETAM, MD., SEPT 16-17. WILLIAMSPORT, SEPT 19-20. SHEPHERDSTOWN, SEPT. 20. BATTLE OF FREDERICKSBURG, VA., DEC. 11-15. "MUD MARCH," JAN'Y 20-24, 1863. CHANCELLORSVILLE, CAMP'N APRIL 27-MAY 6. BATTLE OF CHANCELLORSVILLE, MAY 1-5. ALDIE, JUNE 20. MIDDLEBURG, JUNE 21. UPPERVILLE, JUNE 22. BATTLE OF GETTYSBURG, PA., JULY 1-3. JONES' CROSS ROADS, JULY 10-11 FUNKSTOWN, MD., JULY 14. MANASSAS GAP, VA., JULY 23. RECONN TO RACCOON FORD, OCT 10. BRANDY STATION, OCT BRISTOW STATION, OCT 14. KELLY'S FORD, NOV. 7. DISCHARGED NOV. 10, 1863. TO ACCEPT PROMOTION. APPOINTED 1ST LIEUTENANT 8TH U. S. COLORED INFANTRY, TO DATE FROM NOV. 5, 1863. ORGANIZING REGT. AND DUTY AT CAMP WM. PENN, PHILA., PA., TILL JAN'Y, 1864. ORDERED TO HILTON HEAD, SOUTH CAROLINA, JAN. 16. ATTACHED TO DIST. OF HILTON HEAD, 10TH CORPS, DEPT. OF THE SOUTH, JAN., 1864; TO HAWLEY'S BRIG., SEYMOUR'S DIV. DIST, OF FLORIDA, 10TH CORPS, TO APRIL; TO DIST OF FLA., DEPT. SOUTH, TO AUG.; TO 1ST BRIG., 3D DIV., 10TH CORPS, ARMY JAMES, TO OCT. 2ND BRIG., 3D DIV., 10TH CORPS, TO DEC., 2ND BRIG., 2ND DIV., 25TH CORPS, DEPT. OF VA., AND DEPT. OF TEXAS, TO NOV., 1865. SERVICE: EXP. TO FLA., FEB. 5-25. CAPTURE OF FINNEGAN'S DEPOT, TALLAHATCHIE R. R., FEB. 9. BATTLE OF OLUSTEE, FEB. 20 (IN COMMAND OF CO. AND SLIGHTLY WOUNDED). MOVED TO YELLOW BLUFF, APRIL 16, AND DUTY THERE TILL AUG. ORDERED TO VIRGINIA AUG. 4. SIEGE OF PETERSBURG AND RICHMOND, VA., AUG., 1864, TO APRIL, 1865. BATTLE OF DEEP BOTTOM, AUG. 12. NEWMARKET HEIGHTS, SEPT. 28-29. CHAPIN'S FARM, SEPT. 29-30. DARBYTOWN ROAD, OCT. 13. FAIROAKS, OCT. 27-28. OPERATIONS AGAINST RICHMOND NORTH OF JAMES RIVER TILL MARCH, 1865. REGTL. QUARTERMASTER, NOV., 1864-MAY, 1865. FALL OF RICHMOND, APR. 3. ORDERED TO TEXAS, MAY 26. DUTY AT RINGGOLD BARRACKS, TEXAS, TILL OCT. DETACHED AS POST QUARTERMASTER AT RINGGOLD BARRACKS, ALSO ACTING QUARTERMASTER, 2D DIV., 25TH CORPS, TILL OCT. MUSTERED OUT NOV. 10, 1865.

Note.—The above statement of the military services of the author was furnished by the Adjutant General of the Army from records on file in the War Department. It is substantially correct, but contains two errors. The statement that he was present with his regiment in the engagements at Raccoon Ford, Brandy Station and Bristow Station in October, 1863, and at Newmarket Heights and Chapin's Farm, Virginia, September 28, 29 and 30, 1864, is probably occasioned by the fact that his absence attending the Examining Board in Washington in October, 1863, and in Chesapeake Hospital in September, 1864, was not noted on the muster rolls.

MILITARY SOCIETIES.

The author of the preceding letters counts among the greatest pleasures which he has enjoyed during the years that have passed since the close of the civil war, the privilege of membership in patriotic societies of survivors of the war. Association with men who served the country in its time of peril keeps alive the spirit which actuated these men in their younger days.

In that great society of veterans, the Grand Army of the Republic, his name is on the roll of the George H. Thomas Post, No. 5.

He is a member of the Western Society of the Army of the Potomac, an organization composed of men residing in the west, who served in that army.

In April, 1882, he was elected a Companion of the Military Order of the Loyal Legion of the United States, an organization of commissioned officers of the army and navy who served in defense of the Union during the war of the rebellion. Insignia No. 2321.

In May, 1902, the Illinois Commandery of the Loyal Legion conferred upon him the great honor of electing him its Commander.

By virtue of this election he was made, according to the constitution of the Order, a Life Member of the Commandery-in-Chief of the Military Order of the Loyal Legion of the United States.

The members of these societies take a just pride in the buttons and badges indicating their membership, because the right to wear them cannot be obtained by purchase with money, by political influence or favoritism, by gift of monarch, nor by anything except actual service to the country in war, or inheritance from men who rendered such service.

BATTLES AND SKIRMISHES

IN WHICH O. W. NORTON TOOK PART WITH HIS COMMAND, AS SHOWN BY OFFICIAL RECORDS, WAR DEPARTMENT.

Skirmish at Howard's Mill, Va............April 4, 1862
Siege of Yorktown, Va...........April 5 to May 4, 1862
Hanover Court House, Va...............May 27, 1862
Mechanicsville, Va.....................June 26, 1862
Gaines' Mill, Va.......................June 27, 1862
Savage Station, Va.....................June 29, 1862
White Oak Swamp, Va...................June 30, 1862
Glendale, Va..........................June 30, 1862
Malvern Hill, Va.......................July 1, 1862
Bombardment of Harrison's Landing, Va....July 31, 1862
Groveton, Va..........................August 29, 1862
Second Bull Run, Va...................August 30, 1862
Antietam, Md.......................September 17, 1862
Skirmish at Williamsport, Md........September 19, 1862
Shepherdstown Ford, Md............September 20, 1862
Fredericksburg, Va............December 11 to 15, 1862
Chancellorsville, Va............April 30 to May 4, 1863
Middleburg and Goose Creek, Va...........June 21, 1863
Gettysburg, Penn....................July 2 and 3, 1863
Jones Cross Roads, Md.............July 10 and 11, 1863
Skirmish at Funkstown, Md................July 14, 1863
Skirmish at Manassas Gap, Va.............July 23, 1863
Rappahannock Station, Va.............November 7, 1863
Olustee, Fla........................February 20, 1864
Right of Line near Petersburg, Va.......August 12, 1864
Darbytown Road, Va..................October 13, 1864

LETTER FROM GEN. JAMES C. RICE.

LATE COLONEL FORTY-FOURTH NEW YORK VOLUNTEERS

SUCCESSOR TO COLONEL STRONG VINCENT, IN COMMAND OF THE THIRD BRIGADE.

Army of the Potomac,
Hd. Qrs. 2d Brig., 1st Div., 1st Corps,
Centerville, Va., Oct. 17, 1863.

Major General Casey:

General,

It gives me great pleasure to commend to your most favorable notice, the bearer of this, O. W. Norton, who under my command has proved himself a brave and faithful soldier.

I am, General,
Your most obedient servant,
J. C. RICE,
Brig. Genl. Comdg. 2d Brig.

LETTER FROM CAPTAIN HECHTMAN.

Camp 83d Regmt., Penn. Vols.,
Near Culpeper, Va.,
September 28, 1863.

C. W. Foster, A. A. G.,
    Chief of Colored Bureau.
General,

    Private Oliver W. Norton of my Company, being permitted to appear before the Board of Examination of which Major General Silas Casey is President, it gives me pleasure to make the following statement: He enlisted in my Company August 28, 1861, and since that time has performed his duty honestly and faithfully in every respect, never having been excused from duty a day from any cause whatever. His moral character is exemplary and I am confident that he would do his duty in a more responsible position as well as he has long done it as a Private.

        I have the honor to be,
          Very respectfully,
            Your most obedient servant,
              JOHN HECHTMAN,
    Capt. Commdg. Co. K., 83d Rgmt. Penn. Vols.

ORDER FROM WAR DEPARTMENT HONORABLY DISCHARGING

O. W. NORTON FROM EIGHTY-THIRD PENNSYLVANIA VOLUNTEERS, TO ENABLE HIM TO ACCEPT COMMISSION.

WAR DEPARTMENT,
Adjutant General's Office,
Washington, Nov. 10, 1863.

SPECIAL ORDERS. No. 499.

(Extract.)

....

2. The following named enlisted men are honorably discharged the service of the United States, to enable them to accept appointment in the U. S. Colored Troops:

Private O. W. Norton, Company —, Eighty-third Pennsylvania Volunteers.

....

By order of the Secretary of War:

E. D. TOWNSEND,
Assistant Adjutant General.

Official:
Sam. D. Breck,
Assistant Adjutant General.

Respectfully referred to the Commanding Officer Co. K.
By order of O. S. Woodward, Capt. Cmdg.
M. G. Corey, Lt. & Act. Adjt.

This document bears the following endorsements:

Nov. 17, 1863. $100. U. S. Bounty paid.
D. Taylor, P. M. U. S. A.

Paid in full,
Nov. 17, 1863.
D. Taylor, Paymaster, U. S. A.

HONORABLE DISCHARGE

FROM THE

EIGHTY-THIRD REGIMENT, PENNSYLVANIA VOLUNTEERS.

TO ALL WHOM IT MAY CONCERN:

KNOW YE, That OLIVER W. NORTON, a Private of Captain JOHN HECHTMAN'S Company (K), 83rd Regiment of Pennsylvania Volunteers, who was enrolled on the Twenty-Eighth day of August, one thousand eight hundred and Sixty-One, to serve Three years or during the war, is hereby DISCHARGED from the service of the United States, this Tenth day of November, 1863, at Camp near Kelly's Ford, Va., by reason of SPECIAL ORDER No. 499, WAR DEPARTMENT.

(No objection to his being re-enlisted is known to exist.)

Said Private OLIVER W. NORTON was born in Alleghany County, in the State of New York, is Twenty-Three years of age, Five feet eight inches high, fair complexion, blue eyes, brown hair, and by occupation, when enrolled, a Teacher.

GIVEN at Camp near Kelly's Ford, this Twenty-third day of November, 1863.

WM. H. LAMONT, Major
Commanding the Reg't.

(A. G. O. No. 99.)

COMMISSION

FROM

PRESIDENT ABRAHAM LINCOLN

AS FIRST LIEUTENANT EIGHTH UNITED STATES COLORED TROOPS.

WAR DEPARTMENT.

Washington, Nov. 6, 1863.

Sir:

You are hereby informed that the President of the United States has appointed you FIRST LIEUTENANT in the Eighth Regiment, U. S. COLORED TROOPS, in the service of the United States, to rank as such from the Fifth day of November, one thousand eight hundred and sixty-three.

Immediately on receipt hereof, please to communicate to this Department, through the ADJUTANT GENERAL of the Army, your acceptance or non-acceptance; and with your letter of acceptance, return the OATH herewith enclosed, properly filled up, SUBSCRIBED and ATTESTED, and report your Age, Birthplace, and the State of which you were a permanent resident.

You will report for duty in person to Lieutenant Colonel Wagner, Comdg. Camp Wm. Penn, Philadelphia, Pa.

EDWIN M. STANTON.
Secretary of War.

1st Lieut. O. W. Norton,
8th Reg't U. S. Colored Troops.

This Commission bears the following Endorsement:

Mustered by D. M. W. Brooke,
   1st Lt. 2d U. S. Infy., Asst. Must. Officer.
     Dec. 21, 1863.

APPOINTMENT

AS

REGIMENTAL QUARTERMASTER,

EIGHTH UNITED STATES COLORED TROOPS.

Head Quarters 8th U. S. C. T.,
Ringgold Barracks, Texas,
August 30, 1865.

General Orders,
No. 18.

1st Lieutenant OLIVER W. NORTON, 8th U. S. Colored Troops, is hereby appointed Regimental Quartermaster, 8th U. S. Colored Troops.

He will be obeyed and respected accordingly.

By order of

Col. Sam'l C. Armstrong.
James L. Decker,
1st Lieut. and Adjutant
8th U. S. Colored Troops.

HONORABLE DISCHARGE

FROM THE

EIGHTH REGIMENT UNITED STATES COLORED TROOPS.

TO ALL WHOM IT MAY CONCERN:

KNOW YE, That OLIVER W. NORTON, a 1st Lieut. and R. Q. M., 8th Regiment of United States Colored Infantry, who was enrolled on the Fifth (5th) day of November, one thousand eight hundred and Sixty-three (1863), to serve Three years, or during the war, is hereby DISCHARGED from the service of the United States, this Tenth day of November, 1865, at Brownsville, Texas, by reason of Orders from War Dept., dated Sept. 8th. 1865.

(No objection to his being re-enlisted is known to exist.)

Said OLIVER W. NORTON was born in Angelica, All'y Co., in the State of New York, is 26 years of age, 5 feet, 10 inches high, light complexion, dark eyes, dark hair, and by occupation when appointed, a Soldier.

GIVEN at Brownsville, Texas, this Tenth day of November, 1865.

J. E. LOCKWOOD,
Capt. 116th U. S. C. T. and
A. C. M. 2d Div. 25th A. C.
Mustering Officer.

SAML. C. ARMSTRONG,
Col. 8th U. S. C. T.
Comd'g Regiment.

This document bears the following endorsement:

Paid in full at Philadelphia, December 10, 1865, $550.59.
DAVID TAGGART,
Paymaster U. S. A.

PAPER READ BY O. W. NORTON BEFORE A SOCIAL CLUB IN CHICAGO IN 1875.

Many histories and records relating to our late war have been written, and many more will yet be written, histories that go over the whole ground from the writer's standpoint, histories from the Union side and from the Confederate, histories of armies, of divisions, of regiments, and even of companies, biographies of officers and privates, histories of the volunteers who went from certain towns, histories of hospitals and staff departments—but far the most interesting to the actors and to their friends is the unwritten history which might be made from the experience of the men who think their individual deeds and thoughts not worth the writing, but to whom those army years make up a large part of their real lives.

Army life was not all battle, wounds and death, although the soldier is accustomed in recalling it to think more of such incidents perhaps, than any other. Strange coincidences came now and then to the lives of many. The story of a certain knapsack would be interesting if we knew it all—but we know only the beginning and the end, and some confederate soldier might perhaps supply the missing link if he knew what became of his captured knapsack. Before telling what we do know of it, let me speak of one curious experience in battle which those who participated in probably did not meet again, though they became veterans, and this was their first great battle. At the battle of Gaines' Mill, the second of the seven days battles on the Peninsula in Virginia, the left of the Union army rested just where the rolling broken country terminated in a level plain, perhaps one-third of a mile wide, reaching to the Chickahominy. The creek on which the mill was situated here ran through a deep wooded gully with very steep sides, the fields on either side being cleared and cultivated as near the bank as they could be plowed. Early in the morning position was taken here. One line was placed in the bottom of the gully, and the second on the bank with the gully as a ditch in its front, and instructions given to build a breastwork as rapidly as possible and hold the place at all hazards. The men took off their knapsacks, each company's being placed in a pile by themselves, and soon were fortified in what they felt sure was an impregnable position. The enemy might succeed in reaching the bank of the gully, but only to find a fresh and eager line of rifles waiting for their appearance. In the afternoon they made three separate attempts to drive back our line, and here occurred that singular incident. The line in the gully could see nothing, but were between two fires. Shells and bullets whistled and screamed among the trees overhead, but could not harm them except as some were hurt by falling branches. The roar and din were fearful, but the men below stood steadily with rifles aimed at the top of the bank, waiting for the enemy. Three times they appeared and instantly wavered and fell back as they met the fire of that lower line. Suddenly, however, there was strange excitement. Hurried orders to face to the rear—bullets coming from that direction where our friends had been but shortly before. Our line had been broken farther up the stream, and the enemy had doubled round on us until that regiment in the gully was nearly bagged. There was no escape but the mouth of the bag, now rapidly closing. The men departed hastily from that place, not waiting for further orders, and so that knapsack came to be turned over to Stonewall Jackson. The Eighty-third Pennsylvania had a peculiar knapsack, part of an outfit for a regiment, sent over from France early in the war, and except the regiment thus furnished there were no others like it in the army. It was made of calf skin tanned with the hair on. The time passed on. McClellan was removed from command, reinstated and again removed. Burnside had given way to Hooker when the movement that culminated in the battle of Chancellorsville was begun. The

Confederate army, intrenched on the heights behind Fredericksburg, had its outposts encamped several miles north on the Rappahannock. When the movement began, the regiment that had lost its knapsacks at Gaines' Mill was the first to cross the river above the Confederate outposts, and came marching down on them in a way that gave them little time to strike tents and prepare to move. They fell back hastily to the main army. Marching steadily on, our skirmish line passed through their camp. They found it necessary to examine the tents as they came to them. As one of the Eighty-third Pennsylvania entered a tent, the first object that met his eyes was a hairy knapsack lying on the Confederate's apology for a bed. He seized it with a shout, turned back the flap, and neatly lettered on the inside was his own name, company and regiment, and better than all, as soon as he could examine the contents, he found among some Confederate clothing that he did not care to keep, a little packet of letters addressed to himself and a photograph of the girl he left behind him. The knapsack, the letters and the pictures are all carefully preserved by a family in western Pennsylvania, and the soldier who found it says he always had an idea he should get that knapsack back from Stonewall Jackson, but did not expect it just in that way.

The battle of Chancellorsville was fought almost wholly in the woods called the Wilderness, and was a skirmishing, desultory fight for most of the time. The night before the main battle was one of wonderful beauty in the woods. The men lay on their arms ready for action at a moment's notice. The full moon shone calmly on the scene, and never was a greater contrast, perhaps, between nature and man than was developed that night. At times the rattle of musketry would cease, then one by one, feebly at first but gaining courage from each other, the whippoorwills would begin their song. The woods were full of them, and the night was full of their mournful music. Suddenly the sharp rattle of musketry would be heard in the distance, and rolling along the line, and the frightened birds would cease their singing at once. So they alternated all night, and many of those who were in the Wilderness will recall this as one of the strangest and saddest nights in their army experience.

During McClellan's command the Army of the Potomac was strictly disciplined in the matter of respecting private property. If pigs or chickens came into camp it must be by purchase or clandestinely. Lee's army in its inroad into Pennsylvania were not so particular. They took everything they found that would be of use to them, and made general havoc of the farms along their road. When they were driven back to Virginia and our army followed them, the impression seemed to be general that such orders would not be so strictly enforced when we reached the enemy's territory again. Crossing the Potomac at Harper's Ferry, the first night in Virginia was spent in Loudon County, a few miles south of the Ferry. The Fifth Corps bivouacked on a farm that apparently had been little injured by the war, fences and buildings in good condition. The arms were quickly stacked and preparations for the night began. The fences disappeared like dew before the morning sun. The great straw stacks by the barn were quickly distributed through the camp. The farmer watched these proceedings with looks of dismay, but his language was quite in contrast. He made no protest against anything, but was constantly talking to the men after this fashion: "You-uns are the nicest lot of men I ever saw. Why, they don't touch nothin'. When our fo'ces was here they took everything the people had, but you-uns don't touch nothin'." The straw trailing across the fields rather contradicted his statements, but he persisted in them, shouting now and then to his wife and daughters, who were catching all the turkeys and chickens and putting them into the smoke house. Some one asked him after one of his complimentary speeches if he always shut up his poultry in that way. He was a little disconcerted at first, but replied quickly, "Oh, yes, I always have to shut them up. They wander about so nights." They did wander that night and the old man saw them no more.

On that terrible Saturday night succeeding the battle of Fredericksburg, one brigade of the Fifth Corps had succeeded in forcing their way just after dark to a position within eighty or one hundred yards of the Confederate forts, and there they spent the night. When morning broke they found themselves cut off from the rest of the army which had retired to the town, and protected from the fire of the enemy only by a low rise of ground which sheltered them only when they lay flat upon the ground. The enemy had a line of sharpshooters who busied themselves in firing at every man who showed himself, and they were so near it was dangerous to lift a head above the crest. During the morning detachments of the enemy were seen moving to the left, evidently with the intention of cutting off the brigade and taking them prisoners. The general in command wished to send a message to the division commander to ask for assistance, but hesitated to ask a staff officer to go on a mission that seemed certain death. The only route to the town was over an open plain in full range of all the enemy's sharpshooters, and no one had crossed it alive since morning. A private soldier volunteered to go, and taking the message written on the back of an envelope, and saying a few words of farewell to one of his comrades, with a message for home, he buttoned his coat round him and started. A low shed which stood beside the road protected him from the nearest sharpshooters for a few rods. No grass grew under his feet as he ran. The rifles cracked rapidly and the bullets whistled by him, tearing up the ground by his feet, one passed through his sleeve, another through his cap, when suddenly he fell to the ground, rolled over and was still. His comrades had been anxiously watching him and saw him fall with a thrill of sorrow. The enemy sent up a taunting cheer which seemed to say, "Send another one," but few would care to run the gauntlet with his fate before them, but as they sorrowfully looked where he lay, all at once he sprang to his feet and was tearing over the plain at a speed that took him out of range before the sharpshooters recovered from their astonishment. He had not been hurt at all. His fall was a ruse to stop the firing, which was coming uncomfortably near. He delivered his message and received the answer, and now came the hardest part of his duty. It had been comparatively easy to run down hill, when every step took him farther from danger. Now he must run into it. A part of the way back he followed a railroad cut which shortened the space he must run under fire, but the end of his route was still across the open plain, and unprotected by the shed which had shielded him when he started. But the kind Providence that had protected him before devised help again. One regiment of the brigade was the Twentieth Maine, a new regiment just in the field, and but little drilled. An enthusiastic lieutenant thought it a good time to exercise his men in the manual, and as the soldier peered carefully over the bank of the railroad cut, to reconnoitre the situation, he heard the Maine lieutenant command: "Fire by rank. Rear rank, at the brick house, Aim, Fire! Front rank, at the stone wall, Aim, Fire!" The sharpshooters heard him, too, and during that little exercise kept themselves out of sight. The soldier improved the opportunity and was soon safe behind the knoll with his comrades.

Colonel Strong Vincent commanded this brigade for some time and proved himself one of the most gallant soldiers in the army. When Lee's army started down the Shenandoah on the campaign that ended with Gettysburg, the Union army moved northward, keeping between him and Washington. General J. E. B. Stuart's cavalry moved on his flank on the east side of the mountains and, crossing the Loudon valley, hovered round the flank of our army. Pleasanton's cavalry had been sent to drive them back and had forced them back into the Loudon valley, but could make no headway then on account of the nature of the country, and asked that a brigade of infantry be detailed to assist them. Vincent's brigade was sent, and early in the morning of the twenty-first of June they marched out of the little village of Aldie to the crest of the hill west of the town of Middlebury. The scene that met their eyes was a beautiful one. The Loudon valley at that time had not been disturbed by either army and was the garden spot of Virginia, in all the glory of early summer. A broad turnpike ran directly west across the valley to Ashby's Gap in the Blue Ridge. On either side were fertile farms and good buildings, and all the fences both along the road and at right angles with it were stone walls, and this was the feature that stopped our cavalry. The country was slightly rolling. The enemy had posted a battery of flying artillery on the top of the opposite hill and had a line of dismounted cavalry behind a wall at the foot of the hill between us, and with the main body of their cavalry out of sight behind the hill they waited our coming. Vincent surveyed the scene a moment, then ordered one of his regiments to march to the left and flank this line of skirmishers. This was done as rapidly as possible, and as the infantry came down on them the cavalry had a sudden call to see about their horses and hurried over the hill. Four times this maneuver was repeated. Our cavalry moved up as soon as the infantry dislodged the enemy's skirmishers, but took no part in the action. The infantry were getting tired by their long and exciting march, when they came out on the top of a hill overlooking a valley through which flowed a stream apparently of little depth, although, being fringed by a dense growth of alders, but little could be seen of it. The enemy had retreated beyond this stream, and had placed a heavy pole diagonally across the bridge to prevent our cavalry making a charge. Our skirmishers advanced to the stream, but finding it too deep to ford without wetting their ammunition, had halted, and contented themselves with keeping a desultory firing at such of the enemy as showed themselves. Pleasanton sent an aid to Vincent to say that if he would take that bridge and remove the pole the cavalry would make a charge. Vincent, who was a little nettled that the cavalry had left him to do all the work so far, replied shortly, "Bring on your cavalry, the bridge will be ready." He was a gallant horseman himself and rode a magnificent horse. Sending word to the skirmishers to keep up a lively fire, then starting at full speed for the bridge, drawing his sword and flashing it in the sun, he shouted at the top of his voice and so as to be plainly heard by the enemy, "There they go, boys! Now give them ——!" Well, no matter what he said. Some of our bravest and best were not always particular about their language in such exciting times. The enemy heard it and once more took to their heels. Their officers ran hither and thither trying to stop them, but it was no use. The pole was off the bridge in a trice. The cavalry came thundering down the road and went over the hill with a whoop and cheer that frightened the rebels so that they did not stop until they reached the plain at the foot of Ashby's Gap, and our brigade returned to join the main body of the army.

Both armies moved rapidly northward, and in a few days had crossed Maryland and were in Pennsylvania. Vincent's brigade passed through the town of Hanover at midnight of the 30th of June, on the way to Gettysburg. For more than four weeks they had been on the march, never sleeping twice in the same place. All their experience so far had been in the enemy's country, but now they were among friends. The whole country was aroused. The Union flag was displayed at every house. Groups of girls were on every porch along the route, handkerchiefs waved, the town rang with their patriotic songs, and the men cheered and sang as they marched along, weary with long marches, but buoyant and confident of victory. As the moon rose above the trees, the old battle flag of the Eighty-third Pennsylvania, the leading regiment of the brigade, was unfurled and glistened in the moonlight above the marching men. Vincent removed his hat as he rode behind it, and said to his adjutant who rode by his side, "What death more glorious could any man desire than to die on the soil of old Pennsylvania fighting for that flag?" and the next day he met that glorious death on the field of Gettysburg.

TWO BUGLE CALLS.

O. W. NORTON.

The bugle was much used in the army. The carrying quality of its tones made it possible to convey commands to a great distance in times of quiet, and even in the roar of battle its shrill notes could be distinctly heard. The reveille which waked the soldier from his slumber in camp or bivouac and the order to put out the lights at night were sounded on the bugle. There were calls to breakfast, dinner and supper. Men in camp unfit for duty were summoned to the surgeon's tent by the sick call. The skirmish line in battle was ordered to deploy, to advance, to commence firing, to lie down, to cease firing, to retreat, to rally on the reserve, and to execute many other movements by various calls on the bugle. There were calls for sergeants to report to the adjutant, for officers to report to the colonel, for companies to form for roll-call, for regiments to form line of battle on the colors, to advance in line of battle and to retreat, to change direction in marching, to strike tents and prepare to march, and many others. No cavalryman will ever forget the stirring call of "Boots and Saddles."

When General McClellan was organizing the Army of the Potomac near Washington in the autumn of 1861, the camps along the line were very near together, and the constant drilling, to the sound of the bugle, of the various regiments and brigades often caused confusion in understanding orders. General Daniel Butterfield, who organized a brigade at this time, known at first as "Butterfield's Brigade," saw at an early date the necessity of doing something to prevent this confusion. Butterfield had a genius for military matters, which later secured for him high rank in the Army of the Potomac and in the western armies. He could himself sound the bugle calls when occasion required. Shortly after he assumed command of the brigade, he composed, and taught the writer, then serving as his brigade bugler, a bugle call for his brigade. This consisted of three long notes on one key, and a catch repeated. It was sounded twice before each call for any operation or movement, and indicated to the officers and men that the call to follow was for the troops of this brigade. General Butterfield also prepared different calls for the regimental bugler of each regiment in his brigade. The men were accustomed to sing various words to the accompaniment of the bugle calls when they heard them. Most of these words were explanatory of the meaning of the call, or were jocose comments on the command. When the reveille was sounded men could be heard through the camps singing:

"I can't wake 'em up, I can't wake 'em up, I can't wake 'em up in the morning,
I can't wake 'em up, I can't wake 'em up, I can't wake 'em up at all.
The corporal's worse than the private, the sergeant's worse than the corporal,
The lieutenant's worse than the sergeant and the captain's worst of all.
I can't wake 'em up, I can't wake 'em up, I can't wake 'em up in the morning,
I can't wake 'em up, I can't wake 'em up, I can't wake 'em up at all."

These words exactly fitted the notes of the bugle. When the sick call sounded, the men sang, "All ye sick men, all ye sick men, get your calomel, get your calomel, get your calomel, get your calomel." Sometimes they sang, "Doctor Jones says, Doctor Jones says, come and get your quinine, quinine, quinine, come and get your quinine, qui-i-ni-i-ine."

When, on the march, the general halted his brigade intending to give the men an opportunity for a few moment's rest, the brigade call was sounded, then the call to halt, then a most welcome call of three short notes repeated, to which the great chorus responded along the line, "All lie down, all lie down." When the march was to be resumed the brigade call was again sounded, followed by the less welcome call, "Attention!" To this the men responded in words well suited to the music:

"Fall in ye poor devils as fast as ye can,
And when ye get tired I'll rest you again."

Words were set to many other calls, but one which lasted from Arlington Heights to Appomattox, was the interpretation of the brigade call. To this the men sang:

"Dan, Dan, Dan Butterfield, Butterfield,
Dan, Dan, Dan Butterfield, Butterfield."

The general used to say that sometimes in trying circumstances when the brigade was called up from a too short rest, he thought he could distinguish the words, "Damn, Damn, Damn Butterfield." This is not very probable. The men of that old brigade so much admired their gallant leader that nothing he could do would cause them to use such disrespectful language.

The general calls were used throughout the Union army. The music of the calls was printed in the Tactics where they could be studied and learned by officers whose duty it was to understand them and repeat in words to the men under their command the orders indicated by the bugle. This brigade call was used only by Butterfield's brigade and was not printed in the Tactics.

BUTTERFIELD'S BRIGADE CALL.

Dan, Dan, Dan, Butterfield, Butterfield.

This special call for an organization was useful in many ways. It had no small effect in arousing and maintaining an *esprit de corps* in this brigade, second to none in the army. It was known by all troops of the Army of the Potomac, and the brigade which marched to its music was always respected and welcomed by its comrades in arms as an organization to be trusted, and sure to give a good account of itself under all circumstances.

The rout of the Union army at the second battle of Bull Run was for a time much greater than that which occurred at the first battle, although the men having become veterans, order was more quickly restored. After making a gallant charge which was received by masked batteries and musketry in front, the line also being enfiladed by a large part of Longstreet's artillery, the men fell back in confusion. At the turnpike all trace of organization was lost. Darkness came on and the blockade at the Stone Bridge broke up whatever semblance of order remained. Between the Stone Bridge and Centreville the turnpike was filled with a disorganized mass of infantry, artillery, ambulance and wagon trains. General Butterfield, riding in the midst of the *melee*, ordered his bugler to sound at short intervals his brigade call. It was received with shouts from all directions, and the men of this brigade, rallying to that call in the darkness, were formed into column, and marched into Centreville in better order than that prevailing in almost any other command.

In September, 1889, one of the regiments of this brigade met on Little Round Top, Gettysburg, to dedicate its regimental monument and to hold the annual reunion of the survivors of the regiment. Few of them had seen the battlefield since July, 1863. The writer, attending this reunion, took with him a bugle, and standing among the rocks and trees sounded once more the old Dan Butterfield Call. The men were scattered about over the hill and in the lower ground at its foot, some seeking the rocks where they fought, others going further to see how the position looked from the place where the enemy advanced. When the bugle sounded a great shout came up from the men, who recognized the old familiar call, although many of them had not heard it for a quarter of a century. They came charging up to the spot where the bugler stood, some with tears in their eyes, asking to have it repeated. That familiar sound echoing among the rocks where they had fought brought back, perhaps more vividly than words could do, the memories of the days when they had answered so often to its sound. Few men of the old Third Brigade can hear that call to-day without emotion.

One day in July, 1862, when the Army of the Potomac was in camp at Harrison's Landing on the James river, Virginia, resting and recruiting from its losses in the seven days of battle before Richmond, General Butterfield summoned the writer, his brigade bugler, to his tent, and whistling some new tune asked the bugler to sound it for him. This was done, not quite to his satisfaction at first, but after repeated trials, changing the time of some of the notes, which were scribbled on the back of an envelope, the call was finally arranged to suit the general. He then ordered that it should be substituted in his brigade for the regulation "Taps" (extinguish lights) which was printed in the Tactics and used by the whole army. This was done for the first time that night. The next day buglers from near-by brigades came over to the camp of Butterfield's brigade to ask the meaning of this new call. They liked it, and copying the music returned to their camps, but it was not until some time later, when generals of other commands had heard its melodious notes, that orders were issued, or permission given, to substitute it throughout the Army of the Potomac for the time-honored call which came down from West Point.

In the western armies the regulation call was in use until the autumn of 1863. At that time the Eleventh and Twelfth corps were detached from the Army of the Potomac and sent under command of General Hooker to reinforce the Union army at Chattanooga. Through its use in these corps it became known in the western armies and was adopted by them. From that time it became and remains to this day the official call for "Taps." It is printed in the present Tactics and is used throughout the United States Army, the National Guard, and all organizations of veteran soldiers.

General Butterfield in speaking of the reason for changing the call for "Taps," said that the regulation call was not very musical and not appropriate to the order which it conveyed. He wanted a call which in its music should have some suggestion of putting out the lights and lying down to rest in the silence of the camp, and musing over airs and musical phrases which might better represent this idea, he composed this call and directed its use in the camps of his brigade, the only troops over which he had at that time any authority. It made its way by its intrinsic beauty to a permanent place in the minds and hearts of the soldiers.

In accordance with the custom of attaching words to such calls as had a significance to which words were adapted, the men soon began to sing to this call, "Go to sleep, go to sleep, go to sleep, go to sleep, go to sleep. You may now go to sleep, go to sleep." This was the last regular call of the day or night in camp. About half an hour after the formation of a company for evening roll-call, to which it was summoned by the "Tattoo," this call was sounded as a signal to put out all lights in tents, stop all loud conversation, and everything which would interfere with the quiet rest and sleep of the men. Sometimes they sang, "Put out the lights, go to sleep, go to sleep, go to sleep, go to sleep. Put out the lights, go to sleep, go to sleep."

General Butterfield in composing this call and directing that it be used for "Taps" in his brigade, could not have foreseen its popularity and the use for another purpose into which it would grow. To-day whenever a man is buried with military honors anywhere in the United States, the ceremony is concluded by firing three volleys of musketry over the grave, and sounding with the trumpet or bugle, "Put out the lights. Go to sleep." At the Soldiers' Homes, when the worn-out veterans of the Grand Army of the Republic lie down to their last rest, while their comrades stand about the grave with bared heads, some comrade bids farewell by sounding on the bugle this call to "Go to sleep." At all posts of our little regular army, whether at garrisons or at the distant frontier camps, a soldier who is buried by his comrades receives this last salute. When General Butterfield was buried at West Point a few months ago, the solemn strains of this call bade the last farewell to its author. It consigned to their last rest Sheridan at Arlington, Sherman at St. Louis, Grant at New York and McKinley at Canton.

There is something singularly beautiful and appropriate in the music of this wonderful call. Its strains are melancholy, yet full of rest and peace. Its echoes linger in the heart long after its tones have ceased to vibrate in the air. Like Handel's Largo, it is immortal.

Put out the lights, Go to sleep, Go to sleep, Go to sleep, Go to

sleep. Put out the lights, Go to sleep, Go to sleep.

CORPS BADGES.

O. W. NORTON.

When General Hooker assumed command of the Army of the Potomac early in 1863, he selected General Daniel Butterfield for his Chief of Staff. The army at this time was considerably discouraged and demoralized by the useless slaughter at the battle of Fredericksburg and the melancholy failure of Burnside's "stick-in-the-mud" march. General Butterfield was a firm believer in the advantage of the *esprit de corps* and fertile in resources for producing it. It existed in a limited way in companies, regiments, and possibly in some few brigades, but these organizations lost their identity in the great army. The "Grand Divisions" of "Right," "Left" and "Center," were armies in themselves, and too large to make possible any feeling of unity between their component parts. There had been army corps before, but it seems to have been determined by General Hooker to abandon the "Grand Division" idea and make the Army Corps the unit for military operations.

General Butterfield, believing heartily in the plan of his chief, conceived the idea of giving to each of these army corps a distinctive badge which should be worn only by the officers and men of this corps and distinguish them from all other organizations. Each corps was divided into three divisions, and each division into three brigades. Cloth badges of distinct forms were selected and furnished to each officer and soldier, to be worn conspicuously on the hat or cap. The badge selected for the First Corps was a disc, that for the Second Corps a trefoil (called by the men, "Ace of Clubs"). The Third Corps badge was a lozenge or diamond. The Fifth Corps had the Maltese cross. The Sixth Corps wore the Greek cross, the Ninth Corps a shield, the Eleventh Corps a crescent, and the

Twelfth Corps a star. The Fourth, Seventh, Eighth and Tenth corps were in other armies.

The badges were of three colors—red, white and blue. The badge of the first division of each corps was red, that of the second division white and that of the third division blue. With these badges on the caps of the men it was possible to know at once in what division any man in the Army of the Potomac belonged. The red Maltese cross on a cap denoted that the soldier was a member of the First Division, Fifth Corps—a white trefoil that he belonged in the Second Division, Second Corps. A blue star located him in the Third Division, Twelfth Corps.

When large bodies of troops were moving it was often difficult to distinguish the commander of any given brigade from any of the mounted officers in his vicinity. A staff officer coming from a corps or division headquarters with an order for any brigade commander, would sometimes ride two or three times up and down his line before finding him. In this way valuable time was lost. General Butterfield devised a plan by which the commander of any brigade in the army could be readily found at any time when it was light enough to distinguish a flag. He ordered that each brigade commander should be provided with a special brigade flag which should be displayed at his headquarters tent when in camp, and carried by a mounted man with him wherever he went when his command was under arms. These brigade flags were in the form of an equilateral triangle. No two brigade flags were alike, but each was made up of some combination of the three colors, red, white and blue. The flags of the brigades in each first division had a blue border in whole or in part, with a white center on which was the corps badge in red. The first brigade, first division of any corps had a blue stripe six inches wide on the side of the triangle next the staff, but no stripes at top or bottom. The second brigade had no stripe next the staff, but a blue stripe at top and bottom. The third brigade had a blue stripe on each of the three sides of the triangle. The brigade flag of the Third Brigade, First Division, Fifth Corps had a white center on which was displayed a large red Maltese cross, and was bordered on all three sides with a blue stripe. The brigade flags of the second divisions had blue centers with white badges and red borders. The brigades of the third divisions of each corps had flags with white centers, blue badges and red borders. By means of these flags a staff officer or a general could know without asking any questions, at any time when he could see the flag, the brigade, division and corps of any troops within sight.

The order instituting corps badges in the Army of the Potomac was issued March 21, 1863, and that prescribing flags for the several brigades of this army, May 12, 1863. These orders, as given in the Official Records published by the War Department, are as follows:

Headquarters Army of the Potomac, March 21, 1863.

CIRCULAR:—For the purpose of ready recognition of corps and divisions in this army, and to prevent injustice by reports of straggling and misconduct through mistakes, to its organization, the Chief Quartermaster will furnish without delay the following badges, to be worn by the officers and enlisted men of all the regiments of the various corps mentioned. They will be securely fastened upon the center of the top of the cap.

Inspecting officers will at all inspections see that these badges are worn as designated:

CORPS.	SYMBOL.	COLORS		
		1ST DIV. RED.	2ND DIV. WHITE.	3RD DIV. BLUE.
First	Sphere	"	"	"
Second	Trefoil	"	"	"
Third	Lozenge	"	"	"
Fifth	Maltese Cross	"	"	"
Sixth	Cross	"	"	"
Eleventh	Crescent	"	"	"
Twelfth	Star	"	"	"

The sizes and colors will be according to pattern.

By command of MAJOR GENERAL HOOKER.

S. WILLIAMS, *Assistant Adjutant General.*
Rebellion Record, Series I, Vol. XXV, Part II., Page 152.

Headquarters Army of the Potomac,
Camp near Falmouth, Va.,
May 12, 1863.

GENERAL ORDERS,
Number 53.

EXTRACT.

*   *   *   *   *   *

The flags for the divisions of the different corps of this army will be as follows:

For the first division of each corps, a white rectangular flag, with the symbol of the corps in red.

For the second division of each corps, a blue rectangular flag, with the symbol of the corps in white.

For the third division of each corps, a white rectangular flag, with the symbol of the corps in blue.

For the light division of the Sixth Corps, a white rectangular flag, with the symbol of the corps in green.

The brigades of the first division of each corps, a white triangular flag, with the symbol of the corps in red in the center.

The first brigade, no other stripe or mark.

The second brigade, a blue stripe, six inches wide, next the lance.

The third brigade, a blue border, four and one-half inches wide, all round the flag.

The brigades of the second division of each corps, blue triangular flag; symbol of the corps in white in the center.

First brigade, no other stripe or mark.

Second brigade, red stripe, six inches wide, next the lance.

Third brigade, red border, four and one-half inches wide, around the flag.

The brigades of the third division of each corps, white triangular flag; symbol of the corps in blue in center.

First brigade, no other stripe or mark.

Second brigade, red stripe, six inches wide, next the lance.

Third brigade, red border, four and one-half inches wide, all round the flag.

The Chief Quartermaster will furnish the flags upon requisitions approved by the corps commander.

* * * * * *

By command of
MAJOR GENERAL HOOKER.

S. WILLIAMS,
Assistant Adjutant General.

Rebellion Record, Series I., Vol. XXV., Part II., Pages 470-471.

From the above order it would appear that the flags of first brigades had two colors only, with no stripes. Although I have not been able to find a later order modifying the above, my recollection is that an order was issued making each brigade flag a combination of the three colors, red, white and blue, and that the flags of the first brigades of each division had one stripe next the staff, second brigades two stripes, and third brigades three stripes, with colors as specified in General Order Number 53.

The soldiers very soon became fond and extremely proud of their corps badges. There was a generous rivalry between the men who wore the cross and those who wore the trefoil, the star, or the diamond, and the wearers of each badge were stimulated to maintain the glory of their own organization. Every regiment carried the national colors and some the colors of their state in addition, but these were common to the whole army. Men could not have the same feelings toward other men on account of their membership in the Army of the Potomac as they had toward the men who wore the badge of their own corps or division.

This device of the corps badge was carried to the western armies by the Eleventh and Twelfth corps when they went to join the army at Chattanooga, and was adopted by the corps of that army, and the men along the Mississippi and other sections in the theater of war.

MONUMENT OF EIGHTY-THIRD PENNSYLVANIA VOLUNTEERS.
LITTLE ROUND TOP, GETTYSBURG.

OUR FALLEN COMRADES.

ADDRESS BY O. W. NORTON

AT THE DEDICATION OF THE MONUMENT OF THE EIGHTY-THIRD REGIMENT PENNSYLVANIA VOLUNTEERS ON LITTLE ROUND TOP, GETTYSBURG, SEPTEMBER, 1889.

What man is there of all this assembly whose thought does not go back to-day in tender remembrance of one or more of those four hundred and thirty brave hearts who gave up their lives on some one of these thirty-one battlefields from Yorktown to Appomattox, or in some hospital, where, after the battle, he was carried suffering from wounds that made him envy the fate of comrades to whom the instant summons came with the sharp crack of a rebel rifle or the shriek of the bursting shell?

Is there one who has not some morning shared his coffee and hard tack with a dear friend, gone on the cold and muddy march, or along the dusty, weary way with him, laughing, chatting, singing the old marching songs to lighten the step, and at night, after the battle, lain down alone in the bivouac, the voice of that comrade hushed forever, his body only waiting to be laid with other fallen heroes in that long trench?

Is there one who has not been appealed to by the wife, the mother or the sister of the dear one, for something more definite than the brief official report, "Killed at Gaines' Mill," "Killed at Malvern Hill," "Killed at Gettysburg"?

Is there one whose heart has not bled with sympathy for the friends of his comrade, strangers to him perhaps, as seated under his shelter tent with a cracker box for table, he tried to write something that would comfort the sad hearts, telling how bright and cheerful their dear one had been that last day, how gloriously he fought until struck down, how often he had spoken of the loved ones at home, and asked in the phrase that put death far away, that they might be written to if "anything happened" to him?

Have the years that have passed since brought to us any stronger friendships than those formed by us who "drank from the same canteen"? Those were glorious days when, with the blood of youth coursing through our veins, we consecrated ourselves to the Stars and Stripes, and devoted ourselves to the preservation of the government of the people, by the people, and for the people. We were all willing to die if need be. Some were taken and others left.

It is meet that we come to this holy ground, consecrated to freedom by the life blood of a host of fallen comrades, and bring our wives, our sons and daughters, that with us they may feel the spirit of this place, may know what here their fathers did, and what their mothers whose hearts were on this field suffered; and while we renew our vow of undying allegiance to the government saved by blood, make their vow to preserve it when we have gone to join our comrades.

What shall we say to-day of those who fell in the struggle? A year would not be long enough to mention by name the more than forty men of each company, and recount the glorious deeds of each. Military rank was an accident or incident of the service. It has perished. Privates, captains, colonels, are melted into an army of heroes. Each did his duty in his place and has gone to his reward. We, privates and officers, meet to-day with rank abolished, and as citizens and heirs of the rich inheritance they left us, honor their memory.

Each of us has in his heart the memory of some comrade who fell, dear to him but perhaps unknown to most of the twenty-two hundred and seventy men who from first to last made up the Eighty-third. Not four years of service could suffice to make all the men of the regiment personally known to each other, but that service did suffice to inspire in the heart of every member a feeling of security and invincibility in the line of battle, when, standing to defend or advancing to attack, he knew that the men on his right and left wore on their caps those silver letters "83 P. V." and that touching elbows with the last one on the flank was that other one of "Butterfield's Twins," the Forty-fourth New York.

Some few of the hundreds who fell, by reason of official position, came into personal relation with all. Is there one here to-day of the thousand stalwart bayonets who followed the gallant McLane across the Long Bridge on the first entrance of the Eighty-third into Virginia, who can ever forget him or cease to mourn his untimely fate? His noble presence alone was an inspiration. His faithful drilling of the regiment during the weary months at Hall's Hill had much to do with its later efficiency. When, passing along that restless line at Gaines' Mill, he replied to the men who were tired of watching for the enemy that would not come, "Boys, you will see enough of them before night," his words seemed a prophecy of his own fate.

Who can forget the gentle Naghel, who died beside McLane before he had time to more than begin making a name as Major of the Eighty-third?

To those who saw Lieutenant Plympton White at Gaines' Mill, when the regiment was almost surrounded and summoned to surrender, and heard his scornful "Hell! the Eighty-third Pennsylvania never surrenders"—worthy of Victor Hugo's Cambronne at Waterloo—his sad death in the prison hospital at Charleston will be a tender memory.

In raising here our monument of granite to transmit to those who follow us the story of the deeds of the Eighty-third, we crown it with a tribute in enduring bronze to the one man who above all others seems to personify the spirit of the regiment, of the brigade, of the army, of the people, that poured out its treasure and its blood that this might be forever a free nation. The commissioners of the state very properly refused to permit any personal allusions or inscriptions to be placed on the Pennsylvania monuments.

They stand to commemorate the common deeds of the soldiers of the commonwealth. In their description this statue stands as the "Bronze figure of a Union officer." When the survivors of the Eighty-third, or of any regiment of the old Third Brigade at Gettysburg, think of a Union officer whose figure shall be symbolic, the name of Vincent springs to the front. We honor ourselves in honoring him. He was our ideal. Without previous military training he seemed a born soldier. Turning aside from the ranks of civil life, in a few months he was the more than competent commander of a brigade. Strict in discipline, yet loving his men and jealously guarding their rights, he inspired in them confidence, love and trust. To him the etiquette of the service was a means, not an end. He knew how to ride over it when occasion required. When, at Chancellorsville, the brigade was sent to the extreme right and placed in position to protect the flank, with what magnificent insubordination he dashed up to the brigade commander who ordered him to recall his men from their work of getting timber for a rifle pit to "Dress back about three feet" the left of the crooked line of hastily stacked rifles, and saying with a curt salute, "I must not lose a moment, sir, in fortifying my position," dashed back to stimulate and direct his men, leaving his superior officer muttering a reluctant assent!

When, as the rear guard of that sorrowful retreat from Chancellorsville, we crossed the river to find the roads over which the army had passed turned to fathomless mud, how he scorned the rule that required him to keep his place in line, and led the Eighty-third through woods and fields, reaching camp in time to have supper cooked and men ready to sleep before the balance of the brigade appeared!

• Who can forget the cheers that broke through the solemn decorum of dress parade when the order was published assigning him to the command of the brigade?

What superb generalship he showed at Goose Creek in gauging the morale of the enemy; and when the flanking maneuvre that had driven him across the Loudon Valley failed at last, because the creek was too deep to ford, putting him to rout by dashing at the bridge with sword flashing in air, and, before a man had moved, shouting so as to be plainly heard by the enemy, "There they go, boys; now give them ———!" Well, the rebels did not wait for the balance of the remark. The bridge was cleared, the cavalry thundered over, and the enemy did not stop his retreat until he reached the plain at the foot of Ashby's Gap.

In July, 1863, on this ground we were making history. Assembled here to-day we are making history still. The correct story of Gettysburg has never been, will never be written. None but the actors on the field can tell the story, and each one can tell of his own knowledge but an infinitesimal part. Many conscientious historians have attempted to weave a symmetrical whole from such disconnected threads as they can gather, but their accounts vary as their sources of information. Every man owes to the memory of those who died here his best endeavor to tell truly the story of their deeds, that the historian of the future may have the material out of which to fashion a truer story of Gettysburg.

We may fairly say without fear of contradiction, and without taking a leaf from the laurels of other heroes, that the genius, the devotion, the heroism, the consummate skill of Vincent prevented the turning of our left flank July 2d, held the enemy as in a vise, and preserved to our army the possession of Little Round Top, the loss of which would have meant the loss of our whole position, and a victory for the enemy instead of the defeat which was the beginning of the end.

Full justice has never been done him in any account that I have seen. The Comte de Paris, in his admirable history, says that General Warren, who from his position with the Signal Corps had observed the approach of the column sent by Longstreet to occupy this height, hastened to General Sykes near the wheat field, urging the necessity of placing troops there, and that Sykes sent Vincent's brigade. General Doubleday, in his account, says that General Warren, seeing Barnes' Division, which Sykes had ordered forward, standing formed for a charge to relieve De Trobriand, took the responsibility of detaching Vincent's brigade, and hurried it back to take post on Little Round Top. Neither is entirely correct, and Doubleday almost puts in the mouth of Warren the very words used by Vincent. Although a private soldier, my duty as Vincent's bugler and bearer of his brigade flag that day and during all the period of his command of the brigade, gave me better opportunities than even the officers of his staff enjoyed to see and hear what occurred and was said, for the reason that they were busy transmitting his orders, while I never left him, but was always near enough to hear all verbal orders given and received. The incidents of that day are burned into my memory, and I am glad to-day of the opportunity of giving you my recollections of it. After a long time of waiting for orders in that position in the low ground near the Weikert house, listening to the terrible roar of artillery and musketry in our front, an officer came galloping toward us from the direction of the wheat field. Vincent with eyes ablaze spurred toward him, and as he approached near enough to speak, said in his impetuous way, "Captain, what are your orders?" Instead of answering, the officer inquired, "Where is General Barnes?" If Vincent knew he did not answer. I had not seen him since morning. He was not at the head of his division. If he gave an order during the battle to any brigade commander I fail to find a record of it in any account I have read. The other brigades of the division fought heroically in the line along the wheat field, but the orders appear to have been given by Colonel Tilton and Colonel Sweitzer. Vincent repeated his question with emphasis: "What are your orders?" "Give me your orders." The captain replied, "General Sykes told me to direct General Barnes to send one of his brigades to occupy that hill yonder." Without an instant's hesitation Vincent replied, "I will take the responsibility of taking my brigade there;" and ordering Colonel Rice to follow as rapidly as possible, he dashed at full speed for the hill. The Eighty-third knows how little time there was to spare. Military men would not have criticised him had he directed that staff officer to General Barnes and waited calmly for the order to move to be sent him through the regular channels. Some might censure his assumption of responsibility, but had he waited, that advancing column of the enemy would have been in possession, and not even the Third Brigade could have dislodged it.

Riding rapidly to the summit he came out on the little plateau in rear of the position held later by the Sixteenth Michigan. I followed with the flag. A battery which had been firing at the signal flag a little further to our right opened on us, and he directed me to retire behind the rocks. In a few moments he dismounted, and giving me the bridle rein of Old Jim, went back on foot examining the ground. When the head of the brigade appeared its position was ready. Professional soldiers have pronounced the position chosen by him the finest selected by a volunteer officer during the war. Many an officer ordered to occupy a hill would have formed his main line along the summit, as did Bragg at Missionary Ridge, but he, knowing that the bravest men may sometimes waver before an impetuous charge, placed them lower down, leaving a rallying point and a position above for reserves, should a second line be required.

The momentary recoil of the Sixteenth Michigan when assaulted in front and flank, and the repulse of that assault by the timely arrival of the One hundred and fortieth New York in the place he had left for it, prove the wisdom of his choice.

The line was held, but at what a cost! Throwing himself into the breach, he rallied his men but gave up his own life. Comrades and friends, that was not a bauble thrown away. In the very flower of his young manhood, full of the highest promise, with the love of a young wife filling his thought of the future with the fairest visions, proud, gentle, tender, true, he laid his gift on his country's altar. It was done nobly, gladly. No knight of the days of chivalry was ever more knightly.

When a few hours before, as we tramped along the dusty road in the night, marching to Gettysburg, then unknown to fame, the old flag was unfurled and fluttered in the breeze, he reverently bared his head, and with the premonition of the morrow in his heart, said solemnly:

"What more glorious death can any man desire than to die on the soil of old Pennsylvania, fighting for that flag!"

Some of us wished that those words might be placed upon our monument, but the commissioners would allow nothing but the cold transcript of records in the War Department. May we keep them graven in our hearts and teach them to our children!

This place is holy ground. The glory of the Christ is that He died for men. He died, and we know he is not dead. May we not reverently say that those who have gladly died for men are not dead, but are with us to-day, more living than when they stood to stem the tide of invasion? If we are proud to say that we were in that line on Little Round Top, think you they regret it? With clearer vision than ours their eyes see the glory of the coming of the Lord. They see this broad land a Nation; not an aggregation of petty sovereign states. They look down the coming years and see it peopled with a host of freemen, rejoicing in the result of their sacrifice. They are content.

Let us listen to them to-day. God forbid that this fair land should ever need another such sacrifice, but if it fails to prize its heritage, and must again be purified by fire, may we and our children be able to sing as they sang:

"In the beauty of the lilies Christ was born across the sea,
With a glory in his bosom that transfigures you and me.
As He died to make men holy, let us die to make men free,
    While God is marching on."

POSITION OF EIGHTY-THIRD PENNSYLVANIA VOLUNTEERS ON LITTLE ROUND TOP, GETTYSBURG.

THE THIRD BRIGADE AT APPOMATTOX.

BY GENERAL JOSHUA L. CHAMBERLAIN,
EX-GOVERNOR OF MAINE.

At two o'clock on the morning of April 9, 1865, the Third Brigade, after a feverish march of twenty-nine miles, came to a halt, the rear brigade of the division column, which on such occasions has the hardest place of all. Worn out, body and spirit, by the vexations of a forced march, over a course blocked every half hour by the nondescript and unaccountable obstacles of a lagging column in the road ahead, men made few preliminaries about "going into camp." That peculiar ingredient of humanity called the nervous system held an imperious precedence not only over mind and matter, but over army regulations and discipline. There was no voice and ear for roll calls, and even the command of empty stomachs did not avail with habit or instinct to grope among the jumbled remnants of the too familiar haversacks. Officers and men alike flung themselves right and left along the roadside, whether it were bank or ditch, in whatever order or disorder the column had halted. Horses and riders exchanged positions, the patient animals, with slackened girths, dozing with drooping head just over the faces of their masters. In an instant, as it were, the struggling, straggling hosts were wrapped in misty darkness and silence.

But suddenly and soon the bugles rang out "The General!" Orders came to march within an hour's time. Word had come from Sheridan that he was at Appomattox Station, and that if we could hurry up he could cut the head of Lee's column, then near Appomattox Court House. Such a summons itself gave something of the strength it demanded. Spirit triumphed over body, and seemed to be on the alert before the latter could fully recover its senses. The time given was intended to provide for a meal, but that required also material, which indeed was now so simple as to quality and quantity as to make choice no task. Some of the younger regiments of the division were seen lighting dismal little fires to fry salt pork or steep some musty, sodden coffee. The Third Brigade, made up of veterans, spared their strength until the last for severer exercises. But this time patience did not attain to its perfect work. While sitting on their heels munching crumbs of hard tack and watching the coffee gradually "taking water," so as to produce a black liquid which could be sipped from the black tin dipper, word suddenly came that the Third Brigade was to take the head of the column and must pull out at once. The glimmering daybreak made still more weird the scenes and sounds which betokened that untimely departure, and the glimmering breakfasts must have evoked similar wild sensations for the benighted stomachs of the Third Brigade. But a brisk march with a fight at the end was the best medicine for such a mood. In three hours we were at Appomattox Station, and then learned that Sheridan with the cavalry had pushed on to Appomattox Court House, leaving word for us to follow with all possible dispatch. Indeed, there was no need of orders to this effect, for we now began to hear the boom of cannon ahead, and we knew that Sheridan and our glorious cavalry had cut across Lee's last line of retreat. Every heart beat high. No "obstacles" hindered that march. The head of the Fifth Corps ran past the rear of the Twenty-fourth, which had had the advance in the order of march. It was a triple column. The roads were taken mostly by whatever was to go on wheels, the men of both corps pressing along the fields on each side. We were evidently so near the "front" that General Bartlett thought it time to throw forward a "division" skirmish line, which he and General Griffin followed with characteristic eagerness. I was following with my own brigade and the Second (Gregory's) when there dashed out of a farm road on our right an officer of General Sheridan's staff, who gave me a hurried order to break off from the column at once without waiting for communication with any immediate superiors, and hasten to the support of Sheridan, who was that moment forced to fall back somewhat before the desperate onset of Gordon's old "Stonewall Corps."

Now it was the "double-quick," indeed. This movement of course brought me on the ground our cavalry occupied, and on the enemy's left flank, at nearly the same time at which our skirmish line had struck them in their proper front, the direction of the Lynchburg Pike. Reaching the ground, I wheeled into double line of battle and gradually replaced our cavalry, which galloped off to our right, while the Third Brigade still poured in upon my left. In this way we pressed the enemy steadily back upon Appomattox Court House. There was gallant and wild work done there by the Third Brigade, as well as by the rest of the division.

Gordon had hoped to force his way through our cavalry before our infantry could get up, and reach Lynchburg with the resolute remnant of his famous old corps. But when there burst upon his front and flank these lines of ours they knew so well, that had so unexpectedly kept pace with the cavalry and marched around his retreating front, desperately as he had pressed his march, the veterans of Lee's army took in the situation as by instinct. Their resistance was mechanical and by force of habit or discipline. Their old dash and daring were gone. When our advance struck them at close quarters, they fell back in disorder or rendered themselves up as prisoners. As an example of this feeling, all that was left of an entire brigade surrendered to a single staff officer of the Third Brigade, who dashed up to them with the demand. It may well be believed that our men also were responsive to the logic of the situation. The end was now so near they could see through to it, and they were bound to "be there" themselves. Action there was of the most stirring kind, but of passion nothing. No man wantonly or in excitement struck at the life of his antagonist. It was an example of what is so strangely, and for want of an adequate word, called a "moral" effect. When in the heat of the onset, the flag of truce was seen coming in on our right, some deeper, inner sense seemed to stifle all the others. All was moving with such momentum, that when the order came at length to cease firing and to halt, it was next to impossible to stop the men. They saw well that we held the rebel army at bay, and what the consequence must soon be they did not need to be told, only whatever was to be done, they wanted to be there and have a hand in it. If there was anything to be seen, they had earned the right to front seats at the spectacle. But when at about 4 o'clock in the afternoon the brief, thrilling message was passed along the lines, "Lee surrenders!" there was a tumult as of an ocean let loose. Men went wild with the sweeping energies of that assurance, which answered so much of long-cherished hope and of long-endured suffering that had marked their loyal and brave career. Now that they were no longer allowed to go forward and did not know how to go backward, there was no direction left but to go upward, and that way they took—to the top of fences, haystacks, roofs and chimneys, that they might send their hallelujahs and toss their old caps higher toward heaven. The rebels over across the slender rivulets of the Appomattox were shouting their side of the jubilation, from whatever cause, whether cheering Lee as he rode over to speak a last word to them, or whether in deep truth they were heartily sick of the war and felt that their loyal spirit and manly energies were wasted in a hopeless and perhaps mistaken cause. There is reason to believe the latter feeling was the motive of their exuberant demonstration, whose echoes rolled along the hillsides long after all was silent in our bivouac. For toward evening some of the rations that had been promised us for distribution at 9 o'clock that morning, and from which we had double-quicked away, had now got up and we could finish our breakfasts before lying down in peace at the close of that eventful day; and a certain deeper peace was ours, in that, learning now of the starving condition of our surrendering foes, twenty thousand rations were sent over just as the day was done, into that camp of fellow countrymen we had restored to brotherhood. Fitting token and emblem of the spirit in which that victory was won and that day ended! Here too was possibly one reason for the cheering that echoed in our ears as we fell asleep on that Palm Sunday evening.

All the next day and the day after, measures were being determined as to the actual breaking up of Lee's army, and the return of ours. Grant and Lee had not lingered, after the main points were settled, nor indeed was Sheridan seen again on the field. Generals Griffin, Gibbon and Merritt were appointed commissioners to arrange the final details.

All this while the visiting fever and the exchanging of tokens and souvenirs ran wild through both armies. Stringent measures had to be taken to prevent utter confusion in both camps, especially in ours, as it seemed to be understood that we were the hosts, and it was our "at home" reception. This spirit of exchange shortly passed into the spirit of trade; for our rations, after the best was done, were very short, and for three days afterwards it became necessary to forage the country far and wide to get even raw corn enough for man and beast. So the market "went up" decidedly on all sorts of farm produce. Hard tack was a luxury, and coffee and sugar at a high premium.

How or why it came about I do not know, but on the evening of the 10th of April I was summoned to headquarters and informed that I was to command the parade which was to receive the formal surrender of the arms and colors of the rebel army the next morning. This was an order, and to be received and obeyed without question. One request only I ventured to make of my Corps Commander. It was that, considering this occasion, I might resume command of my old Brigade, the Third, from which I had been transferred in June, 1864, with which I had served up to that time since my entrance into the service. My request was granted, and on that evening I yielded the command of my gallant First Brigade, and went back to my veterans.

General Grant was a magnanimous man, great minded and large minded. He would have nothing done for show and no vain ceremony. He granted to officers the high privilege of retaining their swords, and all men who owned their horses were made welcome to keep them, as they would need them to plough their land. The rebels had begged to be spared the pain of actually laying down their arms and colors in the presence of our troops, and to be permitted to stack them in front of their own camps and march off, and let us go and pick them up after they had gone. But this would be to err too far on the side of mildness. So it was insisted that while the surrendering army should be spared all that could humiliate their manhood, yet the insignia of the rebellion and the tokens of the power and will to hurt, lifted against the country's honor and life, must be laid down in due military form in presence of a designated portion of our army.

This latter office fell to our lot. It gave us no doubt a grateful satisfaction and permitted a modest pride, but it was not accepted as a token that we surpassed our comrades in merit of any kind.

We formed our line of battle on the southern margin of the principal street in Appomattox Court House. Massachusetts on the right—her Thirty-second Regiment, with all that was left to us of her Ninth, Eighteenth and Twenty-second; then Maine—her Twentieth Regiment, with the delivered remnant of her Second and her First Sharpshooters; Michigan next—her Sixteenth, with interminglings of her First and Fourth. On the left Pennsylvania—her One hundred and fifty-fifth holding also filaments which bound us with the Sixty-second, *Eighty-third* (Italics mine.—O. W. N.), Ninety-first and One hundred and eighteenth, an immortal band, which held in it the soul of the famous "Light Brigade," and of the stern old First Division, Porter's, which was nucleus of the Fifth Corps, men among them who had fired the first shot at Yorktown, and others that had fired the last at Appomattox, and who thus bore upon their banners all the battles of that army.

By the courtesy of General Bartlett, the First Brigade,

which I had so long commanded, and the Second, which had been with me in this last campaign, were sent to me and held part in the parade, being formed on another line across the street and facing us. These were, with the exception of the One hundred and ninety-eighth Pennsylvania, composed of New York regiments, the One hundred and eighty-fifth, One hundred and eighty-seventh, One hundred and eighty-eighth and One hundred and eighty-ninth, which in severe service had made themselves veterans worthy the fellowship of those sterling old New York regiments that had fulfilled their time and fame. Names and figures, all of these, dear to every heart that had shared their eventful and glorious history.

As we stood there in the morning mist, straining our eyes toward that camp about to break up for the last march, a feeling came over our hearts which led us to make some appropriate recognition of this great, last meeting.

We could not content ourselves with simply standing in line and witnessing this crowning scene. So instructions were sent to the several commanders that at the given signals, as the head of each division of the surrendering column approached their right, they should in succession bring their men to "Attention" and arms to the "Carry," then resuming the "Ordered Arms" and the "Parade Rest." And now we see the little shelter tents on the opposite slope melting away and carefully folded, being things which were needed by men as men and not as tokens of rebellion. Soon the gray masses are in motion—once more toward us—as in the days that were gone. A thrilling sight. First, Gordon, with the "Stonewall Corps"; then their First Corps—Longstreet's—no less familiar to us and to fame; then Anderson, with his new Fourth Corps; and lastly, A. P. Hill's Corps, commanded now by Heth, since Hill had fallen at one of the river fights a few days before. On they come with careless, swinging route step, the column thick with battle flags, disproportionate to their depleted numbers. As they come opposite our right our bugle sounds the signal, repeated along our line. Each organization comes to "Attention," and thereupon takes up successively the "Carry." The gallant General Gordon, at the head of the marching column, outdoes us in courtesy. He was riding with downcast eyes and more than pensive look; but at this clatter of arms he raises his eyes, and instantly catching the significance, wheels his horse with that superb grace of which he is master, drops the point of his sword to his stirrup, gives a command, at which the great Confederate ensign following him is dipped, and his decimated brigades, as they reach our right, respond to the "Carry." All the while on our part not a sound of trumpet or drum, not a cheer, nor word nor motion of man, but awful stillness, as if it were the passing of the dead. Now and then a gust of wind would spring up from the south with strange greeting; our starry ensigns stiffen and fly out as if to welcome back the returning brothers. The ensigns of rebellion seem to shrink back and strain away from the fated farewell.

So a division at a time covers our front. They halt, face inward, some ten paces from us; carefully "dress" their lines, each captain as careful of his alignment as if at a dress parade. Then they fix bayonets, stack arms, then wearily remove their cartridge boxes and hang them on the pile; lastly, reluctantly, painfully, they furl their battle-stained flags and lay them down; some, unable to restrain themselves, rushing from the ranks, clinging to them, kneeling over them and kissing them with burning tears. And then the Flag of the Union floats alone upon the field.

Then, stripped of every sign of the rebellion and token of its hate and will to hurt, they march off to give their word of honor never to lift arms against the old flag again, and are free to go where they will in the broad Republic.

Thus division after division passes, and it takes the whole day long to complete this deliverance. Twenty-seven thousand men paroled, one hundred and forty cannon and near that number of battle flags surrendered, but only about seventeen thousand stand of small arms. For sometimes a whole brigade, or what was left of it, had scarcely a score of arms to surrender, having thrown them away by roadside and riverside in weariness of flight or hopelessness of heart, or disdaining to carry them longer, only to be taken from them in token of a lost cause. After this it remained only to gather up what was serviceable of this material of war and to destroy the rest. Nothing was left which could be turned to use against the Union armies. The cartridge boxes were emptied on the ground for the most part, burned, and after the troops had withdrawn, at the first dusk of evening, it was a weird and almost sad sight to see the running flame with frequent bursts of lurid explosion along the lines where the surrendering army had stood; then only bits of leather writhing in the gray ashes.

All was over. With the dawn of morning the hillsides were alive with men, in groups or singly, on foot or horse, making their way as by the instinct of an ant, each with his own little burden, each for his own little harbor or home.

And we were left alone and lonesome! The familiar forms that had long so firmly held our eyes, until they almost demanded the sight of them for their daily satisfaction, had vanished like a dream. The very reason of our existence seemed to have been taken away. And when on the morrow we took up our march again, though homeward, something was lacking in the spring and spice which had enlivened us through even the dreariest times. To be sure, the war was not over yet, but we felt that the distinctive work of the old Third Brigade was over. We were soon to be mustered out; but never to be again as if the Third Brigade had not become a part of our lives; a part of our souls. There were "thoughts that ran before and after," memories of things that cannot be told, and new purposes of manly living and hopes of useful service yet, in visions of a broader citizenship and the career of an enfranchised country.

Made in the USA
Lexington, KY
08 April 2017